Understanding the Hospitality Consumer

This book is dedicated to Margaret, and also Roz and the 'girls' Rhiannon, Cerys and Bechan, who between them know more about hyperconsumption than can possibly be good for them.

Understanding the Hospitality Consumer

Alistair Williams

OXFORD   AMSTERDAM   BOSTON   LONDON   NEW YORK   PARIS
SAN DIEGO   SAN FRANCISCO   SINGAPORE   SYDNEY   TOKYO

Butterworth-Heinemann
An imprint of Elsevier Science
Linacre House, Jordan Hill, Oxford OX2 8DP
225 Wildwood Avenue, Woburn MA 01801-2041

First published 2002

British Library Cataloguing in Publication Data
A catalogue record for this book is available from the British Library

Library of Congress Cataloguing in Publication Data
A catalogue record for this book is available from the Library of Congress

ISBN 0 7506 5249 7

For information on all Butterworth-Heinemann publications
visit our website at www.bh.com

Composition by Genesis Typesetting, Rochester, Kent
Printed and bound in Great Britain by Biddles Ltd
www.biddles.co.uk

Contents

Hospitality, Leisure & Tourism Series

v

Preface

Consumption is part of our everyday lives. In contemporary society it encompasses aspects of our lives that were previously thought to be beyond the demands of the marketplace including health, education, religion, culture and politics. All aspects of contemporary society have had to adapt to take account of the wants and needs of ever more 'discerning' consumers. In western society our relationships, standing, self-belief and everyday experiences are seen to be underpinned by what, how and why we consume the goods and services that we do. *Understanding the Hospitality Consumer* seeks to focus on the role of consumption in hospitality and to investigate our understanding of its place in the contemporary industry. The text aims to discuss aspects of consumption within a recognized social context, that is, in relation to the products, services and markets of the hospitality industry.

The aims of the text are to:

1 Introduce and explore the role of consumer behaviour theory within the discipline of hospitality management, in order to assist students in understanding and applying the concepts of consumer behaviour to hospitality contexts and markets.
2 Discuss the principles and research of consumer behaviour and demonstrate how hospitality companies can and do use them in everyday operations.
3 Demonstrate that effective marketing involves focusing organizational activity on the consumer, through identifying factors that are relevant in consumer buying behaviour.
4 Discuss the challenges to traditional approaches to consumption posed by the postmodern hospitality consumer.

The text is interdisciplinary in nature and provides critical analysis of consumer behaviour from a sociological, psychological, economic, historical and media background, while always grounding such analysis within the contemporary hospitality industry.

The study of consumption has grown exponentially, to a point where for many commentators it now comprises the centre of the discipline of marketing, at least in an academic sense. This growth has coincided with a shift in our perception of how consumers act. Traditional approaches to consumption, based in a modernist perspective of rationality, objectivity and analysis, have been challenged by postmodern perspectives, with their focus on ritual, symbolism, communication, globalization and hyperreality.

The text takes as its focus the perspective that effective marketing involves focusing organizational activity on the consumer. Thus the book concentrates on an understanding of determining customer needs, the factors that are relevant in consumer buying behaviour and the effectiveness of many contemporary marketing techniques.

The main feature of existing service marketing literature is its implicit management orientation; little attention has been paid to the consumers of services, particularly with regard to the hospitality industry. Many of the existing consumer behaviour books are written from a marketing perspective and view the consumer as the object rather than the subject of the text. This text investigates consumer behaviour by emphasizing the behaviour of real consumers and then showing how marketers seek to influence their behaviour. This text is an introduction to the study of consumer behaviour within a recognized social context, that is, in relation to the products, services and markets of the hospitality industry. In addition, the text maintains a particular focus, the factors that influence why people buy particular products or services. Within the text we will consider such aspects as social and cultural influences, psychological influences and marketing influences that can have an impact on purchase behaviour.

The approach taken is to section the book into three parts. Part One introduces the subject area through placing the consumer in a general context, before continuing by considering the specific social context relating to the consumption of products and services of the hospitality industry.

In Part Two we investigate the key perspectives that are seen as being complementary to an understanding of consumer behaviour. First, the core feature of consumer behaviour, consumer decision-making. This is undertaken through a consideration of generalized models of decision-making, including an investigation of many of the seminal models which have been developed in consumer decision-making, such as those provided by Engel, Blackwell and Miniard (1995) and Foxall and Goldsmith (1994), along with models specifically developed for investigating the consumption of hospitality goods and services, such as those by Teare (1998). We then consider the characteristics that impact upon consumer decision-making, first by considering the core literature on individual psychological variables to consumption, such as perception, personality, learning, memory and motivation, and second considering the range of cultural and social influences on consumer behaviour. Here we consider the influences on the individual of the family, small and large groups and society in general. We also consider the role played by culture and other forms of social influence.

Part Three concludes the book by considering the value of consumer behaviour research as applied to the contemporary hospitality industry. Within this section we seek to address three key issues within contemporary hospitality consumer behaviour. First, we investigate the relationship between marketing, with its perceived management orientation, and consumer behaviour, which should be concerned primarily with emphasizing the behaviour of real consumers. Few authors would argue that marketing occupies a central position in the hospitality business environment and within hospitality education the proliferation of publications and the centrality of marketing on all undergraduate and postgraduate degree programmes clearly demonstrates that marketing is in the ascendancy. The question that has to be addressed is 'why have companies so readily adopted the discipline of marketing, and what are the repercussions of this for the study of consumption within the hospitality industry?'

Second, we consider the argument that we are witnessing significant social and cultural shift in terms of consumption, and in particular the consumption of hospitality goods and services, this shift being epitomized by postmodernism. In essence, if postmodernists are correct, people raised in a postmodern society are different from those raised in an earlier modernist era. As a result today's consumers are radically different from yesterday's in terms of taste, sensibilities, values and attitudes, as they have been raised in different eras, that is, the latter at the tail end of modernism and the former at the beginning stages of postmodernism. We will seek to argue that, given some of the issues raised by postmodernism, what is needed for the contemporary hospitality industry is an alternative way of looking at consumers and markets, one that is truly consumer led.

Third, we consider some of the issues raised by using postmodernism as an alternative paradigm for researching customer behaviour in the contemporary hospitality industry.

The difficulty of determining research agenda for investigating postmodern consumer behaviour, given the three key themes traditionally associated with postmodernism – the disintegration of universal forms of knowledge, the rise of simulacrity and hyperreality, and the move to an era of conspicuous consumption – are assessed. The argument that at present no paradigm for consumer behaviour that allows hospitality organizations to investigate postmodern consumption, and that consumer research, particularly in the hospitality field, lacks a systematic framework of conceptualization and analysis for the explanation of situational influences on consumer choice is evaluated. This part closes by identifying a range of potentially appropriate research agendas.

Figures and tables

Figures

Hospitality, Leisure & Tourism Series

Tables

Case studies

PART 1

Setting the Context for the Study of Hospitality Consumption

An introduction to the consumption of hospitality services

Key themes

- The study of consumption has grown exponentially, to a point where for many commentators it now comprises the centre of the discipline of marketing, at least in an academic sense. This growth has recently coincided with a shift in our perception of how consumers act.

- This chapter introduces and explores the role of consumer behaviour theory within the discipline of hospitality management, in order to assist students in understanding and applying the concepts of consumer behaviour to hospitality contexts and markets.

- Many of the existing consumer behaviour books are written from a marketing perspective and view the consumer as the object rather than the subject of the text. This text investigates consumer behaviour by emphasizing the behaviour of real consumers and then showing how marketers seek to influence their behaviour.

- This text is an introduction to the study of consumer behaviour within a recognized social context, that is, in relation to the products, services and markets of the hospitality industry.

An introduction to a discipline of consumer behaviour research

Increasingly we are referred to as consumers, whether we are parents, train users, hospital patients or, in the context in which we are primarily interested, users of hospitality services including bars, hotels, clubs and restaurants. *Understanding the Hospitality Consumer* seeks to focus on the role of consumption in hospitality and to investigate our understanding of its place in the contemporary industry. The text aims to discuss aspects of consumption within a recognized social context, that is, in relation to the products, services and markets of the hospitality industry.

The study of consumption has grown exponentially, to a point where for many commentators it now comprises the centre of the discipline of marketing, at least in an academic sense. Consumption is a part and parcel of everyday life; areas that were previously free of issues in respect of the marketplace have had to adapt to cope with a world where the consumer is paramount. For many people success is measured in terms of how well we are doing as consumers; consumption pervades all aspects of our everyday life and can be argued to structure all of our experience. As Miles (1998: 1) suggests: 'Our city centres are more remarkable as sites of consumption than they are as cultural centres, our homes might be described as temples to the religion of consumption, our lives apparently amount to little more that a constant juxtaposition of diverse consumer styles and tastes.'

This growth has coincided with a shift in our perception of how consumers act. Postmodern perspectives have challenged traditional approaches to consumption, based in a modernist perspective of rationality, objectivity and analysis, with their focus on ritual, symbolism, communication, globalization and hyperreality. How and what we consume have become increasingly significant, as ways in which we and others construct individuals. As Miles (1998: 1) argues, 'It (consumption) is ubiquitous and ephemeral; it is arguably the religion of the late twentieth century'. The complexity of consumption has also increased, as Lash and Urry (1994: 59) suggest: 'It (contemporary consumption) results in a French waiter serving a German business traveller in a New York restaurant advertising world cuisines. The traveller will jump into a taxi driven by a Pakistani immigrant, get her shoes repaired in a shop owned by a Russian Jewish émigré, and make her way to the latest Broadway musical direct from London.' In contemporary society it is increasingly clear that we are no longer characterized by our relationship to work, previously modernism had seen the characteristics and experiences of work as being key to the ways we as individuals were construed, with people's relationship to work seen as being the fundamental determinant of their experiences (Miles, 1998). Within such a perspective consumption is seen largely as a result of production, not a cause for it. Increasingly, however, the consumption of goods and services, such as hospitality, are seen as playing an important role in who we are, how we construct our lives and how we relate to others.

Commercial hospitality companies make a massive contribution to our economy, however, it is argued (Teare, 1994: 1998) that understanding of the interactions between consumers and suppliers is limited. These interactions, coupled with the unpredictability of consumer behaviour as a result of individual differences and the ways in which we categorize consumption decisions, makes the study of consumer behaviour a complex undertaking. However, it is clear that if in hospitality we wish to meet the expectations of our consumers we need to understand the needs, motives and preferences that generate those expectations. To do this we need to investigate the complexity of influences that consumers experience during the decision process (Teare, 1998).

This chapter is an introduction to the study of consumer behaviour within the hospitality industry, with a particular focus on investigating what consumption is and why has it become such a central feature of contemporary society, how the phenomena has been investigated, why we need to use theory to investigate hospitality consumption and what the relationship is between marketing and consumer behaviour. The chapter will also discuss, albeit briefly given the complexities involved, the nature and scope of the hospitality industry.

Contemporary hospitality

Within this book it is not intended to consider in any detail the ongoing discussions regarding the definition of 'hospitality' as it relates to our industry as these arguments are better rehearsed elsewhere, notably in Lashley and Morrison (2000). However, it would be remiss not to define the industry that this text is primarily concerned with, and to consider the ways in which those definitions will be used throughout this text.

Defining the hospitality industry is not as straightforward as one would imagine, indeed, a number of approaches to defining hospitality are available, the choice depending upon your preferred perspective. Traditional definitions have tended to focus upon the economic activities previously associated with the hotel and catering industries (Lashley and Morrison, 2000).

Such definitions tend to be very semantic in nature, for example The Joint Hospitality Industry Congress (1996: 13) define hospitality as 'The provision of food and/or drink and/or accommodation away from home'. Similarly Pfeifer (1983: 191) defines hospitality as 'Offering food, beverage and lodging, or, in other words, of offering the basic needs for the person away from home'.

Attempts have been made to widen out these definitions to encourage consideration of the non-economic relationships that are a feature of hospitality (Brotherton and Wood, 2000). These more evidential definitions are useful in that they encourage greater depth and scope in analysing what we mean by the 'hospitality industry', and thus it is this wider definition that I intend to use in order to define the context of this book. Brotherton and Wood (2000: 141) define hospitality by drawing together a number of key characteristics ascribed to it, including:

- a concern with producing and supplying certain physical products; namely accommodation, food and drink
- involvement in an exchange relationship, which may be economic, social or psychological in nature
- a combination of tangible and intangible elements, the precise proportion of each varying according to the specifics of different hospitality encounters
- association with particular forms of human behaviour and interaction
- an activity entered into on a voluntary basis by the parties involved
- an exchange which takes place within an intermediate time frame, and one which reflects the close temporal connection between production and consumption.

Drawing these characteristics together Brotherton and Wood (2000: 143) define the hospitality industry as 'Comprised of commercial organisations that specialize in providing accommodation and/or, food, and/or drink, through a voluntary human exchange, which is contemporaneous in nature, and undertaken to enhance the mutual well being of the parties involved'. While this definition is clearly more useful than the earlier semantic forms it does not readily identify the types of organizations with which this text is concerned, a point highlighted by Brotherton and Wood (2000: 143) themselves when they suggest 'The detail of those activities and organisations that should, based, on this [the above] definition, be included in the hospitality industry requires further thought'.

It is my intention within this text to consider hospitality through its widest possible connotations. Hospitality clearly has a very close relationship with the study of tourism and leisure, and I do not wish to be constrained to the semantic notions of hospitality as being concerned with the study of food, beverages and accommodation. With the exception of travel perhaps, most other aspects of tourism, for example, can be seen to be related to hospitality. It is with this focus in mind that, within this text at least, the hospitality industry will be considered to include, but not be limited to, hotels, restaurants, bars, clubs, entertainment venues, fast-food outlets, leisure venues, cafés, events, food-services, resorts, cruise ships, indeed almost anywhere you can have a good time and there is some relationship with food, drink or facilities.

Defining consumer behaviour

It is useful to begin any analysis by defining the key terms used, which in our case means considering what we mean by the term 'consumer behaviour', and investigating its use in the consumption of hospitality services. The first distinction we should make is that between 'consumers' and 'customers', terms that are often used interchangeably. In general, however, 'customer' is used to describe someone who makes a purchase, that is, with customers there is usually an element of exchange. As Gabbott and Hogg (1998: 9) suggest 'There is a construction on the term "customer" which implies a simple economic relationship between a business and a buyer, i.e. that the relationship is based on monetary exchange'. 'Consumer' is a much wider term, which recognizes that it is not necessarily based on any form of financial exchange. As we discussed at the beginning of the chapter it is common today, for example, to refer to the consumption of hospital or education services, for which no direct financial exchange takes place.

A second issue that we need to address is that using the term 'customer' tends to focus on the individual who undertakes the purchase decision. However, it is clear in hospitality environments this may not be the same person who consumes the service. If we look at fast-food restaurants, for example, it is clear that the consumers of children's meals are not the people who act as the customer. Similarly in bars and public houses the person who buys the drinks may not be the person who consumes them.

Gabbott and Hogg (1998: 10) suggest that consumer refers to a higher level of behaviour encompassing a wide range of relationships, defining consumer behaviour as 'A wide range of activities and behaviours, the processes involved when individuals or groups select, purchase, use or dispose of products, services, ideas or experiences'. The difficulty with this definition is that in trying to cover all possible aspects and relationships, it tends to vagueness and is of limited practical use. It does, however, reinforce the fact that consumer behaviour is a difficult discipline to define, particularly in hospitality where purchases can tend to demonstrate significant emotional involvement. Horner and Swarbrook (1996: 4)) opt for a simple form of definition, settling for defining consumer behaviour as 'the study of why people buy the product they do, and how they make the decision'. The problem with this definition is that again it focuses on the exchange relationship as being a feature of consumption, which increasingly is seen as too limiting. This focus on exchange is avoided to some extent by Wilkie (1994: 132) who defines consumer behaviour as 'the mental, emotional and physical activities that people engage in when selecting, purchasing, using, and disposing of products and services so as to satisfy needs and desires'.

One of the most useful definitions of consumer behaviour is that offered by Engel, Blackwell and Miniard (1995: 121) who refer to it as 'those activities directly involved in obtaining, consuming and disposing of products and services including the decision processes that precede and follow these actions'. The concept of consumer needs and wants has also been incorporated into definitions of consumer behaviour, for example in that of Solomon (1996: 43) who, in a definition similar to that offered by Gabbott and Hogg (1998) defines it as 'the process involved when individuals or groups select, purchase, use, or dispose of products, services, ideas or experiences to satisfy needs and wants'.

Having provided a range of definitions, we will now move on to consider why there has been such an upsurge in interest in consumption and what the implications of this are for the hospitality industry.

Why now, and what about hospitality?

It is clear that today's society, at least western society, is characterized more by consumption than production. Most of us enthusiastically embrace the consumer society and are keen to partake of the opportunities it affords. As Ritzer (1999: 34) states: 'There is little question that (western) society is increasingly characterized by what could now be termed hyper-consumption, and that most people are increasingly obsessed by consumption'. It is clear that consumption plays an ever-increasing role in western society; to some indeed it would appear that consumption defines western society (Ritzer, 1999). As more and more basic production is taking place in developing, and therefore cheaper, nations, consumption has taken a central position in society. So this leads to the questions why has there been a growth in interest in consumption and what are its implications for the hospitality industry?

A number of authors have produced accounts charting the rise of consumption, including Benson (1994), Miles (1998) and Ritzer (1999); Gabriel and Lang (1995) in particular have a very comprehensive description detailing the growth of consumption. It is not my intention here to go into depth regarding this matter; those interested in reading more about the historical development of consumption studies are directed to one of the books highlighted above.

If we first consider the growth of consumption, most authors argue that it can be explained by a number of key factors, including:

1 *The economy.* Recent movements in the economies of most developed countries, that is, movements in the 1980s and 1990s, have led to upturns in stock market prices and very low unemployment, leaving people with unprecedented levels of disposable income. In addition it has led to growth in the number of people able to take advantage of early retirement opportunities, people who have the resources to become active consumers. The result is that people want and can afford more goods and services, and for many people consumption of services such as hospitality has become a major form of recreation. From a supply perspective, companies, especially those quoted on the world's stock markets, recognize that in order to be seen to be doing well it is necessary to show substantial profit increases year on year. Economic growth has also got significant political implications which governments are keen to exploit as they recognize the social benefits of consumption (Miles, 1998).

2 *The growth of the youth market.* The youth of today are experienced consumers, and companies market directly to them, recognizing their role in the family decision-making unit. As Goodman (1997: 21) argues, 'The marketplace has turned kids into short consumers'. This is increasingly true within the hospitality industry. Consider fast-food restaurants and theme parks, for example; children and young people have become increasingly important consumers of hospitality services. In the UK the growth of child-friendly public houses has been a dominant feature of the sector since the late 1980s. All

the major public house retailers have a version of the public house as child activity centre, based around Greenalls' original Jungle Bungle concept. Funky Forest, Deep Sea Den, Charlie Chalks, Brewsters and all of the myriad other variations have been developed specifically to encourage children to pressurize parents into frequenting their particular offer; there is even a term for it today – *pester power*.

In a similar manner the fast-food industry directly markets to children, through its children's meals. To the children the food offer is largely irrelevant; the promotional gift, or *premium*, is the key. These gifts, almost always linked to the latest fad, fashion or film release, ensure huge profits to the fast-food companies, who charge premium prices for the meals. As Cross (1997: 1) argues: 'Today, adults know little or nothing of these products because they are part of a distinct children's culture that is marketed directly to children on television and at the movies'.

3 *Technological change*. Ritzer (1999) suggests that technological change is probably the most important factor in the growth of consumption, citing the development of transportation links such as cars, motorways and jet travel as being of prime importance in this growth. Also included are developments such as television and delivery technology, which are necessary to expedite mass advertising. However, no technological change has been as important in the growth of consumption as the computer, which is seen to link most of the other developments. If we consider the typical hotel stay, for example, computers will be used by both the consumer and the supplier at all stages of the stay.

4 *Social change*. As has been discussed, contemporary society is characterized by consumption rather than production, as was previously the case. All aspects of contemporary life are the focus of consumption, including most relationships and encounters we undertake on a day-to-day basis.

5 *The mass media*. The importance of the role of the mass media in fuelling contemporary consumption is without doubt, as consumption relies on the media to disseminate its messages and to mould its images. Through advertising, meanings are attached to commodities which are then seen as key to success and happiness. The cumulative effect of advertising is to associate goods and services, in particular brands, with meanings, and significant research has been done on the power of advertising and the mass media, some of which we will consider later in this book. Whatever the arguments about the power of advertising, however, it should be remembered that companies such as McDonald's, KFC and Burger King spend

billions of pounds every year seeking to convert consumers to the, for example, McDonald experience, and often irrevocably breaking traditional eating cultures at the same time.

6 *Facilitating means.* The growth of sophisticated means for exchange is seen as one of the key factors in the growth of consumption, as it removes a natural barrier to growth, limited resources at the individual level. The growth of credit cards, store cards etc. allow everyone the freedom to consume, with the widespread availability of credit an important factor in the growth of consumption. Where earlier generations saved until they could afford to buy an item with cash, today's consumers operate on the 'buy now, pay later' principle, made possible by widely available credit. The growth of mail order, television shopping channels and, increasingly significantly, the Internet, has also fuelled the growth in consumption, products are more widely available and, in an age of mass media, are more widely advertised. If we consider booking a holiday, for example, to the traditional high street travel agents we now have to add the travel hypermarkets, the magazines and newspapers, World Wide Web (WWW) sites such as e.bookers and the satellite television companies. Sky alone currently has three travel channels enabling consumers to book direct. These new facilitators of travel consumption have done much to fuel the huge growth in tourism, often paid for using credit cards.

7 *Globalization.* Most of the changes highlighted above have been accompanied by increased globalization, 'A process whereby the common currency of consumption plays a key role most evidently through the influence of multinational companies' (Miles, 1998: 11). This growth in globalization is clearly visible within the hospitality industry, where companies such as McDonald's have grown at a rapid rate. The first McDonald's opened in 1955 and by 2000 McDonald's had over 30 000 stores in more than 100 countries, including China, Russia, India and Israel. In 1991 less than 25 per cent of McDonald's restaurants were outside the USA; five years later this had risen to over 40 per cent and these stores accounted for more than 50 per cent of sales. Currently more than 80 per cent of new stores are built outside the USA. Other examples abound: Hanoi has Baskin-Robbins, TGI Friday, KFC and McDonald's; Paris, seen by many as the centre for western gastronomy, has seen its famous boulevard, the Champs-Elysées, come increasingly to resemble an American mall, complete with Planet Hollywood, McDonald's, Burger King and the Chicago Pizza Pie Factory.

In an interesting reversal to the more often seen American-led globalization of markets, Prêt-a-Manger, a UK-based sandwich company, has recently opened a store in New York's

Times Square (albeit following a decision by McDonald's to acquire a substantial shareholding in the company).

The second question this leads us to is what are the implications of this growth in interest about consumption, for the hospitality industry? The answer appears to be significant. As consumers we are able to gamble in casinos that double up as amusement parks, such as many of those in Las Vegas. The Mirage for example incorporates a 50-foot aquarium (complete with sharks) behind the registration desk, it also has a 1.5 million gallon dolphin habitat and a zoo. We can holiday on cruise ships that encompass floating hotels, casinos, leisure clubs, amusement arcades and sports clubs. One of the largest cruise ships currently afloat, the *Voyager of the Seas*, incorporates a huge casino; a five-story theatre; a full-size basketball court; a golf course (complete with sand bunkers); a rock-climbing wall and a theatre-size ice rink. Alternatively we are able to eat in restaurants such as the Rainforest Café or Planet Hollywood where settings, staff, the food and the ambience replicate the world of the rainforest or the movies respectively. Or we can shop in malls that encompass entire amusement parks, such as the Mall of America or the Edmonton Mall. Edmonton Mall, which among other things incorporates a sunken pirate ship, is the largest single tourist attraction in Canada, a country that offers the Niagara Falls among its many other tourist attractions (Ritzer, 1999). We are also able to consume differently in today's consumer society; we are more likely to eat alone, women use public houses and clubs in single-sex groups without any of the previously attached stigma, we are able to eat a much wider range of food offers (at all times of the year, seasonality no longer applying) and hospitality has become much more fragmented and obtainable. The growth of markets such as budget hotels, for example, has opened up the hotel sector to many who were previously disenfranchised, either by cost or experience.

It is fair to argue that hospitality by its very nature is in the vanguard of the growth of interest in consumption. Hospitality venues such as bars, restaurants, hotels, theme parks, casinos, etc. offer a multitude of ways in which people can consume. The value of this market is significant and grows year on year. Ritzer (1999) refers to the growth in outlets for consumption as 'the new means of consumption' or more lyrically 'cathedrals of consumption', going on to highlight a substantial number of hospitality offers as examples of these cathedrals. Among these he includes theme parks such as Disneyland; casinos such as those in Las Vegas; cruise ships, for example those operated by companies such as Royal Caribbean; the fast-food industry, for example

McDonald's; themed bars and restaurants, what Ritzer refers to as 'eatertainment'; and adult entertainment venues such as Dave & Busters. It is clear that the growth of interest in consumption and the subsequent upsurge in research within this area has substantial implications for the hospitality industry. This will be further considered in subsequent chapters.

The value of theory in researching consumer behaviour in hospitality

The unpredictable nature of hospitality consumption has much to do with individual preference and the ways in which we categorize decisions. In order to identify relationships, which occur during decision-making, researchers have developed models and frameworks portraying these relationships. These models seek to simplify our theoretical understanding of consumer decision-making. They seek to represent complex variables in order to make them easier to understand. As Teare (1998: 76) suggests 'Models seek to simulate or approximate as realistically as possible the complications of consumer preference, choice and purchase behaviour'. The question this generates is how useful and relevant are such theories in exploring hospitality consumption? Teare argues that theory can be considered valuable if it performs any one or more of the following functions:

- as a means of classifying, organizing and integrating information relevant to the factual world of business
- as a technique for thinking about marketing problems, and a perspective for practical action
- as an analytical tool kit to be drawn on when required for solving marketing problems
- in order to derive a number of principles, or even laws, of marketing behaviour.

As can be seen from Teare, theories can be considered as a means of bringing together facts in order to comprehend them, and by combining a number of facts into theory a framework is created which aids understanding and anticipation.

Consumer behaviour is a field that incorporates a number of disciplines and thus what may often appear to be conflicting theories in order to investigate and explain this behaviour. As we see in Part One of this book, consumer behaviour can be considered multidisciplinary in origin, however, as we shall see in later parts, consumer behaviour can also be seen as interdisciplinary, in that disciplines can come together in order to provide new insights to the ways in which we consume hospitality. A key concern within hospitality marketing is seeking to understand how or why consumers use particular goods and services, and, as we see during the course of this book, this issue is a challenging one. There are many varied reasons, some of which may not be conscious ones, why people consume as they do. To seek to identify patterns of behaviour given such a scenario is clearly a complex undertaking and theories are used to simplify and 'confirm' some of this complexity. Chapter 3 considers consumer decision-making models in detail, first by looking at generalized models of consumer decision behaviour, and then by looking at a number of models that have been generated specifically in relation to hospitality consumption.

The development of consumer behaviour research

It is suggested (Belk, 1995; Gabbott and Hogg, 1998) that the development of an academic discipline within the area of consumption began with the marketing departments in the business schools of the 1950s. Belk, in an extensive analysis of the emergence and transformation of consumer behaviour research, suggests that marketing courses were taught in American universities from the turn of the twentieth. century. However, it was not until the early 1930s that academics in this area began to consider themselves as marketing scholars, rather than econo-mists. Though, as Belk suggests, while from this time there was a formal academic separation of marketing from economics, ideologically the two disciplines continued to be joined.

Statt (1997) dates the emergence of consumer research, as a distinct discipline, to the mid-1960s, suggesting that the main impetus for its development was the practical issue of helping marketing managers understand how the social and behavioural sciences could help in finding specific causes of consumer behaviour and, in particular, consumer buying decisions. According to Statt this focus on what the consumer would do under certain specified conditions became known as the positivist approach. Statt argues that such a positivist approach makes a number of assumptions about consumer research, namely:

1 All behaviour has objectively identifiable causes and effects, all of which can be isolated, studied and measured.
2 When faced with a problem or decision, people process all the information relevant to it.
3 After processing this information people make a rational decision about the best choice or decision to make.

It became clear, however, that this perspective leaves a lot of human behaviour unaccounted for. As people are continually in relationships with others, particularly in our own field of hospitality, the act of consuming is more complex than simply one of buying and selling at a rational level. While such an analysis is acceptable at a simple level, it is clear that in complex economies it limits our understanding of consumer behaviour. In particular, such an analysis makes little allowance for the fact that in complex economies price is not the dominant factor that motivates choice. In addition, increasing use of media and other technologies which make huge amounts of information available to consumers has an impact on our behaviour. Finally, the positivist approach leaves open the question of an individual's capacity to process large amounts of information, prior to making decisions. It is clear that the positivist school of thought, with its emphasis on rationality, ignores the symbolic aspects of consumption. However, the relationships in which we are involved are important in understanding consumer behaviour because they affect the buying decisions and consumption patterns of everyone involved. As such, consumer behaviour has to be understood within the context of human interaction. This has become known as the interpretivist school of research, and is based on a set of assumptions which include that:

- cause and effect cannot be isolated because there is no single objective reality that everyone can agree on
- reality is an individual's subjective experience of it, as such each consumers experience is unique
- people are not simply rational information processors or decision makers; this view takes no account of emotion.

The interpretivist school argues that buying behaviour has to be interpreted in the light of a person's whole consumer experience. Behaviours adopted by individuals are formed in response to the society within which we operate and the roles that we adopt or which are assigned to us. These roles must be incorporated in any understanding of the ways in which we consume.

The positivist and interpretivist schools of thought have come to be seen as complementary to each other (Statt, 1997). The role of prediction and control is seen as trying to isolate cause and effect in behaviour, while at the same time the importance of understanding the complexity of consumer buying behaviour is emphasized. Contemporary reviews of the literature would indicate three broad approaches to consumption – the economic, positivist (rational) or cognitive consumer, the behavioural, interpretivist consumer (learning) and the experiential consumer (postmodern):

1 *The economic consumer.* As discussed earlier, the fundamental assumption here is that consumers are logical and adopt a structured approach to consumption. Consumers are expected to make rational decisions, based on an analysis of potential benefits and losses. Using such a model a consumer seeking a beer would investigate all the potential options and consume at the cheapest location. This model assumes that consumption is a series of tasks, which can be seen as a problem-solving exercise, comprising a series of distinct stages. This model generated much of the early literature in consumer behaviour, including many of the consumer decision models, which we consider in Chapter 3.

2 *The behavioural consumer.* This model is based on the view that consumption is a learned response to stimuli, that is, consumers learn to consume as a response to punishment or reward, approach or avoidance. The model is based on the assumption that there is relationship between experience and subsequent behaviour.

3 *The experiential consumer.* This focus rejects a structural response to experience. Within this school of thought consumption is beyond explanation or prediction. Aspects such as choice, decision and learning are seen as modern constructs and are replaced by postmodern constructs such as fantasy, hedonism or symbolism (Gabbott and Hogg, 1998). Postmodern approaches to consumption will be considered in greater depth in Part Three of this book.

Research within consumer behaviour developed in order to assist firms to market consumer goods more successfully, with early studies including tea consumption, film going, shoe purchasing and noodle-eating (Fullerton, 1990). However, as Belk (1995) notes, marketing at this time stressed objective service and product benefits and as such did not stray far from the economic perspective of 'rationality'. Belk suggests that the economic emphasis in consumption studies declined during the 1950s when the focus moved to that of motivation research. However, this change did not last long and motivation research rapidly declined in academic respectability. A number of causes are suggested for this decline, including a belief that motivation research manipulated the subconscious desires of consumers, and the growth of scientific experimentation within the field (Stern, 1990). Scientific experimentation was founded on the methods and concepts of psychology, and focused on examining the effect of physical features such as pricing, product design and packaging on consumers, using forms of scaled responses. Belk (1995) suggests that the growth of scientific experimentation led to a 're-rationalization' of the dominant view of the consumer, with the result that information processing models of consumer behaviour came to the fore. These models perceived of the consumer as acting like a computer, gathering and processing information in a rational manner in order to assist in making decisions. While some effort was made to incorporate aspects of culture, group processes and social influence, texts from this period are largely formed in terms of the consumer as information processor (Howard and Seth, 1969; Nicosia, 1966).

From the 1970s onwards the discipline of consumer research has grown to be one of the major areas of academic activity, contributing much of the research activity within marketing departments. However, as Belk (1995: 60) suggests, 'much of this consumer research retains the strong rationality biases inherited from economics and the strong micro biases inherited from marketing'. The value of consumer behaviour research is advocated by numerous authors as typified by Swarbrook and Horner (1999: 3) who suggest 'The subject of consumer behaviour is key to the understanding of all marketing activity, which is carried out to develop, promote and sell hospitality products'. From the 1980s onwards there has been a shift in the dominant perspectives within consumer research. Belk (1995) suggests that a major cause for this shift has been the move towards multi-disciplinary research in the area, which has led to departments broadening their membership to include anthropologists and sociologists, among other disciplines. As membership of these departments widened, the appeal of laboratory and anonymous scaled attitude measures declined. The result was a move away from a perception of the consumer as an automaton, receiving inputs and, through a process of maximization, producing outputs. The new consumer was perceived as a socially construing individual participating in a multitude of interactions and contexts. Within such a perspective the family is not a decision-making consumption unit, but a consumption reality involving hegemonic control, core and peripheral cultures and subcultures and relationships. Similarly if we consider goods and services within the paradigm of new consumption studies a product such as a hotel is not simply a system of sleeping and eating rooms, but can be seen as a venue for fun, prestige, power, sex, etc.

Belk's argument is taken up by Campbell (1995) when he suggests that, during the 1980s and 1990s, developments both within academia and within society at large have resulted in the sociology of consumption taking centre stage. As we have previously discussed, this may be the result of a commonplace view that contemporary society is grounded in consumption, rather than as previously in aspects of production. The use of the term 'consumer culture' is now widely expressed in a range of aspects of everyday life. Such a focus on a consumer society is taken to suggest that not only is the economy structured around the promotion and selling of goods and services rather than their production, but also that members of such a society will treat high levels of consumption as indicative of social success. As a result consumption will be seen as a life goal for members of such a society. This argument is confirmed by Ritzer (1999: 2) when he states: 'Consumption plays an ever-expanding role in the lives of individuals around the world. To some, consumption defines contemporary American society, as well as much of the rest of the developed world.'

Within the hospitality industry, and in hospitality education, consumption and consumer behaviour has not been well represented. The focus within hospitality has long been on marketing planning; witness the numerous textbooks that are available to students. In the few cases where consumer behaviour has been taken as a key focus of a book it is dealt with from a marketing perspective, viewing the consumer as the object rather than the subject of the text. Given that the prescribed focus of the hospitality industry is supposedly on the consumer, this seems to be a major oversight. A very small number of hospitality-based consumer behaviour texts are available, the best of which are probably those by Bareham (1995), which focuses on the consumption of food, and, albeit more in the field of tourism studies, Swarbrook and Horner (1999). In addition, Teare (1990; 1994; 1998) has written a large number of articles within this area, but many of these are firmly based in a modernist perspective of cognitive decision-making. In the main, however, consumer behaviour has been dealt with in one chapter of hospitality marketing textbooks; clearly, this is inadequate for such a complex phenomena.

When writing this text I have sought to avoid some of the difficulties indicated above. This text investigates consumer behaviour by emphasizing the behaviour of real consumers and then showing how marketers seek to influence that behaviour. The book, unlike many existing texts, is interdisciplinary in nature and provides critical analysis of consumer behaviour from a sociological, psychological, economic and historical background, while always grounding such analysis within the contemporary hospitality industry. In addition, the text takes the perspective that effective marketing involves focusing organizational activity on the consumer. Thus the book concentrates on an understanding of determining customer needs, the factors which are relevant in consumer buying behaviour and the effectiveness of many contemporary marketing techniques.

Summary

The chapter introduces and explores the role of consumer behaviour theory within the discipline of hospitality management, in order to assist students in understanding and applying the concepts of consumer behaviour to hospitality contexts and markets. This has been undertaken through defining consumer behaviour, considering the context of this book, that is, the contemporary hospitality industry, investigating a number of the reasons for the huge growth in interest in hospitality consumption and considering some of the means that have been used to research what is clearly one of the most important phenomenon of the contemporary industry. Many of the themes introduced within this chapter will be explored in greater detail throughout the remainder of this book.

Consuming hospitality services

Key themes

- Increasing attention has been paid in recent years to the marketing and consumption of services such as hospitality, a change brought about due to recognition that services are increasingly important in economic terms.

- Despite substantial evidence to the contrary, however, much marketing and consumer behaviour literature within hospitality management is predicated on the belief that goods, products and services are essentially the same and can be investigated as such.

- This chapter considers the consumption of hospitality services through an investigation of the contemporary literature, focusing on the ways in which the hospitality offer differs from that of physical goods.

Hospitality as service

Despite recent arguments, which suggest that services are increasingly important features of economic performance, there continues to be a debate as to whether the consumption of services, of which hospitality consumption is a part, differs significantly from that of consumer goods. As Gabbott and Hogg (1998:2) argue: 'Despite the myriad of evidence to suggest that services are becoming critical to economic growth in most developed economies, thus requiring some fairly substantial reflection from both business and government, marketing and its related disciplines seem remarkably insulated from this trend.' This debate has increased in importance, given the enormous growth in the service sector within the world's advanced industrial economies. As this growth has been fuelled by increasing living standards in western economies and rapid technological development, it is anticipated that the service sector will continue to thrive. Service industries are playing an increasingly important role in developed economies and now account for over 70 per cent of employment in many instances.

As this debate has arisen it is necessary for us to consider its implications for the consumption of hospitality services. In particular we need to investigate the reservations expressed as to whether hospitality services really are different or distinctive in consumption terms, especially to consumers. In doing so we will seek to answer a number of questions, including:

- Are the benefits consumers receive from consuming hospitality services more difficult to evaluate than those for physical goods?
- Is the process of developing, planning and delivering hospitality services significantly different from that for physical goods?
- How do we explain the relationships inherent in the 'service encounter'?
- Is all hospitality homogeneous and can it all be investigated in the same way?
- Do consumers behave differently when consuming services, such as hospitality, than when consuming physical goods?

Literature on the consumption of services, as distinct from it appearing as an afterthought in marketing textbooks, is a relatively new and very limited field. As Gabbott and Hogg (1998: 5) argue: 'There are very few examples of published works, which refer explicitly to the consumption characteristics of services. There would seem to be an assumption that consumer behaviour related to goods is the same for all products, i.e. the difference between goods and services is not significant to the consumer.' An appreciation of the difficulties posed by the consumption of services has largely developed during the last thirty years, with most contributions to the area having been developed since the late 1970s. Prior to this period services marketing was dealt with as an add-on to the marketing of goods. In much contemporary marketing literature, however, the marketing of services has been elevated to the position of an academic discipline in its own right. Despite this, many academic texts still make reference to the marketing of goods and services as if they were interchangeable. Within the discipline of hospitality management this problem is very evident, hospitality consumer behaviour and marketing texts largely comprise traditional concepts derived from the literature on goods and applied with little contextualization for the specific characteristics of hospitality (Calver, 1994; Teare, 1995).

I do not intend within this book to discuss in depth the evolution of services marketing or hospitality marketing and/or the role that services play in contemporary western economies. This subject has been the focus of many texts, including those by Zeithaml and Bitner (1996), Lovelock (1996) and Bateson (1996), and anyone wishing to pursue this aspect of services is directed to these texts. This chapter focuses on the demands that the consumption of services, with their associated characteristics, place on consumers of hospitality.

The nature of products, goods and services

Products

Central to all forms of marketing is some understanding of the concept of 'product'. As a result within the literature the concept of product has been extensively defined and evaluated. For example, Enis and Roering (1981: 17) define product as 'Any bundle or combination of qualities, processes and capabilities (goods, services and ideas) that a buyer believes will deliver satisfaction'. In a similar vein Gabbott and Hogg (1998: 20) suggest that 'Product is multi-dimensional and dependent upon how the buyer responds to different facets of the offering'.

One of the early key texts concerned with defining products and services was that by Levitt (1986) in which product is defined as a complex cluster of value satisfactions. Levitt considered product as having five elements or levels, starting with a central *core benefit*, defined as the essential benefit the customer is buying. Around this core Levitt identified four additional product levels: the *generic product*, the *expected product*, the *augmented product* and the *potential product*. Each of the elements Levitt identifies describes a different dimension of the product and, therefore, a different relationship with the consumer. When we are considering the case of the consumption of hospitality, however, we are only considering one of the possible product classes – that of services. This leads us to the question 'how, if at all, is the consumption of services different from that of other goods?'

Goods and services

As we have previously stated, there has been a discernible shift in the marketing and management literature towards an acknowledgement that services are distinctive and deserving of consideration in their own right. This has been fuelled by the enormous growth in service industries within western economies and their subsequent growing importance in economic terms. For example, it is argued that service industries now account for over 70 per cent of employment in many western economies (Gabbott and Hogg, 1998; Lovelock, 1996; Rust and Oliver, 1994).

Since the late 1970s a significant body of literature has grown up which seeks to challenge the orthodoxy that goods and services are one and the same, and to establish that services are different to other products and, as such, present specific challenges to marketers. This argument is supported through literature by authors such as Shostack (1977), Berry (1980), Bateson (1996) and Gabbott and Hogg, (1998). Within the hospitality sector these arguments have been rehearsed by authors such as Buttle (1986; 1992) and Crawford-Welch (1994). The argument exists due to the perceived differences between services and goods. As Shostack (1982: 51) observes: 'The difference between goods and services is more than semantic. Goods are tangible objects that exist in both time and space; services consist solely of acts or processes, and exist in time only. Services are rendered, goods are possessed. Services cannot be possessed; they can only be experienced, created or participated in.' This lack of ownership by purchasers of services is also emphasized by Kotler (1994: 111) who suggests 'Services encompass any activity or benefit that one party can offer to another that is essentially intangible and does not result in the ownership of anything'. Berry (1980) also follows this line of reasoning, suggesting that services are identified as deeds, performances or efforts, whereas goods are devices, things or objects.

Gabbott and Hogg (1998) suggest that the literature within services marketing can be seen to fall into three distinct schools, exemplified by the work of Lovelock (1981; 1996), Rushton and

Carson (1989) and Rust and Oliver (1994). These schools of thought can be considered bipolar in nature and are indicated in Figure 2.1. The first school (Lovelock, 1981; 1996; Mill, 1986) suggests that goods and services are intrinsically different and that the application of models, concepts and theories developed for goods cannot be applied with any confidence to services. They argue that the inherent differences between goods and services (Kotler, 1994; Shostack, 1982) mean that we must develop unique processes for services management. As such management within hospitality services needs new tools, techniques, strategies and structures in order to be effective. This body of knowledge argues services management must develop its own theoretical and conceptual approaches, which parallel those for other products. At the other extreme are those authors who argue that all marketing is situation specific and allows for only limited generalization, within common situational boundaries (Rushton and Carson, 1989).

Finally, there is a middle ground represented by the body of authority which suggests that whatever differences there are between goods and services, are of a limited nature and thus marketing practice, developed for goods, can be modified to serve the purposes of services (Rust and Oliver, 1994; Sasser, Olson and Wyckoff, 1978). Such authors argue that the differences between goods and services are exaggerated and provide little insight in understanding either of them. In addition, it is argued that customers do not buy physical experiences; they buy expectations or value satisfaction. As such it makes little difference whether the item purchased is physically present or not. This argument implies that marketing concepts and theories can be applied regardless of product type. However, it also concedes that there are a number of distinct characteristics displayed by services, which require these concepts and theories to be modified.

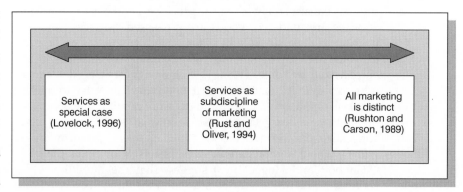

Figure 2.1 Bipolar representation of the service/goods marketing debate

According to Gabbott and Hogg (1998) it is this latter school that has largely been responsible for the development of the discipline of services marketing, to the stage whereby it now has its own conferences, journals and research base (see Fisk, Brown and Bitner, 1993, for a description of the way in which the discipline has grown). The problems of determining even the existence of a distinct discipline of services marketing is reflected in a wider argument, which considers whether there is such a thing as a service, which is sufficiently distinct from a good(s), as to require marketing. Authors such as Levitt (1976), Shostack (1982) and Kotler (1994) argue that we should not consider a separate service industry; there are only industries with more or less service elements. Such authors see the issue as one of a continuum from pure service products through to pure tangible products, the distinction as seen here would be between products where the core is a service and products where the core is a physical good.

An alternative to this perspective is offered by Rust and Oliver (1994) who suggest we consider all purchases as services, some of which involve a physical product, others that do not. Rust and Oliver's argument is based on the premise that all products, whether they are goods or services, deliver a service. As such a drink refreshes us; the drink is the physical product that delivers that service and, in addition to the physical product, we buy the service element (communication and the environment) and the service product (the drink's specifications). They argue all products are made up of this mix of elements, centred on the physical product, which is present for goods and not for services.

Despite these valid contributions, it is increasingly clear that a case exists for considering the consumption of services as distinct from those for goods, a case promulgated on the evidence that there are a number of fundamental characteristics of service products, which distinguish them from goods. However, a further problem within this issue of goods and services is identified by Gabbott and Hogg (1998: 26) when they state: 'While the management of services has been recognized as a distinctive activity, the consumption of services has never been disentangled from the goods literature.'

If we are to accept that there is a separate discipline of services consumption and to consider the ways in which it impacts on the consumption of hospitality services, we need to identify what the characteristics of hospitality as a service are that make it different from other products. However, as we have already discussed, the first problem we meet is that of determining a usable definition for services. Kotler (1994: 111) suggests the definition: 'Services encompass any activity or benefit that one party can offer to another that is essentially intangible and does not result in the ownership of anything.' The intangible aspect of services also features in the definition offered by Gronroos (1990: 27) who describes them as 'An activity or series of activities of more or less intangible nature that normally, but not necessarily, take place in interactions between the customer and the service employee and/or physical resources or goods and/or systems of the service provider, which are provided as solutions to customer problems'.

While this is a convenient catch-all definition, it does not help us to understand the consumption of hospitality services in any meaningful way. The easiest way around these definitional problems appears to be to return to the issue of identifying those characteristics that define the nature of services such as hospitality, based around the characteristics and dynamics of service environments. The service characteristics of hospitality include their intangibility, their temporal nature and their heterogeneity, while hospitality service dynamics are seen to include the simultaneous nature of production and consumption, short channels of distribution, the difficulties inherent in ensuring reliability and consistency, demand fluctuations and imprecise standards (Crawford-Welch, 1994).

Traditionally the characteristics of service have been classified under five main headings, namely: *intangibility, inseparability, heterogeneity, perishability* and *lack of ownership*:

1 *Intangibility.* Insubstantial, ethereal or without physical presence, this is probably the single most important factor, which distinguishes services from goods. As we have discussed, while it is possible to describe the nature and performance of physical products using objective criteria, this is very limited in the case of services. Intangibility has two dimensions – the inability to touch an item and the mental difficulty in accepting a concept or idea. Consumers cannot see, touch, hear, smell or taste hospitality services; they can only experience their performance. For example, if we consider the case of visiting a bar with friends it is clear that we can partake of a number of physical sensations, for example taste, sound, touch, etc. The whole performance of being in a bar with friends, however, is clearly much more than the sum of these sensations, and as such can only be experienced as a totality. As Gummesson (1987: 22) stated: 'Services are something which can be brought and sold but which you cannot drop on your foot.'

Services are often described as deeds, performances or efforts in order to differentiate them from goods, which are described using tangible nouns such as object or device. In this way it is argued that even though the performance of services is supported by tangibles, the essence of their performance is ephemeral; services are an abstract concept for consumers, meaning that they are highly subjective. The result is that customers have to search for tangible clues associated with a service in order to evaluate it.

If we consider the ways in which we use a hotel, for example, it is clear that while there are a number of tangible elements to its use (for example the bed, the restaurant, the bar, the food, etc.) the overall consumption is made up of more than simply these tangible aspects. It would, for example, include the atmospherics, our relationships with staff and other customers, our ongoing feeling of (dis)satisfaction, etc.

2 *Inseparability*. This refers to the lack of distinction between delivery and use, due to services being produced and consumed simultaneously. Linked to this is the role of the customer in service encounters, wherein they become part of the service, particularly for other customers. Consider visits to clubs, bars and restaurants. Our interactions with other customers and staff are as much a part of the experience as are the physical items we consume. Services are performances in which consumers voluntarily participate with producers, and the inseparability of the service from the consumer leads to problems in standardization, as both may alter the way in which the service is delivered. Due to inseparability it is impossible for hospitality organizations to standardize output and gain economies of scale in the same way that firms producing goods can. Hospitality services by their very nature need to be customized and focused on the needs and wants of consumers.

3 *Heterogeneity*. This refers to the ability to develop uniformity and standardization. Services are seen as heterogeneous, that is, variable, while goods are more uniform. As hospitality services are performed it is difficult to conclude with any certainty that people will perform in the same way during any two service encounters, particularly given the number of variables at play. Hospitality is delivered by individuals; therefore, each consumer is likely to receive a different service experience and this has clear implications for consumers and producers. As a result of this in-built variability, during the early days of hospitality management literature much store was put on seeking procedures for 'industrializing' services in order to achieve uniformity in service delivery (Lockwood and Jones, 2000). While such efforts to industrialize the hospitality industry were understandable from a control perspective, their

modernist stance always seemed likely to fail. Efforts to compare and contrast restaurants and bars on the basis of square footage, etc. (Ball, 1994) while ignoring the context within which they operated can in many ways be seen to be misguided.

4 *Perishability.* This means that services cannot be stored in the same way that goods can, with the result that unused capacity is lost for ever. The perishability of services such as hospitality means that demand fluctuations cannot be managed in the same way that it can for goods; consumers cannot simply stockpile services against future need. From a consumer perspective the time at which an act of consumption is made can be critical, the experience of using a restaurant or bar at a peak trading time is completely different to that experienced during a quiet period. Hotels and restaurants have traditionally recognized this feature of the industry by targeting different markets at weekends to those targeted during the week.

5 *Ownership.* As discussed earlier, this results in the customer only gaining access to the activity or facility, not gaining ownership of anything at the end of the transaction. Services are seen to offer satisfaction rather than tangible items, which can be demonstrated to others. If we consume a holiday, we have the benefit of travel, accommodation, food, location, etc. but we do not own these. According to Gabbott and Hogg (1998) the lack of ownership stresses the finite nature of hospitality services, that is, there is no enduring product only benefits.

It is suggested (Baker, 1995) that the original distinction between products and services was based on the view that goods are produced and services are performed. However, as we have seen, this rigid view has in many ways been superseded by the view that both goods and services have elements of tangible and intangible characteristics. Contemporary authors argue that consumers are not buying goods or services, but the value/ satisfaction of the offer. Buttle (1992), for example, applies Levitts's (1981) definition to hospitality services, arguing that customers seek intangible benefits regardless of whether the product is tangible or not. He uses the example of a restaurant meal to support this argument, suggesting that it is characterized by aspects, which are both tangible (for example, the food) and intangible (for example, the atmospherics). Buttle refers to the sum of these experiences as the 'catering product'. This approach is supported by Nightingale (1985) who describes hotels as a composite of activities and interactions each of which has physical and emotional content. If we consider a typical hospitality encounter, we can identify the characteristics that it is suggested make services sufficiently different from products as to warrant their own discipline within the field of marketing. First, in the majority of cases service operations are small-scale activities, albeit that many operate as part of large-scale organizations. If we consider a chain restaurant such as TGI Friday, for example, despite being part of a multimillion pound organization the restaurant itself is likely to be of a limited nature, especially when compared with Whitbread's myriad other activities. Second, service encounters provide a form of 'social role', as Czepiel, Solomon and Surprenant (1985: 9) suggest: 'Service encounters are a form of human interaction important not only to their direct participants and the organizations that sponsor them, but also to society as a whole'.

Finally, services include a high level of human interaction in the delivery of the service itself, commonly consisting of interactions between contact personnel and customers and between customers and other service users. Consider the complex interpersonal relationships that are occurring with every service encounter in the thousands of bars, restaurants and hotels that form part of the hospitality industry. Services such as hospitality are seen as having a people rather than a technology focus. This characteristic is seen by both service providers and authors in the field of services marketing as the key feature of services, as Baron and Harris (1995: 10) argue: 'In a service business you're dealing with something that is primarily delivered by people to people. Your people are as much a part of your product in the consumer's mind as any other attribute of that service. People's performance day in and day out fluctuates up and down. Therefore the level of consistency that you can count on and try to communicate to the consumer is not a certain thing.'

Given the weight of the arguments that hospitality services possess certain distinguishing features, which make them fundamentally different to goods, we will be considering consumer behaviour utilizing in the main literature that supports the development of a services discipline. As we will see during the course of this text, according to such an approach, the consumption of hospitality is more complex than that of goods, due to the characteristics identified.

Consuming services

In services marketing the point at which consumers come into contact with the service company is critical to success, and this service encounter has become known euphemistically as 'the moment of truth' (Carlsson, 1987). This moment, combining expectation, experience and knowledge in an interaction between consumer and staff, has been investigated by many authors including Bitner (1992), Hui and Bateson (1991) and Bateson (1996). Bateson (1996) drew a diagrammatical distinction between the visible and invisible parts of the organization, which sought to represent the combination of factors involved in the service encounter (see Figure 2.2), emphasizing that for many hospitality consumption activities the consumer is unaware of many of the organization's activities.

Aspects of interpersonal interaction between the service firm employees and consumers and considered critical in hospitality consumption, have been considered by a number of authors, including Czepiel, Solomon and Surprenant (1985) who identified them as:

1 *Service encounters have purpose and are not altruistic.* This excludes interactions, which are not goal orientated and are not intended ultimately to lead to financial reward. It can be argued that, in hospitality services, encounters happen which are not goal orientated and which do not directly lead to financial reward; for example, housekeeping. In such situations it is the overall service encounter which must be considered, not each individual exchange.

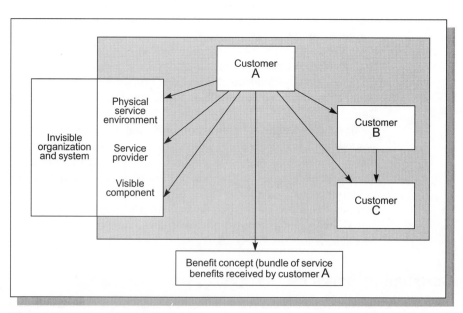

Figure 2.2 The servuction system
Source: adapted from Gabbott and Hogg (1998)

2 *Service encounters do not assume prior acquaintance.* As service encounters happen in contexts in which the interacting parties do not necessarily know each other, the normal rules of social exchange do not apply and strangers can converse without threat. It is common for customers in hospitality locations such as bars, restaurants and hotels to strike up conversations with service staff and other customers. Compare this with the behaviour of people on trains and buses where they stoically avoid meeting one another's gaze, never mind seeking a conversation.

3 *The service encounter provides behavioural boundaries.* The service being delivered constrains the details of the encounter and the aspects of the product form the boundaries for behaviour demonstrated. When working in a hotel an employee may not like a guest but will be necessarily polite and friendly during the service encounter. Similarly most, but not always all, customers understand and respect the boundaries to their relationships with staff.

Czepiel, Solomon and Surprenant identified the above characteristics in order that we might identify what we mean by service encounters. Understanding hospitality encounters involves us in an appreciation of a complex set of behaviours, which vary from service to service, defined by Klaus (1985) as an 'epiphenomenona'. As we have discussed, given the complexity of understanding the variables that go towards the hospitality encounter it is not surprising that it has proven impossible to define the attributes of good and bad service; suffice to say we all know them when we experience them.

In addition to the characteristics of services that we highlighted earlier it is suggested that the particular nature of services such as hospitality offers a number of dimensions which impact on consumer behaviour. These have been identified by various authors (Gabbott and Hogg, 1998; Lovelock, 1996; Zeithaml and Bitner, 1996) as time, physical proximity, participation, degree of involvement, degree of customization, service providers and setting. Each of these is now considered in more detail.

Time

Time is the first continuum upon which hospitality consumption can be discriminated. Hospitality is mostly concerned with service encounters, which are long, complex and involve a number of individual but linked interactions. Within hospitality, customers go through a number of service encounters, interacting with the same or a number of members of staff many times during the course of the service. If we consider the case of a hotel stay, for example, these encounters could go on for many days or even weeks. All these interactions will offer the consumer different experiences over a long period of time. It is these individual encounters within the overall service that are likely to be the key to whether individuals have a good or bad experience. Within hospitality, however, the dimension of time is highly differentiated. In the hotel stay example, the duration of time in which encounters can occur could be anything up to a couple of weeks. Compare this with the more limited time available in a busy bar or fast-food encounter.

Physical proximity

Zeithaml and Bitner (1996) identify three types of service encounter in terms of physical proximity: face to face, remote and remote personal encounters (such as those via a telephone or video link). As the personal contact element of hospitality is so central to its performance it is clear that the aspect of physical proximity becomes a key feature. The effect of having the hospitality provider and the customer in close physical contact, such as the face-to-face encounters that occur in reception areas, enables a great degree of customization of the service. This richness of the service experience is removed by moving towards a remote encounter, such as the automated, quick checkout billing systems routinely seen in many busy hotels, such as those at airports and those that primarily cater for the business sector. In such systems guests check their own bills on in-room televisions, porter their own luggage to the exit, before paying by credit card at a machine in the foyer. Such an automated routinized system does not allow for any customization or on-selling to take place. The developments taking place in e-commerce are a demonstration of the increasing availability of remote encounters, often only reverting to remote personal encounters when systems fail or consumers are seeking to customize specific offers. It is becoming commonplace for customers to book whole holidays on the World Wide Web, including flights, hotels and even sightseeing tours.

Participation

Hospitality service by its very definition involves customers in the product, albeit to varying degrees dependent upon the type of service being consumed. Participation is seen as being closely related to aspects of customization and physical proximity, in that increasingly customers are required to co-produce the service. If we again consider the automated billing systems in hotels, it can be seen that they reduce the need for reservations staff at peak times, staff that would perhaps not be needed later in the day. In a similar manner, customers in many restaurant chains such as Harvester are encouraged to fill their own salad bowls; the message to customers is a positive one, that is, you can select your favourite ingredients in whatever proportion you choose, however, this does not mask the fact that you are doing what was once a role of service staff.

Degree of involvement

Engagement has been widely used within consumer behaviour as a means of explaining choice and behaviour, and has recently been applied in a similar manner to services. It can be argued that different degrees of engagement are made by customers in respect of different types of service and also intra-multiple service encounters (Gabbott and Hogg, 1998). For example, it would seem a safe argument that consumers demonstrate higher levels of engagement with decisions about hospitality services such as restaurants and bars, than about utilities such as the supply of electricity. Similarly, consumers are likely to be more engaged in areas such as leisure facilities and restaurants than at check-in in hotels. The issue of involvement is a significant one within hospitality consumption and is discussed in greater depth later in this text.

Degree of customization

The degree of customization can be seen in two ways: the degree to which a customer interacts with the service (dependent upon the degree to which a customer can intervene in the service) and the degree to which a service is altered for specific customers (dependent upon the degree to which a service can be customized). The ability to customize services is often shown as a positive one, however, it is dependent on a number of variables such as the degree of knowledge customers have, the confidence customers have in the service provider and the risks involved in adapting standard goods and services. If we consider booking a holiday, for example, our knowledge is often limited to what the service provider gives us, as a result we tend to accept their 'expert' knowledge and would be unlikely to initiate the risk of customizing the service against their advise.

Service providers

Hospitality staff are critical in creating the experience consumers have of the service, to the extent that, as Zeithaml and Bitner (1996: 304) argue, 'the offering is the employee'. The employee is seen by consumers as embodying the attributes of the organization, so restaurants are judged by the performance of the host, the server and the billing staff, and these in turn are directly affected by such factors as expertise, attitude and demography (Czepiel, Solomon and Surprenant, 1985). The difficulty for hospitality firms in accepting the notion that 'the offering is the employee' is that, despite their best endeavours, their employees cannot be considered as standardized. Practices such as rote learning of responses has left hospitality firms such as McDonald's ('Do you want fries with that?') open to ridicule and are thankfully declining in popularity. Hospitality employees need to be able to express their individuality' after all, it is for many central to their role, especially in such venues as bars, restaurants and clubs.

Setting

Setting is seen as either encouraging approach or avoidance responses among consumers. However, this aspect of the service encounter is regarded as very difficult to research (Gabbott and Hogg, 1998), due to the difficulty in isolating environmental factors from other variables associated with the service encounter. In hospitality the physical design, atmospherics, ongoing activities and other aspects of the environment become very confusing for researchers of consumer behaviour. As a result very little research is available to aid understanding of the impact setting has on the behaviour of consumers of hospitality services.

It was the complexity of these aspects of the service encounter that led Klaus (1985) to describe them as an epiphenomenona, in that services are not prescriptive nor definitive but ephemeral. As such it is clear that the service encounter is central to an understanding of consumer behaviour in hospitality.

Summary: conceptualizing hospitality services

The first issue in conceptualizing the hospitality industry is to accept that it is not necessarily, or indeed very often, transaction based. Hospitality consumption comprises multiple interactions, often with very many people, some of whom may be consumers themselves, the whole of which forms an experience for the consumer. As such, hospitality services are not finite; they are chaotic and unpredictable, changing in nature for each consumer on a continuous basis, wherein even the basic set of products evokes different responses in different consumers. Hospitality as a service comprises a series of events randomly grouped together, each of which, regardless of size, can affect the consumer's overall perception of the service. Consumers of hospitality services do not necessarily make evaluations based on the sum of these experiences, but may generate an overall perception of the service based on one single episode in an encounter that comprises hundreds. As a result, for example, a hotel may deliver the promise they made but consumers will respond not to the overall performance of the service, but to a single incident in a bar on one night of their stay, and this event will have a disproportionate effect on their evaluation of the overall stay. For many hospitality practitioners and academics, this seeming chaos has encouraged a concentration on the individual components of the service encounter. This has been demonstrated by the desire to identify manipulable characteristics in order to seek control of the service environment. However, this fails to take account of two factors: first, the imbalance consumers place on individual events within an overall service encounter and, second, the lack of control that can be instigated once the service is put into the public domain.

As we indicated at the beginning of this chapter it is clear that the western world is currently embarked on a transition from an industrial to service-based economy. This has serious repercussions for managers in service industries, such as hospitality, the key one of which is how do consumers understand and interpret the messages they receive about services. This is considered in greater depth in the coming chapters.

The Key Perspectives Seen as Complementary to an Understanding of Hospitality Consumer Behaviour

Frameworks for considering hospitality consumer decision-making

- Hospitality consumer decision-making is a dynamic, complex phenomenon, in order to aid our understanding of it a range of explanatory models have been developed.

- Consumer decision models are abstract conceptions of reality; they simplify the variables involved in order to make them easier to explain.

- If we are systematically to investigate the hospitality environment in which we operate, then it is necessary that we understand the ways in which we make choices as individuals and groups.

- The study of hospitality consumer decision-making is concerned with the need to explain and make intelligible the environment in which such decisions are a continuous emphasis.

An introduction to consumer decision-making

The study of decision-making is at the centre of a number of disciplines, including economics, politics, systems theory, sociology and psychology. The study of decisions is concerned with choices in a complex environment, and each of these disciplines could argue a valid case that the focus of the processes involved lies within their area of study. The need to investigate the decision process is largely self-evident; if we are systematically to investigate the world in which we operate, then it is necessary that we understand the millions of choices we make as individuals and groups. The ordering of these decisions from individual and discrete, to comprehensible patterns, makes it more likely we are able to explain and replicate them. The study of decision-making is concerned with the need to explain and make intelligible the environment in which such decisions are a continuous emphasis.

There are four primary types of decisions that consumers of hospitality goods and services must make and these are highlighted in Figure 3.1.

Financial allocation involves choices of how to spend the moneys we have available, whether this is in the form of ready cash, credit cards or other borrowings. These decisions are made continuously, with individuals and households allocating spending for various hospitality goods and services. Individuals differ

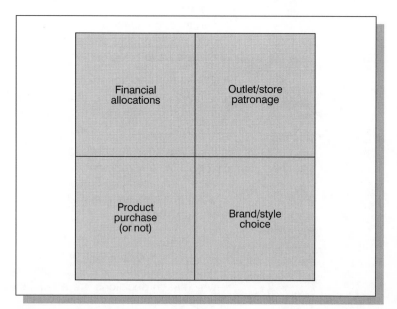

Figure 3.1 Hospitality decision types

as to how much consideration they give to budgetary constraints, some undertake extensive planning while others rarely give much thought to financial matters. The bulk of consumers, however, fall somewhere in between, budgeting for some purchases, for example holidays, while making other purchases in a more ad hoc manner.

Purchase or not decisions often reflect choices made with respect to individual products or between competing purchases, and it is this area of consumer behaviour that is of major interest to hospitality researchers. Researchers are interested in how these decisions are made. What influences these decisions? How are non-decisions made? How do consumers decide between alternatives? And other questions related to the purchase of hospitality goods and services. Once the consumer has decided to purchase goods or services the final two categories come into play.

Outlet/store patronage refers to the decision as to which outlet hospitality consumers will use to obtain their goods and services. In the contemporary hospitality market, as distribution channels have proliferated, this choice has become more complex, with contemporary consumers able to obtain goods and services from a wide range of distribution outlets, including retail stores, mail-order sites, satellite television and other forms of media, among others.

Finally, *brand and style decisions* refer to the specifications of the goods and services chosen, and again this area of consumer behaviour has received considerable attention by hospitality consumer researchers. Indeed, most recent consumer marketing literature has focused upon exploring consumers' brand and style decisions (Wilkie, 1994).

Modelling consumer decision-making

The unpredictability of consumption as it relates to hospitality lies in individual differences and the ways in which people categorize purchase decisions (Teare, 1998). In order to identify the interrelationships between influences, researchers develop frameworks or models, which are intended to portray the perceived relationships and thus enrich our understanding of the consumers' decision processes. Such models 'Represent the often-complex array of factors (or variables) which influence consumer decision-making. In essence models seek to simulate or approximate as realistically as possible the complications of consumer preference, choice and purchase behaviour' (Teare, 1998: 76).

The intention of developing models of decision processes and consumer behaviour is to attempt to identify, in a simplified

Hospitality, Leisure & Tourism Series

manner, the relationships between factors that influence behaviour. As Jennings and Wattam (1998: 133) argue: 'The idea that we can adopt a view of the world, examine it and discover its characteristics is at the heart of simulation.' Models are abstracts or simplifications of aspects of the 'real' world. The purpose of models is to simplify and identify aspects of decisions in order to make them more accessible for investigation. If, as an example, we consider the purchase of a meal, we first need to have some concept of what we value in a meal. We then need to identify a working definition of how we intend to judge one meal against another, for example taste, cost etc. and, having identified the criteria, we need to order these such that we can make our decision. This, in essence, is the modelling process – the act of simplifying reality in order to assist in the decision process, an activity that we are constantly engaged in from trivial decisions such as what sauce to have with our pasta, through to those decisions which fundamentally alter the way in which we interact with our environment. Models are essential to all investigations of consumer behaviour, whether they are models that consider the ways in which we structure and interpret the world or models used by researchers in order to explain the world.

Jennings and Wattam identified a number of reasons for building models or for simulating complex problems and these are indicated in Figure 3.2. Models can be developed in a number

Inevitable	There are no permanent dividing lines between facts about the system, and the beliefs held about that system. Models are theories, laws, equations or beliefs which state things about the problem in hand and assist in our understanding of it
Economic	The compression of the system into model form allows information to be passed, assessed and quantified, so that the ideas and beliefs contained within the model can be altered or modified at will. Thus there is a lower risk and use of resources than when experimenting with actuality
Simplification	When we build a model, of necessity, we overgeneralize and simplify in order to make clear those complex areas within the task at hand. By simplification we can ensure a close examination of those parts of the system that may prove contentious, or where an improvement in existing working is required.

Figure 3.2 Why build models?
Source: adapted from Jennings and Wattam (1998)

of ways, with the type of presentation being dependent on the systems we are trying to model and the purpose of the model, typically models can be constructed as:

- *descriptive models*, which provide a qualitative description and explanation of the systems we are trying to model; in other words they can be seen as a word picture of the problem
- *predictive models*, which are developed in order to estimate future performance, for example data collected over a period of time can be analysed to predict expected value
- *mechanistic models*, which describe the behaviour of a system, given inputs, outputs and the transformation process
- *empirical models*, which are generated by adding data to mathematical models, for example regression analysis or cost-benefit analysis
- *steady state models*, which map a system's average performance against time, for example in statistical analysis
- *dynamic models*, which seek to represent fluctuations of performance with time
- *local models*, which describe the individual sub-systems that form the model and thus the system.
- *global models*, which describe the whole model and thus the whole system.

It is anticipated that models assist us in investigating consumer behaviour in two ways. First, they allow for description, explanation, prediction and (some would argue), ultimately, control of consumer behaviour. Second, such models assist researchers in developing more adequate hypotheses and theories in respect of the relationships that influence consumer behaviour. However, as Bareham (1995: 3) suggests, 'most models of consumer behaviour are a long way from fulfilling either of these (intentions); most models are simply descriptive'. Such a view is supported by Swarbook and Horner (1999: 3) who suggest, 'The problem with the academic discipline of consumer behaviour is that while many general models have been advanced, there has been little empirical research conducted in order to test these models against actual behaviour patterns'.

This is particularly true in the hospitality sector where research on consumer behaviour is in a very early stage of development. However, despite their limitations it is apparent models have value in aiding our understanding of hospitality consumption. For example, it is generally accepted that their use is in appreciating the variety of factors that can have an influence on what would appear to be simple consumption decisions. Consumer behaviour models, which are often repre-sented as elaborate flow diagrams, simplify and abstract what it is assumed happens in reality. The formulation of the model facilitates the understanding of the problem itself and gives pointers to its solution. In summary, models allow researchers to test assumptions, ideas and alterations to the problem scenario itself.

Defining consumer decision-making

Before we can continue to consider in detail the dominant perspectives in consumer decision-making, we need to identify what we mean by the terms 'decision' and 'decision processes'. As we have already indicated, decision-making is an activity that is commonplace and undertaken by all individuals. As such it may appear unnecessary to define what we mean by the concept of a decision. However, it is the very commonplace nature of decision-making that necessitates our defining the subject because, as Jennings and Wattam (1998: 1) suggest, 'Our involvement in decision making often leaves misconceptions concerning the process that has taken place . . . it is such a vital and complex process that it justifies academic study and critical examination'. In many cases decision implies 'an act of choice between alternatives' (McGrew and Wilson, 1982: 4), however, most authors confirm that the act itself is not as static as the everyday conception of decision implies. Decision-making sug-gests the connotation of decisiveness, yet many decisions are taken over long periods of time and may involve many stops and starts during the process. It is considered that the decision is in fact the end-state of a complex dynamic process, consisting of a series of connected stages of activity, not a discrete action. In essence, when we refer to a decision we are referring to the 'final definitive solution in a problem solving process' (McGrew and Wilson, 1982: 4), whereas when we refer to the decision process we are referring to a framework that suggests decision-making is a sequence of activities, of which the decision itself is one stage (Wilkie, 1994).

Complexity in decision-making

When we discuss decision-making it is easy to view decisions as a homogeneous phenomenon; in reality, however, they vary enormously. One of the most important areas of difference is that of complexity in decision-making. Many decisions are simple in nature and thus easy to make, while others are more complex and thus more difficult to interpret. The nature of the decision process is different for both these cases, as aspects such as involvement, effort, time, learning and complexity all come into play. As we discuss later, the level of involvement is crucial in determining the type of decision process consumers undertake. High levels of involvement suggest that consumers will expend resources undertaking the decision, treating it as important, comparing brands, outlets, prices and styles. Where consumers demonstrate low levels of involvement, however, the decision processes will be entirely different; less effort will be given to information searching, limited comparisons will take place and consumers are more likely to buy on impulse.

In addition to involvement, the complexity of the decision process is influenced by the frequency of purchase, with many purchase decisions being repetitive in nature, whereas others are infrequent. Where consumers repeat decisions they are able to learn from their previous decisions, and this learning shapes their future actions. As a consequence, consumers are able to make a choice in full knowledge of the available options. Many authors have commented on this continuum of decision processes, Wilkie (1994), for example, refers to the continuum as containing three types of process:

1 *Extensive problem-solving*, which requires significant effort, takes time and is complex. Consumers need to understand and evaluate the features and attributes of particular hospitality service; they must develop a criteria for selection and they need to undertake extensive information searches. For many people, choosing their annual holiday would constitute a scenario requiring extensive problem-solving.
2 *Limited problem-solving*, which is an intermediate form of decision-making where typically the consumer has some information about the service but is unfamiliar with specific brands, styles, options or choices. The emphasis here tends to be on information searching. This category encompasses a wide range of decision-making and, according to Wilkie, characterizes most decision behaviour. The selection of venues such as restaurants exemplifies this type of decision for many people.
3 *Routine behaviour* is seen as the least complex form of decision-making. Consumers understand the services on offer, are aware of the options and have developed likes and dislikes. As a result consumers undertake limited information searches and decisions are reached quickly, such as when we frequent a local for an evening drink.

Generalized models of consumer decision-making

In considering the consumer decision process, it is often conceived of, and in particular modelled, as a process which is tidy and has in-built logic. However, as Jennings and Wattam (1998: 9) suggest, decision-making is a broad, complex, wide-ranging phenomenon with 'processes, which are difficult to identify and . . . model'. Wilkie (1994) suggests that implicit in the idea of a decision process is an element of staging or procedure, and argues that this view has become the dominant perspective on consumer behaviour in the last twenty years. As such it is assumed that the decision process involves a series of key stages, with most authors suggesting these would include the aspects identified in Figure 3.3. According to Wilkie (1994: 17), 'implicit in these stages is the concept that a consumer's selection would precede purchase, which would in turn precede usage and disposition'. The decision process framework, as envisaged by authors such as Wilkie, stresses that pre-purchase, purchase and post-purchase activities are all important features of the purchase process. This basic model can be developed further (Figure 3.4) to form a generally accepted normative model of the decision process. It identifies logically the steps taken in making a decision, and has become identified as a model which defines how a decision should be made.

The normative model assumes that the decision maker has an identifiable set of goals and objectives which can be developed in

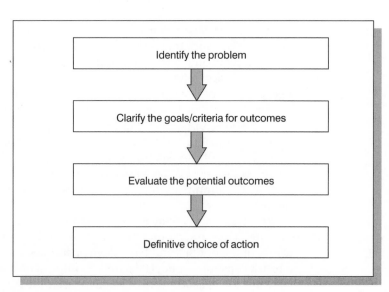

Figure 3.3 Stages in the decision process

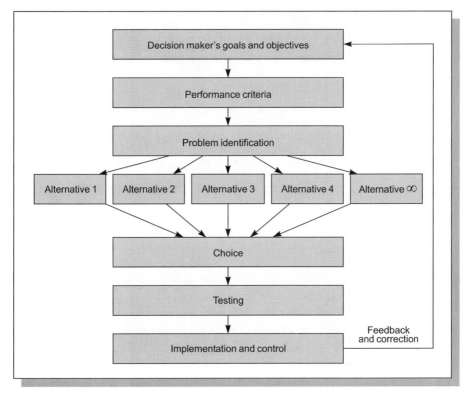

Figure 3.4 A normative model of consumer decision-making

order to provide definitive criteria, that is, clear definitions of how those objectives are to be measured. This leads to the defined problem identification, which in turn, it is suggested, leads to a search for alternative outcomes, conducted using a variety of means including memory, creativity, etc. Having considered the outcomes available a choice is made, which is then tested against the criteria prior to implementation, before the final activity, that of monitoring the decision in order to ascertain its development, is undertaken. As we discuss later, in reality this sequential approach is a very simplistic way of viewing consumer decision-making; the making of decisions is actually much more complex.

Comprehensive models of consumer decision behaviour attempt to encompass the wide range of factors that have an influence on decisions to consume. One of the seminal texts in this area and one which, although considerably updated, remains a key text in the field, is that of Engel, Kollatt and Blackwell (1968). The model's value, however, is limited by the fact that it

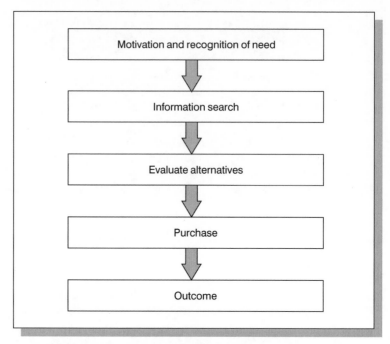

Figure 3.5 Basic Engel, Kollat and Blackwell (EKB) model of consumer decision-making

is descriptive rather than predictive, and was developed primarily to consider the purchase of high-risk items. The basic model is highlighted in Figure 3.5.

Stage 1: motivation and recognition of need. This is seen as the commencement of the decision process, for example, a person needs to purchase food to assuage hunger. Engel, Blackwell and Miniard (1995) recognize a number of key determinants of need, including individual differences, environmental influences and information stored in the memory. These are wide-ranging determinants that encompass a variety of social, cultural and individual factors, some of which are indicated by Figure 3.6.

Stage 2: information search. The second stage is the search for information about possible purchase choices, the extent of which may be a feature of how important or routine the decision is seen to be by the decision maker. Potential sources of information are considered, including the media, friends, relations or other significant influences, with external messages dominated by a range of marketing sources, including sales persons, point of sale material and other forms of advertising, etc.

Stage 3: alternative evaluation. Having considered the range of alternatives available, the potential consumer then evaluates each in terms of gains and losses, this consideration being based on the range of criteria that the consumer has developed as being important to the particular decision. These criteria, it is suggested, stem from more general beliefs, attitudes and intentions that the decision maker holds. However, as Foxall (1992) suggests the act of consumption is not a simple single activity; it is a complex selection involving subdecisions regarding time, place, method of payment, etc.

Stage 4: consumption and outcome. Having evaluated the outcomes, the consumer chooses the product and as a result is either satisfied or dissatisfied. At this stage the level of satisfaction is open to change, the consumer may, for example, overstate the positive features in order to reduce anxiety. Alternatively, the consumer may regret making the choice and therefore accentuate the negative aspects of the product.

It should be recognized that this model, while forming the basis of many future developments within decision-making, has been widely criticized; in particular the model is seen as being too complex and having limited predictive capacity. In addition, it is suggested that the model does not define relationships that occur within the decision process (Bareham, 1995). However, the model is a useful introduction to the subject of consumer decision-making as it does emphasize the role of environmental

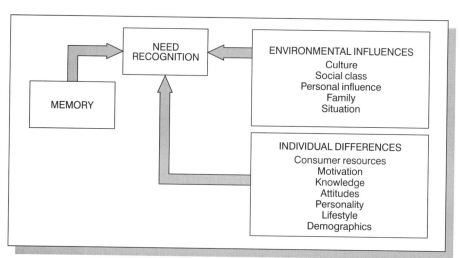

Figure 3.6 Social, cultural and individual factors which impact on consumer decision-making

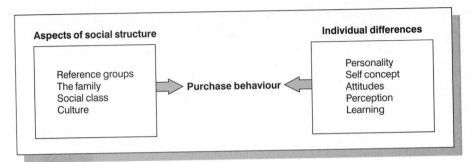

Figure 3.7 Foxall's model of purchase behaviour

and social influences on decisions; also the model can be seen to consider the internal decision processes and to link all of these within one overview.

Foxall (1980) further considered the EKB model, focusing on the clusters of factors that it is suggested influence purchase behaviour, in order to simplify these relationships. Foxall focused on identifying aspects of social structure and individual difference within the decision process as identified in Figure 3.7.

Hospitality decision making

The models considered up to this point have been general models of consumer behaviour. Within this text, however, the focus of consideration is concerned in particular with consumer choice as it relates to the choice of hospitality services, for example the use of public houses, the choosing of a holiday or the choice of restaurant to frequent. A number of studies have been undertaken into the variables that have an effect on our choice of food and drink. Shepherd (1989), for example, listed a range of these factors, dividing them into three categories, namely *physical* (for example, geography, seasonality, economics and food technology), *social* (for example, religion, custom, class and education) and *physiological* (for example, heredity, allergy, diet, acceptability and nutrition). A second author, Shepherd (1989), developed a generalized model of food choice suggesting that there were two major sets of influences, individual differences and the food itself, which in turn combined to have an influence on acceptance or rejection behaviour.

Other authors have suggested similar models, many of which demonstrate common features, including those of Khan (in Shepherd, 1989) and Randall and Sanjur (in Shepherd, 1989). These models all include such features as the identification of cultural and socio-economic factors, personal and individual characteristics such as age, gender and personal circumstance, and factors that are intrinsic to the food itself, for example taste, appearance and preparation.

The models discussed, along with a number of similar models of general consumer decision processes, are instrumental in identifying and defining components of the decision process and the nature of the relationships, which may occur. However, the same criticisms can be made for these models as for the more generalized models identified earlier in that they are descriptive and, in essence, list the factors that it is suggested affect purchase behaviour, without suggesting how they could be used in a predictive capacity. In addition there is a danger inherent in many of these models that drawing arrows connecting boxes in this manner may indicate causal relationships that may not be apparent (Bareham, 1995). As a result attempts to validate these models have met with only limited success and their utility remains questionable. In particular, their complexity and unreliability as a means of predicting behaviour give cause for concern.

Generalized models of hospitality consumption

As has been indicated by many of the models outlined above, it is suggested that consumers form a hierarchy of expectations and needs, related in part at least to the environment in which the decision is made. The difficulty with an investigation into consumer decision processes in hospitality, as highlighted earlier, is that the environment in which decisions are made is one that demonstrates high levels of variability and intangibility within the service itself. Within hospitality the period of consumption can range from one of a few minutes in the case of a fast-food product, to one lasting several days and nights when one considers hotel stays. It is clear that, given such a wide and complex range of possibilities, consumer wants and needs will be varied, dependent upon such factors as situation, circumstance, expenditure, etc. Teare (1998) suggests that hospitality services have both physiological and psychological roles to fulfil, with the consumer concerned with the desire to satisfy basic functional needs such as thirst and hunger, alongside more complex needs such as identity, group membership, status, etc. However, as hospitality services can vary chronologically as previously discussed, a sophisticated form of consumer evaluation is required, due to the accumulation of a succession of transient experiences and interactions. Teare goes on to develop a hypothetical model of the consumer decision process for hospitality services, focusing on the proposition that, as hospitality services are largely undertaken for social reasons, the decision process is likely to be characterized by joint and family decision-making and thus may involve greater degrees of caution. Figure 3.8 demonstrates this model. Teare (1998: 79) argues that hospitality consumption should be defined beyond generalized models, as models of hospitality consumption need to reflect 'the relatively high investment cost of hospitality services, given that the return on investment (in the form of benefits derived) is

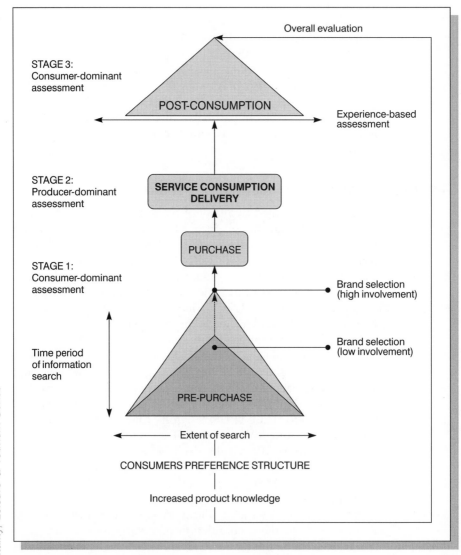

Figure 3.8 The consumer decision process for hospitality services
Source: adapted from Teare (1998)

mainly intangible . . . that satisfaction is derived from transient impressions and experiences . . . (and) the consumer's psychological state of mind is likely to affect the way in which the consumer approaches subsequent purchase decisions'. Teare's model is essentially a three-stage model based around pre-purchase behaviour, purchase behaviour and post-purchase behaviour, and we will consider each of these stages in some detail.

Pre-purchase stage

At this stage hospitality consumption decisions can first be seen to be a continuum from complex decision-making through to habit. Consumers are required, on the one hand, to base decisions on complex cognitive processes of information search and evaluation, while, on the other hand, little or no decision processing seems to take place where a consumer is satisfied with a particular product and purchases it regularly.

This bipolar aspect is dissected by a second continuum – risk, that is, those products that are seen as high-involvement purchases and those that are seen as low-involvement purchases. These two continua can be seen to generate four types of consumer purchase processes (Figure 3.9).

The first of these processes, complex decision-making, takes place when involvement is high and decision-making occurs. Examples might include a choice of holidays, restaurants or theme parks. However, these might also include choosing a bar, if the decision is sufficiently important to the consumer. For complex decisions, consumers require time to search for information and to process it in detail. They use this information to

	HIGH-INVOLVEMENT PURCHASE DECISION	LOW-INVOLVEMENT PURCHASE DECISION
DECISION-MAKING (information search extensive)	COMPLEX DECISION (holidays, restaurants, theme parks)	LIMITED DECISION (beer brands, bowling alley, cinema)
HABIT (limited information search)	BRAND LOYALTY (hotel chain, pub brand, fast-food outlet)	INERTIA (snacks in bars, beer brands (for some people))

Figure 3.9 A continuum of hospitality consumer purchase processes

evaluate and consider alternatives, applying specific criteria, for example, in the case of hotels, price, location and service quality.

When the consumer makes a choice in low-involvement conditions, it is likely to be characterized by limited decision-making. Some decision processes will be undertaken, as consumers may have little experience of the service, however, the information search is likely to be limited with few brands being evaluated. In addition, where involvement is low, brand loyalty may be limited. Examples in hospitality may include venues such as cinemas, where the choice of film on offer may be more important than the venue itself.

Complex or even limited decision-making may not occur every time consumers make a purchase; when the choice has become repetitive consumers learn from previous experience and tend to buy the brand that has given most satisfaction in the past. Such brand loyalty is the result of repeated satisfaction and/or a strong emotional commitment to a particular brand. Brands proliferate throughout the hospital industry and are a key feature of the contemporary industry. Indeed, as we discuss later in this book, it could be argued that in many ways brands define the contemporary industry.

The last-choice process is that of inertia – low involvement with the product and no decision-making. Inertia suggests consumers purchase the goods and services that they do because it is not worth the time or effort to seek alternatives. Within hospitality, examples of inertia are perhaps limited. However, for some people, myself included, the choice of beer brand consumed, for example, could be considered inertia as it tends to be a repercussion of my choice of public house.

The pre-purchase stage within hospitality consumption is influenced by a number of factors, including the consumers' preference structure, issues in respect of information searching, prior knowledge, the level to which consumers are involved with products and services, and levels of perceived risk. However, before any of these come into play the need for a decision or the recognition of a problem has to exist.

Problem recognition represents the start of the decision process. It is at this point that consumers perceive the need for hospitality goods and services, and become motivated to consume. Other stages in the decision process cannot be undertaken until a problem has been recognized. It is argued Wilkie (1994: 482) that 'problem recognition takes place when consumers perceive a gap or discrepancy between their current state and their desired state'. Wilkie goes on to suggest that problem recognition is caused by one of two factors: either a change in the desired state

Changes in Desired State	Changes in Current State
■ New need circumstances ■ New want circumstances ■ New products available ■ Purchases of other products ■ Marketing inputs	■ Depletion of stock ■ Dissatisfaction with current stock ■ Decrease in finances ■ Increase in finances ■ Marketing inputs

Figure 3.10 Key stimulators of problem recognition
Source: adapted from Wilkie (1994)

or a change in the current state of the consumer. Figure 3.10 demonstrates the major causes of these changes according to Wilkie.

Major causes leading to changes in the desired state ● ● ●

1 *New need circumstances* arise from changes in our daily circumstances whereby new categories of consumer need arise, for example when we have children the types of hotels and restaurants we use differ from those we use in our late teens.
2 *New want circumstances* notes some distinction between wants and needs; often new circumstances can create new wants, for example new friendships may lead us to want to travel overseas or to begin to frequent the theatre, etc.
3 *New products* are continually being put on the market by companies keen to encourage new purchasers. The act of marketing encourages problem recognition for products consumers had perhaps not previously considered; this increases our desired state for the new product. The huge growth in the alcopops (spirit-based soft drinks) market can be seen to be the result of licensed retailers marketing their new products in an aggressive manner.
4 *Purchases of other products* often lead to instances of problem recognition, for example if we are in a bar having a drink we are likely to recognize the opportunities for consuming meals or snacks, playing the slot machines or putting our favourite music on the jukebox.
5 *Marketing inputs* are primarily aimed at affecting our levels of desired state; so, for example, the advertising of summer holiday brochures twelve months before the intended departure increases our desire for our next holiday. Another example

would be that television advertisements for beer products are often screened between 8.30 pm and 9.00 pm in order to affect the behaviour of watching consumers.

Major causes leading to changes in the current state • • •

1 *Depletion of stock* refers to using up the available supply of goods or services, through consumption, and is the most common cause of problem recognition. For example, if we are hungry we recognize the need to eat, and head to the nearest McDonald's or food outlet of our choice.

2 *Dissatisfaction with current stock* occurs when we perceive that our current goods and services are inadequate to meet our needs. Traditionally, clothing and fashion are common examples, and within the hospitality industry fashionable bars and restaurants are equally valid examples.

3 *Decrease in finances* encourages us to reduce spending, usually through a reduction in discretionary purchases. Thus decreases in finances lead us to spend less in bars and restaurants, opting for cheaper meals and perhaps consuming at home.

4 *Increase in finances*, by comparison, allow us to rethink our spending patterns positively, opting for more expensive holidays, restaurants and leisure activities.

Preference structure • • •

By preference structure we are referring to the individual differences between consumers of hospitality products and services that are deeply embedded in aspects of personality, socialization, perception and learning, and combine to define our preference structure. Teare (1994) suggests three factors define consumer behaviour within the preference structure: cognition (the mental processes of knowing, perceiving and judging, cognition enables individuals to map a subjective view of the world which is based on personal beliefs, values and experience), learning (changes in behaviour which arise from the acquisition of skills, knowledge and evaluation) and motivation (the general drivers that direct consumer behaviour towards the attainment of needs and goals). If we consider hospitality consumption, preference structure is likely to be influenced by such aspects as cultural norms and values, family influences, reference group influences, financial standing and perceived social status. These aspects form and are influenced by differences within the consumer's own personality, lifestyle, perceptions and motivations. Considerable research has been undertaken in order to explain buying behaviour in terms of these characteristics, however, the empirical evidence is weak, as Kassarjian and Sheffet (1981: 181) argue: 'the correlation or relationship between personality test scores and consumer behaviour variables such as product choice, media exposure, innovation, segmentation, etc., are weak at best and thus of little value in prediction'.

Information searching • • •

The extent of the pre-purchase search behaviour undertaken by hospitality consumers is largely determined by individual preference, availability and accessibility of the information, and the range of acceptable purchase options. This is again related to factors such as perceived benefit, brand preference, power, knowledge, perceived risk, experience, finance, time available and the range of alternatives. As we have stated previously, search activity is likely to be greater when consumers believe a purchase is significant; less so when the purchase is routine. If we consider consumers buying holidays, it is likely that they will spend a significant proportion of time searching for information, given the perceived risk and the amount of money they will be spending. If we compare this with using a bar or restaurant, the perceived risk is likely to be significantly lower, the spend will be significantly lower and, thus, the information search is likely to be more limited. In addition, the extent of the information search can vary, dependent upon whether the information searches take place in the external environment or are limited to an individual's long-term memory. This process is largely determined by the type of consumption we are making, for example, loyalty, brand awareness, impulse buying, etc. all impact upon the decision process. Routinely, studies suggest that consumers do not engage in extensive information searches; however, this should not be taken as evidence that consumers lack concern. It may simply indicate that they feel confident with the information they have.

Traditionally, when we refer to consumer information searching, it is with the understanding that the information will reduce consumer uncertainty. However, in some instances information can lead to increases in uncertainty as consumers learn more about goods and services; thus increased availability of information can lead to dissonance among consumers. Consider, for example, the feeling engendered when we go into a restaurant, which has a huge range of menu items from which we have to choose, then an equally wide selection of wines for our consideration. In such situations it would not be surprising for consumers to demonstrate a certain lack of dissonance.

Information is seen to serve consumers in a number of different ways (Evans, Moutinho and Van Raaij, 1996), for example:

1 Consumers may expect to take better decisions after information acquisition and processing.
2 Information is seen to reduce perceived risk.
3 Consumers may be more confident after using information.
4 Information processing identifies desirable alternatives and rules out undesirable options.
5 Information is used as a defence mechanism in justifying a decision after it has been made.

Consumer information can be generated from one of two sources, either an internal or external search of information. Internal information, as stored in our memory, uses information from previous learning and experience that may be suitable for similar decisions. External sources of information employs information generated from mass media, retailers, conversations with others and observation. We discuss information searching in more detail in later chapters. It is generally assumed that more information leads consumers to make a 'better' decision, due to an expectation that decisions are based on reasoning, rationality and documentation. However, as we shall see, consumer decisions are often based not on reasoning or rationality but on affective factors such as branding. Despite this, research suggests (Evans, Moutinho and Van Raaij, 1996) that consumers feel more confident after acquiring information, even if they do not use the information to reach a decision. For example Jacoby et al. (1974) found that consumers use only a small part of the information that is available to them, however, they are more confident if a significant amount of information is made available.

Prior product knowledge • • •

Familiarity with a given product of service is likely to increase the confidence consumers have about the purchase decision; where consumers have little or no previous experience of hospitality services this is likely to generate significant information searching. When consumers are determining which restaurant to use their previous experience can be seen to be highly influential in the decision.

Product involvement • • •

Product involvement is difficult to determine, as it comprises factors such as interest, emotion, arousal and attachment. Within hospitality this variable as much as any other characterizes the complexity of the decision process. It is perceived that low-involvement purchases involve mostly passive information processing, whereas purchases with high personal involvement, such as those involving status and value, warrant far greater levels of information processing. Assael (1998) suggests that involvement depends on several factors:

1 *It is important to the consumer.* This is more likely when it links to the consumer's self-image, it has symbolic meaning tied to the consumer's own values, it is expensive or it has a vital functional role.
2 *It has emotional appeal.* As we see later, consumers do not only look for function in products, they seek emotional benefits from their choices. For many people having been to a Planet Hollywood restaurant offers kinship with other like-minded individuals, which goes far beyond the functional benefits of eating a burger in a themed restaurant.
3 *It is continually of interest to the consumer.* Fashion-conscious consumers, for example, have an ongoing interest in bars and clubs; they know which are in and which are out, and make choices as a consequence.
4 *It entails significant risk.* This might include financial risk, emotional risk, physical risk or social risk. For many people the purchase of their main annual holiday represents a significant risk on many of these factors, and as such can be seen to be a high-involvement choice.
5 *It is identified with the norms of a specific group.* As we consider later in this book, products can be seen as badges for some consumers. This explains the huge merchandising opportunities for companies such as Disneyland Paris or Planet Hollywood. It is important for consumers to be able to badge their choice, and due to the temporal nature of the product itself this can only be done through the use and wearing of merchandising which confirms the purchase.

Purchase/consumption stage

The outcome of evaluation is an intention to purchase/consume or not to purchase/consume. If the intention is to consume, it is likely a number of other choices now come into play. If we consider the choice of hotel to stay in, for example, we now have choices such as how to pay for our stay – cash or credit – or we may have to decide which services to opt for and which to decline – for example, do we want a dinner, bed and breakfast rate, or simply a room rate.

The decision may be made not to consume, or the decision process may be terminated or interrupted before its conclusion. For example, by the time we have evaluated all the options when choosing a hotel, the situation may have changed and no room be available. Assael (1998) suggests that a number of factors might lead to consumers delaying decisions or choosing not to consume, including a lack of time to make the decision, an emotional response to the product, a concern about the social risk of the purchase, an ego risk, worry that the product may not work, a lack of adequate information on which to base their choice or a belief that better value will be obtained at a later stage.

Rules in decision-making • • •

Decision rules refer to the guiding principles or frameworks that develop as we become experienced consumers. A number of these basic strategies, known as heuristics, have been identified, they operate as rules of thumb, aiding in the decision-making process. Heuristics provide guidance while we are making decisions; they do this through offering short cuts to decision-making by allowing us to use only part of the information available, acting as simple guidelines that we use to reduce mental efforts in processing information. While it is recognized that such short cuts bias the decision process by not allowing consumers to use all the available information, we appear willing to accept such a limitation as a means of dealing with a complex world. As a result consumers are said to *satisfice* their decision-making, that is, to settle for less than the optimal decision. Where a hospitality product, such as a hotel, which has given us satisfaction in the past, is subsequently chosen again, this can be seen as a relatively simple choice process. If when choosing hotels we subsequently opt for this same hotel, it may become established as part of a buying sequence; it thus becomes a rule, which can be applied to subsequent decisions. This is a simple form of heuristics. While as individuals we use a number of heuristics, three general heuristics are most commonly identified (Bazerman, 1998), namely:

1 *The availability heuristic.* This suggests that we assess the likelihood of an event happening by the degree to which occurrences of the event are readily available in our memory. Thus, events that evoke emotion, are vivid or easily imagined, will become more accessible from memory than an event that is difficult to imagine, vague or unemotional. For example, the

subordinate with whom a manager has contact is most likely to receive a negative appraisal, as the manager is more likely to be aware of his or her errors.

2 *The representativeness heuristic.* This suggests we assess the likelihood of an event's occurrence by the similarity of a recurrence to stereotypes of similar occurrences. Thus, for example, we predict a person's performance based on the performance of others whom that person represents to us, or we predict the performance of a service based on the similarity of that service to past successful and unsuccessful services.

3 *The anchoring and adjusting heuristic.* This suggests we make assessments by starting from an initial value and adjusting this to yield a final decision, with historical precedents often generating the initial value. For example, managers when considering salary adjustments take as the start point not what the job is worth, having undertaken some form of job evaluation, but what the present incumbent or most suitable applicant is earning.

Heuristics are the cognitive tools we use to simplify decision-making; we adopt them because on average any loss of quality of decision is outweighed by the time they save. However, it should be recognized that they represent a flawed decision process; we are not weighing up all of the available information and, more often than not, we are not even aware that our decisions are being influenced by these guidelines.

Problem framing • • •

Studies have demonstrated that the way in which we frame problems has an impact on the decisions we arrive at. Consumers are sensitive to the way in which they perceive a problem and in the connections they make; even minor amendments to the framing of problems can have a significant impact. Typical studies demonstrate that reference points impact upon a decision process; for example, we are more willing to pay premium prices for drinks in a hotel than in a supermarket, as our reference points are different for both these situations. When we are making decisions outcomes are evaluated relative to a reference point; consequently the location of that reference point is critical to the way in which we perceive likely outcomes. The concept of framing, linked to that of prospect theory (Bazerman, 1998), has enormous implications for the study of consumer decision-making. In trying to investigate the ways in which consumers operate, these inconsistent reasonings complicate our understanding. As Dawes (1988: 273) suggests:

'there is much uncertainty in the world, one of our basic choices is whether we accept that uncertainty as a fact or try to invent a stable world of our own'.

Post-consumption stage

Levels of satisfaction provide the link between expectation and experience, and relate directly to repurchase decisions. Satisfaction is seen to occur where consumers' expectations are met and there are limited signs of dissatisfaction. It is seen to be measured against experience and norms. Satisfaction reinforces positive attitudes towards a product, leading to a greater likelihood of repeat consumption. By contrast dissatisfaction will lead to negative attitudes and will lessen the likelihood of repetition. Thus, we are unlikely to return to a restaurant where we have experienced a poor meal or low levels of service quality.

In many cases, having made a decision consumers may feel insecure about their choice. Such post-purchase dissonance is uncomfortable for people and so there is a tendency to try to reduce doubt through confirming the benefits of the decision reached. One of the ways in which we can understand post-purchase evaluation is through cognitive dissonance theory (Festinger, 1982). Used in this way dissonance theory suggests that marketers should seek to reduce dissonance by ensuring consumers have a ready supply of positive information post-consumption. This may, for example, include additional product information and positive advertising, warranties and guarantees, comprehensive complaints handling procedures, reassurance about the quality aspects of the consumed item and following up the purchase with direct contacts in order to ensure consumer satisfaction. An example of this is common in many hotel companies today, where, once you have settled into your room, guest services contact you to ensure that your room is satisfactory and you have everything you need. As hospitality is often a high-risk, high-involvement product, it is imperative that strategies are put into place to ensure that consumer dissonance is minimized. Strategies such as those identified above are designed to change consumer attitudes towards the hospitality service by reducing post-consumption insecurity.

However, in addition to the strategies businesses put in place in order to reduce dissonance, people also introduce their own strategies for reducing any feelings of insecurity they may display. Wilkie (1994) suggests that they do this in a number of ways including:

- by ignoring dissonant information
- by selectively interpreting any information about their chosen product
- by lowering their levels of expectation
- by seeking out positive information about their chosen product
- by seeking to convince others they have made a good choice, and thereby convincing themselves.

If we consider the choice of a holiday, for example, having made our decision and purchased our holiday we will have certain expectations from it. If when we arrive our room is worse than expected we will experience dissonance. However, if other aspects of the holiday exceed our expectation and therefore overall the disparity between our prior expectations and subsequent performance is limited, we experience an assimilation effect. As a result we tend to ignore the defects of the service and overemphasize the positives, in order to reduce dissonance. However, if, for example, in addition to the room failing to meet our expectations the food in the restaurant was also below standard, a contrast effect may take place. In such a scenario consumers magnify poor performance, so that, even if the rest of the hotel was well above expectation, the focus is on the poorly performing aspects.

Consumer satisfaction has become a key objective for contemporary organizations, and has become one of the most researched areas within marketing and consumer behaviour. This is in a large part a result of research that tends to suggest that the financial benefits of loyal, satisfied customers can be considerable. Lashley (2000: 13) for example suggests that, 'whilst estimates differ, every sector of the hospitality industry reports that there are substantial savings to be gained from existing customers'. Lashley goes on to quote Carpenter (1992) who estimated that in the hotel sector it costs seven times more to attract new customers to a business than to retain existing customers. Other research within this area, conducted by Leach (1995), argues that the costs of dissatisfied customers can be very high, estimating that in 1995 it cost an average of more than £11 000 for each customer lost to a business. Consumer satisfaction/dissatisfaction refers to the emotional response we generate as consumers when we evaluate goods or services, and Wilkie (1994) suggests it has five key elements:

1 *Expectation* that is generated during the pre-consumption stage, as consumers develop an understanding of what they expect from goods and services. It is these understandings or

expectations that are taken forward by consumers into the consumption and post-consumption stages.

2 *Performance* is experienced during consumption, when consumers perceive performance on the dimensions they consider important.

3 Comparison is undertaken when consumers compare expectation and performance.

4 Confirmation/disconfirmation is the result of the above comparison.

Consumer satisfaction/dissatisfaction is in most cases relatively straightforward. Consumer satisfaction is likely to occur when performance meets or exceeds expectation. However, if performance falls below expectation, dissatisfaction occurs. In reality, of course, the situation can be much more complicated, depending upon factors such as the level of experience consumers have with the services they choose and the degree to which consumers are able to set expectations or determine performance. If, for example, we regularly use a restaurant and have developed an expectation of the very high standard of service one receives, any decline from this point is likely to be noted, this would not be the case were this our first visit.

Should consumers be dissatisfied the question is what action do they take? The answer seems to be that there is a range of activities they initiate, from at the extremes doing nothing through to making a formal complaint to an outside agency, such as an ombudsman. Within this range, however, are actions that can directly impact on hospitality businesses, such as avoiding the service in the future or passing negative comments about the service to friends and others. Linked to this aspect is the question, what leads people to complain when they are dissatisfied with a service? The answer appears, however, to be complex, involving such issues as the level of dissatisfaction, the importance placed on the service by the consumer, the likelihood of redress and the personal characteristics of those involved (for example, research suggests that educated people are more likely to seek redress).

Summary

Consumer decision-making is central to our understanding of how consumers behave. However, it is not a uniform process. It involves active and passive information searching, cognitive aspects such as information processing and issues such as dissonance and satisfaction. Factors such as habit, involvement and complexity further cloud our understanding of the process.

In order to aid our understanding of this complex phenomena, a range of models have been developed which seek to identify the factors involved in consumer decision-making and the relationships between them. The purpose of these models is to provide description, explanation and, ultimately, prediction of consumer behaviour. The models accomplish this through providing conceptual and theoretical frameworks that allow researchers to test a range of alternative explanations. Most models of consumer behaviour, particularly those developed as generalized models of hospitality consumption, take the form of computer flow diagrams, and provide little more than a description of the likely factors involved. They are valuable in that they offer an organizational framework describing the decision process, which aids discussion of what is clearly a complex phenomenon. However, as Bareham (1995: 13) states, 'most models can be criticized as providing no more than a description of a range of influencing variables. There is a danger that the mere drawing of boxes and arrows, which show links between variables, may imply causal relationships which do not exist'. This warning should be borne in mind as we continue to investigate consumer behaviour in the hospitality industry.

Individual processes in consuming hospitality

- The focus of this chapter is on the hospitality consumer as an individual, investigating how cognitive processes influence consumer behaviour.

- We will consider such aspects as perception, personality, learning, memory, meaning, motivation and trait theory, and how these impact upon hospitality consumer decision-making.

- We will consider how hospitality consumers acquire, organize and interpret the messages that hospitality companies send out through their advertising, pricing structures and visual and other forms of stimulus.

- We will seek to answer the questions why do hospitality consumers behave in the ways that they do? How do hospitality consumers interpret the world of hospitality? And how do we learn and retain our understanding of hospitality consumption?

Introduction

In this chapter we focus on the hospitality consumer as an individual, investigating how our cognitive processes influence our consumption behaviour, within the chapter we will consider such aspects as perception, personality, learning, memory, meaning, motivation and trait theory, and how these impact upon the hospitality consumers' thought processes and thus the consumption decisions they make. The value of investigating the hospitality consumers' cognitive, or mental, processes is that they are argued to be the building blocks of consumer behaviour, that is, 'the internal processes that guide us in our actions as consumers' (Wilkie, 1994: 121). As such, it is argued, investigating aspects like motivation (why hospitality consumers behave as they do) or perception (how the external world gets translated into the world as we perceive it) will help us to better understand hospitality consumer behaviour. As Wilkie (1994: 121) argues: 'as a set, these topics provide us with a powerful base of knowledge. Also as we shall see, each of these topics . . . holds significant implications for us as managers and as consumers'.

Elsewhere within this book we consider hospitality consumer behaviour through social and cultural perspectives. These influences can be seen to be external to the consumer, and thus the individual consumer has little control over them. What we are investigating within this chapter, however, are motives, values, needs and perceptions, constructs that are internal to the hospitality consumer. For example, extensive research has been undertaken to investigate whether individuals with certain personalities – those traits and behaviours that differentiate us from each other – consume certain products or brands. We consider the implications of this research to an understanding of hospitality consumer behaviour. Similarly the link between many of the aspects identified above and behaviour, an important one given the vast sums of money that hospitality companies spend trying to influence and change our behaviour, is investigated. As a result this chapter considers a wide-ranging and varied set of internal psychological processes, which it is argued, may have an impact on hospitality consumer behaviour.

Consumer motivation

'Motivation asks the question why? About human behaviour, a small word perhaps, but an enormous question' (Statt, 1997: 138). For example, why do some people prefer McDonald's hamburgers, while others prefer Burger King, or why do some people prefer one five-star hotel brand over another? While these appear to be simple questions, answering them requires us to understand an extremely complex phenomenon. Even defining what we mean by motivation can be problematic. For example, the *Dictionary of Psychology* describes motivation as 'an extremely important but definitionally elusive term'. According to Evans, Miutinho and van Raaij (1996: 20) motivation is 'an activation, drive and/or reason to engage in a certain behaviour and to maintain that behaviour. Motivation determines the direction and the strength or intensity of behaviour'. While Statt (1997: 95) defines it as 'a general term for any part of the hypothetical psychological process which involves the experiencing of needs and drives, and the behaviour that leads to the goals which satisfy them'. Statt goes on to suggest that the key terms in defining motivation are *needs*, *drives*, *goals* and *satisfies*. It is argued that consumption is the result of three factors multiplied by each other: the ability to consume, the opportunity to consume and the motivation (the need or desire) to do so.

- Ability includes such factors as knowledge, physical ability and resources. For example, if we are considering the motivation to consume at McDonald's, we would ask does the consumer know about McDonald's, are they able to get to McDonald's and do they have the resources to consume there?
- Opportunity in our Macdonald's example would focus on the questions, is there a McDonald's in the location? When does it open? etc.
- Motivation is the final part of the equation. Why do we want to consume a McDonald's? What wish, need or desire will we fulfil by doing so?

As the above suggests, it is important to realize that motivation is only one of the elements that contributes to consumer behaviour. We may be highly motivated to consume a McDonald's hamburger, however, if there is not one in our locality or if it is closed when we are motivated to consume, motivation cannot lead to behaviour. Similarly we are unable to consume hospitality products about which we have no knowledge.

Motivation and need

Motivation theory has played a part in hospitality education since the development of the discipline more than forty years ago. As a result there can be few people, having graduated from that system in the intervening years, unaware of theories such as Maslow's (1954) needs hierarchy. In essence Maslow argued that an individual's behaviour is directed to satisfying a sequential set of needs, a needs hierarchy. This hierarchy he demonstrated as a pyramid, with each person's behaviour being targeted to the attainment or satisfaction of each level of need, before moving on to the next unsatisfied level. According to Maslow, 'each successive level in the hierarchy must be sufficiently satisfied before the next level becomes operational' (Bareham, 1995: 68). The needs represented in Maslow's hierarchy range from basic physiological needs, such as food, shelter, rest and sex, through middle-order needs such as the need for security and social needs, up to the top of the hierarchy as represented by the need for self-esteem and self-actualization. The full needs hierarchy as envisaged by Maslow incorporates:

Level 1: Physiological needs. These are the demands that our bodies put on us in terms of survival and include air, water, food, etc. They are seen as pre-potent needs as they must be satisfied before other needs are activated, something that happens by and large within our culture. However, there are arguments that addictions, for example, can motivate individuals to ignore these seemingly pre-potent needs.

Level 2: Safety needs. This category refers to safety in its broadest sense, that is, incorporating both physiological and psychological aspects of safety, such as familiarity and predictability. In most cultures institutions such as religion and education are designed to provide both physical and psychological safety. Thus for most of us these needs are not activated.

Level 3: Love and belonging. This category refers to the need to feel a sense of belonging, the absence of which can lead to depression and loneliness.

Level 4: Esteem. This level reflects the need for individuals to evaluate themselves positively, and is considered both as inward directed (competence and confidence in ourselves) and outward directed (the evaluations we receive from others). Esteem is seen to encourage self-confidence and capability, while a lack of esteem is seen to lead to feelings of inferiority and helplessness.

Level 5: Self-actualization. This refers to the fulfilment of our individual potential, being everything we could be. At this stage, Maslow suggested, people are motivated by ultimate values, what he referred to as metamotives, such as truth, beauty, justice and unity. Once an individual has achieved self-actualization they are seen to have achieved complete fulfilment.

Two factors dominate Maslow's needs hierarchy: deprivation and gratification. If an individual is deprived in terms of satisfying a need, this dominates their behaviour until the need is met. Once this happens and gratification is achieved the next step on the hierarchy is activated and this need then dominates their behaviour, until it too is gratified. Maslow's hierarchy should not be seen as a rigid framework; it was only meant to represent a loose hierarchy, as Statt (1997: 98) suggests, 'Although lower level needs are more easily satisfied, or satisfiable, than higher level ones, more than one level of need can be experienced at the same time'. Maslow (1954) also suggested that people can be influenced by higher-order needs before lower-order needs have been entirely satisfied. In terms of consumer behaviour this suggests that people may be willing to trade needs in a certain areas against needs in others.

Maslow's hierarchy has attracted widespread criticism, despite its pervasiveness throughout investigations of consumer motivation, most of which focus on the lack of evidence to support his arguments. Despite this, the needs hierarchy has been used extensively as a framework for investigating motivation, and continues to be represented in most texts on consumer behaviour. In addition it has been adapted, modified and applied in a number of other motivation models, including the ERG (existence, relatedness and growth) model and Reisman et al.'s (1960) needs model, among others. Despite the controversy, Maslow's hierarchy is seen by many to offer valuable insights into consumer behaviour. In particular it is interpreted as suggesting that once people's physiological and safety needs have been met, they are free to focus on social, psychological and self-actualization needs, offering huge scope for marketers. Individuals responsible for hospitality marketing have often used Maslow's hierarchy in practical terms as a framework for marketing activities, with specific goods and services being targeted at specific hierarchical levels. For example:

- *physiological* – accommodation, food and drink
- *safety* – accommodation, female-friendly services such as separate female-only floors in hotels
- *self-esteem* – luxury or high-status goods and services such as 5-star plus hotel rooms, champagne, butler service in hotels
- *social* – members-only clubs, Club 18–30 and other holiday companies for like-minded people
- *self-actualization* – hospitality educational programmes, conferences and seminars.

Motivation is a complex concept, it cannot safely be inferred from behaviour. For example, if we consider two groups of people eating in a restaurant and then if we were to infer motivation from behaviour, both groups would be motivated by the same thing. However, we know that it is possible that one group has gone into the restaurant because it is lunchtime and they are motivated by hunger. The second group, however, may be using the restaurant as a venue for an informal business meeting, thus the motivation that has driven their behaviour is clearly different from that of the first group. The same behaviour in this case has its origins in different motivations. Similarly, when we peruse the menu board in McDonald's, we could be motivated by considerations of price, but equally we could be considering the range of offers available, again similar behaviour having its origins in different motivations.

This aspect of motivation is further complicated by the fact that consumers may have multiple motives for their behaviour. The study of consumer motivation is complicated as any particular motive can usually be satisfied by any number of different types of behaviour acting alone or in combination with other behaviour. If we consider going to a bar, we could be there to assuage our thirst, to meet new friends, to meet old friends, to see a new bar or to take a break from other activities, and all or some of these motives might be acting in combination to create the behaviour of spending time in the bar. How can we interpret and understand consumer behaviour in such a complex scenario? As we have stated previously, simply observing the behaviour of consumers in such scenarios does not enable us to determine the motives that are at play.

Motivation can be demonstrated as either a positive aspect or a negative one: with positive motivation we seek positive moods, pleasure, social approval, etc., while for negative motivation we seek to escape negative situations, for example pain, pessimism or discomfort. This view of motivation was first suggested by the Gestalt psychologist Kurt Lewin (1935), who suggested that as a result of positive and negative (what he referred to as approach and avoidance) motivational forces, conflict could arise. Where these motivational forces are equal three situations will arise:

1 *Approach–approach conflict*: a common form of conflict where a consumer has to choose between two or more desirable outcomes; for example, do you holiday at the beach or in the mountains? Do you stay at the Holiday Inn or the Hilton? As both of these choices are positive, consumers are seen to want to make the decision and thus obtain the benefits.

Hospitality, Leisure & Tourism Series

2 *Avoidance–avoidance conflict*: the opposite situation to the above. Here consumers have to choose between two or more equally undesirable options. Having chosen your holiday, for example, you have to decide how to pay for it – cash or credit card. Arguably both are equally unappealing and thus consumers are seen to move away from both alternatives.

3 *Approach–avoidance conflict*: here the conflict is between a positive and a negative outcome. A typical example would be the holiday of your dreams (positive) being at the very limits of your budget (negative). Consumer behaviour here is seen as being influenced by the strength of the opposing forces, with much marketing and sales activity aimed at strengthening the positive or approach forces or weakening the negative avoidance forces.

In addition to the above, it is suggested that motivation can be derived internally (from within the individual), for example instinct, need, drive or emotion, or from the external environment (based on the attractiveness of environmental stimuli) (Evans, Moutinho and Van Raaij, 1996), resulting in a matrix encompassing four basic motivation types, as indicated in Table 4.1.

Motivation	Internal	External
Positive	Pleasure, comfort	Attractive goods and services, attractive situations
Negative	Pain, discomfort	Unattractive goods and services, unattractive situations

Source: adapted from Evans, Moutinho and Van Raaij (1996)

Table 4.1 A typology of motivation

Internal and external motivation ● ● ●

Early literature on motivation focused on the effect of internal, primarily physiological, drives on behaviour. These drives, with their origin in the gratification of the lowest forms of need, that is, hunger, thirst, reproduction, etc., were seen as pushing behaviour, and thus were visualized as negative motivations. More recent views of motivation consider the attractiveness of objects as a source of motivation and therefore behaviour. External motivation suggests that objects, for example, hospitality goods or services, are attractive to consumers and that the desire to own or experience them is a motivating force.

Clearly the assumption that motivation is either internal or external is a simplistic one, as in many if not most instances motivation is a combination of both factors. Hospitality goods and services can be seen to offer both internal (physiological factors such as food and drink) and external (the attractiveness of experiencing the services) forces that motivate.

Conscious and unconscious motivation • • •

Motivation can be seen as one of the psychological features of our lives that we are largely unaware of, along with aspects such as learning, our sense of our own personality and the ways in which we construct the world around us. As Statt (1997: 105) suggests, 'there are times when we literally do not know why we did something, we usually try to think up plausible reasons, but they will simply be ways of justifying our behaviour'. As a result of our unconscious motives we may be unable to identify and thus record our motives for some forms of behaviour. A number of authors have referred to our subconscious motives within a three-level framework: conscious (consciously aware), pre-conscious (not consciously aware of, but can be brought to the surface if it can be located) and unconscious (deeply embedded, not available to be brought to consciousness). Within consumer behaviour and marketing this factor has been taken on board and consideration given to how it can be made to work positively for organizations.

Motivational research, the studying of unconscious consumer behaviour, has developed a significant following since its inception in the 1950s despite the fact that we mock many of its more contentious suggestions; for example, the idea that a sports car has the same unconscious meaning to a man as having extramarital sex, that the act of baking a cake symbolizes childbirth for women and that ice-cream represents a nurturing mother. Contemporary motivational research, which is significant in scale and arguably more sophisticated than in earlier forms, is a key forum for generating advertising ideas for many agencies. Motivational researchers believe that consumption motives can be determined through indirect methods such as in-depth interviews, focus-group interviewing or projective techniques (techniques which seek to identify underlying motives for behaviour, motives that consumers may not be aware of).

There have been many significant criticisms of motivational research, many of which have been fuelled by the media when it headlines findings such as giving blood symbolizing a loss of potency to men, or that using instant coffee generated a deep-seated fear of disapproval in women, related to their roles as homemakers. Most of the criticism has been related to the value of research based on an individual's interpretation of qualitative judgement. However, motivational research also considers the questions, can needs be created and, if so, should they be? These are difficult ethical questions for many people. Significant research has been undertaken into whether it is possible to create needs in individuals. However, when considering this research, authors such as Statt (1997: 107) conclude: 'there is no evidence whatsoever that anyone can create a need in a consumer. What advertising and marketing can do is try to stimulate an existing need, or channel it in another direction towards one product or brand rather than another, but the results are still pretty unpredictable'.

Involvement

We discussed briefly in Chapter 3 the concept of involvement. Here we will consider how involvement impacts on the consumer at an individual level, primarily concerned with the relationships consumers develop with hospitality goods and services. As Statt (1997: 101) suggests, 'it refers to the personal importance that a given product in a given situation has for a particular individual. What does it do for the needs and values that are the behavioural expression of his or her self-image'. It is argued that the greater involvement individuals have with hospitality products and their perceived benefits, the more motivated they are to consume them. In terms of involvement, motivation is determined by the way in which individual consumers interpret hospitality goods and services. Involvement is seen to be a result of three factors: antecedents, properties and involvement outcomes.

1 Antecedents are the personal, product and situational factors that precede involvement and limit its scope:
   (a) *Personal*: personal factors include self-image, needs, drives, values, fantasy, etc. and the extent to which they can be translated into consumption. People who have high involvement with bars and clubs, for example, will perceive them as demonstrations of their lifestyle, others with low involvement will simply see them as a forum for drinking and dancing.
   (b) *Product*: we react to hospitality products in different ways as a result of the way in which we as consumers perceive

them. For example, the more identifiable hospitality services are, the greater is the scope for consumers to develop involvement with them. In addition consumers increase involvement where elements of risk are involved, in essence the reason branding hospitality services has been so successful – it combines the identification of hospitality services with the potential for reduced risk.

(c) *Situation*: levels of involvement are also influenced by the situation in which we consume. For example, we are more likely to be highly involved when we are taking our partners out to an expensive restaurant for dinner, than when we are popping into McDonald's for a quick lunch. An expensive restaurant date suggests an important relationship and, thus, routine activities such as eating and drinking become significant.

2 Properties of involvement refer to the feelings that hospitality consumers experience when involved with goods and services and that lead to behaviour. From our example above, when we are highly involved in planning our dinner date it is likely we will spend significant periods of time searching for information and evaluating it prior to making our decisions. We become more engaged to the service than when we are making what can be regarded as low-involvement decisions.

3 Outcomes of involvement depend upon the relationship between the antecedents of involvement and properties of involvement.

A good deal of research has been undertaken which attempts to determine scales of involvement for various goods and services. However, to date few if any have produced meaningful results.

Semiotics

Semiotics refers to the meanings we give to symbols and signs, both at a conscious and unconscious level. We operate in an environment full of signs and symbols and we interpret them vicariously, whether we are aware of it or not. Rituals of the key hospitality activities of eating and drinking are among the most common forms. Formal dinner settings have numerous tools for eating, all associated with various types of food, despite the fact that in reality most of us could manage with just a simple knife, fork and spoon. Similarly, when we consume food we go through rituals of how it should be sequenced, with particular courses in specific order. Such ritual and symbolism is culture based and thus varies from one to another. On the occasion of my first 'real northern' family Sunday lunch I was somewhat taken aback to

Hospitality, Leisure & Tourism Series

receive a plate with Yorkshire pudding sitting alone and somewhat forlorn on it. The Todd family tradition required Yorkshire pudding to be served as a separate course, a tradition I subsequently heartily partook of on many occasions.

Semiotics is used in marketing to suggest activities that cannot easily be put into words. So, for example, hotels are not simply shown as places to eat, drink and sleep, but are shown to be places of leisure, fun, prestige, sex, etc. Semiotics, because of its non-verbal nature, is of prime importance to hospitality consumption, especially when we consider contemporary and postmodern hospitality consumers, which we return to in later chapters.

Learning and memory

Learning is 'the relatively permanent process by which changes in behaviour, knowledge, feelings or attitudes occur as the result of experience' (Statt, 1997: 77) and, as this definition suggests, it is a complex phenomenon to study. Traditionally, learning is associated with two schools of thought – the behaviourist approach and the cognitive approach.

Behaviourism

Behaviourism was traditionally rooted in the thought that what you see is what you get. Behaviourism operated by experimenters providing stimuli and noting responses to them. What happened in between these stages was not a concern in early behaviourism. Today behaviourism is generally subdivided into two main areas – classical conditioning and operant conditioning – and within these areas the investigation of what happens between stimuli and response is a key activity. Classical conditioning is most closely associated with Pavlov, whose work, which was undertaken by observing the effect of stimuli such as buzzers, bells and lights on dogs at meal times, demonstrated that, given time to learn, dogs would respond to conditioned stimuli (bells etc.) with conditioned responses (for example, salivation). This led to the realization that it should be possible to use conditioning to change people's behaviour in a desired direction, something that marketers had always sought to do. What marketers, such as those in hospitality, try to do is to associate particular goods and services with images that are attractive to consumers. The launch advertisements of Bass's beer product, Caffrey's, are a case in point. The product, a light beer, was sold with images of raven-haired Irish maidens, Irish street urchins, a rolling Irish coastline and a typical Irish village with wild horses in the street. Considerable research has been undertaken to try to evaluate the effectiveness of classical conditioning in marketing, with mixed results. It is clear that under laboratory conditions subjects can be seen to be affected by stimuli to behave in a desired manner. However, this is a long way short of proving that in the more complex wider environment outside the laboratory the same results can be obtained.

Operant conditioning, associated most closely with the work of Skinner, takes classical conditioning a stage further, suggesting that subjects experiment within their environment, thus demonstrating operant behaviour. Skinner demonstrated that the behaviour of subjects can be shaped using conditioning techniques – a process known as instrumental conditioning. Skinner, using research on rats, demonstrated how they could learn to act in order to obtain reward (in his research rats learnt to press a bar to obtain food). Operant conditioning can be seen to operate widely in hospitality consumer behaviour. For example, TGI Friday often offers customers waiting at the bar for their table a sample of the latest menu offering as a taster. Future purchases of the product depend on the consumer's response to it. If the response is rewarded by liking it, the consumer may consume it again, if not he or she will not. Other techniques include introductory offers, free gifts, free samples, etc. A recent addition to the hospitality marketing tool kit, which is associated with operant conditioning, is that of the numerous loyalty schemes that are operated by hospitality companies. These schemes, widely offered by companies such as Forte hotels, Holiday Inn, Bass Taverns, etc., aim to reward the consumer for purchasing their products. In the longer term the hope is that hospitality consumers will become so conditioned to the goods and services they consume that they will continue even when the rewards are reduced or cancelled altogether. The same concerns arise as to the value of operant conditioning as classical conditioning, in terms of empirical evidence supporting its value. As Statt (1997: 85) suggests 'it might be argued that behaviourism provides a description of the behaviour involved rather than an explanation of how and why the consumer came to make the decision'.

The cognitive school

This school focuses on learning as knowledge, incorporating factors such as insight, memory and modelling. The learning that takes place in operant conditioning is based on trial and error; if we repeat an activity a number of times we are able to learn how to accomplish it successfully. However, much of our learning is a result of insight, an understanding of how solutions can be generated, which does not rely on repetitive trialling. Insight allows us to apply solutions generated for one occasion to a wide range of other problems, through an understanding of the relationships between means and ends. Cognitive learning focuses on the role of learning, insight and understanding, factors which allow us to solve problems even when we have never experienced them before, an understanding of behaviour that is more complex than learning as habit.

Memory

Memory is a key factor in learning. It enables us to retrieve our learning when we need it, the process known as remembering. Memory is important in hospitality consumer behaviour in that it enables consumers to recall or recognize previous experiences. Thus when we are deciding where to go for a coffee, we use our memory to recall previous pleasant experiences in order to aid our decision. In a similar manner, if we are trying to decide what hotel to stay at, memory allows us to recognize brands in hotel directories. As memory is important to hospitality consumption companies use a range of techniques to ensure that our learning is meaningful and useful, including such tactics as:

- repetition – repeating the message a number of times so that we learn it, hence the number of repetitions of holiday company advertisements in August and September)
- visual images – visuals are used in adverts as they appear to be easier for us to encode to memory; I would refer again to the television adverts for Caffrey's described above
- self-referencing – the relation of advertisements to people's own lives; Harvester Steak Houses, for example, ran a series of advertisements using 'real' families and their experiences
- coding – the putting of information into coded chunks for easier retrieval. Hotel companies such as Forte use easy to remember telephone numbers for central reservations as it is easier for us to recall 0800 (which most of us would recall as the freephone number) 40 40 40, that is, Forte Forte Forte, than a random set of numbers, for example 86492304894).

Personality

Personality represents a second set of characteristics that it is argued can contribute to our understanding of hospitality consumption. Like many terms, 'personality' is a common one used freely in everyday speech, for example, when we refer to someone as having a pleasant or unpleasant personality. In the field of consumer behaviour, however, personality has a specific meaning. It refers to the patterns of behaviour demonstrated by an individual, patterns we have learnt to recognize from previous experiences of dealing with people. Statt (1997: 63) defines personality as 'the sum total of all the factors which make an individual human being both individual and human; the thinking, feeling and behaving that all human beings have in common, and the particular characteristic pattern of these elements that makes every human being unique ... stresses the important role of unconscious processes that may be hidden from the individual but are at least partly perceptible to other people'. Put simply, theories of personality attempt to explain why people behave in the way that they do, based on the concept of a complete person. It is argued that our personalities develop as a result of the ways in which we respond to the things that happen around us. For example, we are all affected by general influences simultaneously, whether these are economic, social or cultural. However, we each have a unique predisposition to react to these influences as a result of our individual upbringing, a result of the influence of our families, our education, our peers, etc. Our personality results from the unique way in which each of us then internalizes these influences. As Bareham (1995: 146) states: 'differences exist between each of us because each of us internalizes these two sets of influences in different ways. The unique set of characteristics which each of us has influences the way in which we behave. These characteristics are relatively stable and are used to identify our particular personality'.

A number of personality theories have been used to describe hospitality consumption, with the most common being psychoanalytical theory, self-concept, social/cultural theory and trait theory.

Psychoanalytical theory

The psychoanalytical approach to personality is most closely associated with the work of Freud, emerging from his work as a psychotherapist. Freud suggested that our personalities are at least partly made up of subconscious influences, suggesting that there are three forces at play, the interaction between which determines our personality, and thus our behaviour. These three forces he labelled:

- *the id*: the intuitive, subconscious element, which forces us to gratify our basic needs, for example sex, survival, food, etc. The id is a powerful drive that requires immediate satisfaction, usually considered as part of our unconscious state

- *the ego*: considered to be our rational, conscious state, this acts as a manager for the id, attempting to attain the needs of the id in a socially acceptable manner. Self-image is closely associated with the ego, which is seen to manage the conflict that arises between the id and the superego
- *the superego*: is considered to equate to our conscious and represents the internalization of the norms and morality of society. Like the id it is usually unconscious and as individuals we are unaware of its workings, the superego acts to suppress the desires of the id, not through managing it, the task of the ego, but by generating guilt.

The id, ego and superego constantly interact with each other and are thus frequently in conflict. In the ego this conflict appears as anxiety, but we are unaware of the source of this anxiety as the conflict between the id and the superego is unconscious. Where the ego is able to resolve conflict between the id and the superego the resultant personality is seen to be balanced and well adjusted. Where either the id or the superego are dominant they influence the individual's personality and they feel anxious or neurotic. The conflict between the id and the superego determines our personality and thus our behaviour. Freud believed that childhood was crucial in shaping personality, as conflicts that were not resolved at that time result in defence mechanisms to reduce tension and influence behaviour in adult life.

In terms of hospitality consumer behaviour the importance of the psychoanalytical approach is its emphasis on the unconscious as the cause of behaviour. For example, if we need to eat lunch, why is it important to some people that the lunch be consumed at a Burger King and for others at a McDonald's. If all food outlets satisfy our hunger then what significance do these particular outlets have for the consumers who use them? The problem is that as the psychoanalytical approach suggests that we are unaware of many of our motives; even if we ask consumers they may not be able to explain the true reasons for their choice. As a result, in many cases marketers have stopped trying to extol the benefits of certain hospitality services, preferring instead to align their products with consumer lifestyles or wished lifestyles. The development of psychographics as a means of segmenting markets, including those for hospitality products, reflects the desire to express personality differences in a consumer or marketing context. The argument is that as personality reflects patterns of need, it is possible to identify products that are suited to satisfying certain personality types. However, as we discuss in Chapter 7, the value of psychographics as a segmentation model is not proven. Psychoanalytical approaches are 'crude, uncertain and difficult to verify' (Statt, 1997; 67) with the result that, while still popular for much marketing and advertising, and still a strong influence in terms of the belief that consumers have unconscious desires, they have lost the cache they enjoyed at their peak.

Self-theory

The central theory in self-concept is that individuals have a concept of who they are (the actual self) or who they would like to be (the ideal self). The concept of self is related to psycho-analytical theory, the ego and the superego, and is seen as a component of personality. Self-concept develops unabated throughout our lives, with the development taking place as a result of our interactions with others and from the feedback we receive during the interaction process, and as such our concept of self is never completed, it can always be altered by social and environmental factors. It is generally accepted that as con-sumers we do not have a single actual self, as consumers we have multiple roles, for example, husband, father, executive, volunteer, etc., each of which is dominant dependent on the context.

Self-concept is important to our understanding of hospitality consumption because of its subjective nature. It is based on the premise that as consumers we buy the hospitality goods and services that encompass the characteristics we believe we have, or we would like to have or we would like others to think we have. An individual's self-concept is determined by the view they have of themselves and that view may be very different from the one identified by many forms of consumer research. Thus the way in which researchers interpret an individual's behaviour may not be the same way that the individual interprets it, a result of which is that a good deal of marketing activity is undertaken to appeal to an individuals sense of self. Thus business hotels in the 1990s used to emphasize the fact that their rooms were 'your office away from home', whereas current advertisements focus on the holistic contemporary executives who are more than just their work, emphasizing the leisure opportunities available for their relaxation.

In addition to the actual and ideal self Belk (1988) identified what he referred to as the extended self, suggesting that our possessions are linked to our self-concept, as what we wear and own, we are. According to the extended self theory, products have symbolic value to us, they badge us and say something about the way we perceive ourselves – a theory that is in many ways linked to that of symbolic interactionism. We discuss the symbolic role of products in more detail in later chapters; however, it is clear that marketers have used symbolic roles of consumption for many years. For example, in hospitality lavish entertaining is usually symbolized by images of champagne and lobster.

Criticisms of the self-concept in relation to hospitality consumption focus on the understanding that it is evident largely in the conscious state, whereas as we have discussed much of our consumption activity may be unconscious in nature. Despite this, however, self-image remains an important aspect of hospitality consumption, in particular when we consider services such as themed restaurants, cruise liners, restaurant merchandising, our choice of alcoholic beverages, etc. In the past many studies have tended to suggest that consumers buy products they rate as similar to themselves. Indeed, the importance of the self-concept was highlighted by Foxall (1992: 196) when he stated: 'of all the personality concepts which have been applied to marketing, self-concept has probably provided the most consistent results and the greatest promise of application to the needs of business firms'.

Social/cultural theory

This theory is also referred to as neo-Freudian psychoanalysis, as it is largely derived from the work of the successors to Freud in this field. They differed from Freud in two key respects: first, they believed that social and cultural variables (related to the ego) were more important than biological drives (those related to the id) in the development of our personalities and, second, they undertook their research away from the clinical context of Freud's work. Horney (1958) suggested that personality was a mechanism we develop to cope with anxiety and identified three orientations she suggested we develop in order to function in our relationships with others. These orientations have since been widely used by researchers seeking to understand consumer behaviour, usually through some form of personality scaling mechanism, and are described as:

1 *The compliant orientation*: which as the name suggests includes people who tend towards compliance, dependency and a need for affection/approval. Compliant individuals tend to be conformist and easily dominated. As such it is argued they are good targets for advertisers, as they will consume in order to avoid causing offence.

2 *The aggressive orientation*: which includes people who demonstrate a need for power, are achievement orientated and

manipulate others. In marketing terms they are seen to consume products that make them look or feel more complete.

3 *The detached orientation*: which includes people who are independent, self-motivated, and self-reliant and who avoid developing emotional ties with others. In terms of consumer behaviour they are seen as disinterested in the views of others, unaware of brands and disinterested in buying the right, or 'in' things.

Reisman (1960) developed Horner's work, identifying three categories of individuals related to those listed above: tradition orientated with values based in the past (related to the compliant orientation above), outer directed with values determined by the views of others (the aggressive orientation) and inner directed with a sense of the value of their own perspective (the detached orientation).

From a hospitality consumption perspective it should be noted that while social/cultural theory is still widely used in market research, little if any significant evidence has been offered that it is possible to identify our 'orientations' in such a way as to be useful in determining behaviour. As Statt (1997: 70) suggests 'generally this line of research has not been as fruitful as it looked like being in the 1960s'. Despite this, much contemporary marketing seeks to exploit these theories and they have had a strong influence on the development of segmentation models based on lifestyle, as we discuss later in this book.

Trait theory

Trait theory suggests that personality comprises a set of traits, either physiological such as height or weight, or psychological such as intelligence or imagination, that are used to describe our predispositions to behave in a particular way. As a result, it is argued, it is possible to develop a set of personality inventories, the analysis of which suggests the way in which an individual will consume. While it is suggested many people share the same traits, they are unique in that the strength of each trait will vary for each individual. Trait theory suggests that personality can be measured and that underlying personality traits, which are seen as stable, can be used to explain hospitality consumption. Thus if we are able to identify consumers with particular profiles we will be able to identify the hospitality products they are likely to consume. The theory is built around a statistical procedure known as factor analysis, the most common ones being the 16PF (personality factors) scale developed by Cattell (1989), and the EPI (Eysenck personality inventory) (Eysenck and Eysenck,

1964). The EPI suggests, for example, that if we are looking at the use of bars or nightclubs we should seek to identify individuals who scored highly on the extrovert scale on the EPI test, as these individuals are more likely to be sociable, active and requiring stimulation, features we associated with such venues.

Trait theory suffers from similar criticisms to most of the other theories of personality, despite widespread use of the theory there is little empirical evidence to suggest it has value in determining consumer behaviour. As Statt (1997: 74) argues, 'attempts to find practical applications for this kind of personality theory have been no more successful than those for any other theory ... the results are questionable or perhaps meaningless'. Statt suggests this may be because the theory was derived for a clinical purpose and 'bastardized' for consumer research, that the attempt to reduce consumer behaviour to correlations between products and personality is simplistic or that personality, while a complex phenomena, is only one element of consumer behaviour.

Personality measures were originally developed as a means of identifying patterns of behaviour in a clinical context, applying measures developed for this purpose to an understanding of consumer behaviour per se, never mind that of hospitality goods and services, is clearly problematic. As Kassarjian (1971: 415) suggests: 'instruments originally intended to measure gross personality characteristics such as sociability, emotional stability, introversion, or neuroticism have been used to make predictions of brands of toothpaste or cigarette. The variables that lead to the assassination of a president, confinement in a mental hospital or suicide may not be identical to those that lead to the purchase of a washing machine'. Despite its limitations, however, Wilkie (1994) suggests that we should not conclude that personality has no influence on hospitality consumer behaviour but, rather, that it is only one influence among others. Wilkie argues that a number of personality measures have been found to offer some value to our understanding of consumer behaviour, including those that study patterns of behaviour, those that focus on consumption-related needs, those that investigate physiological differences and the self-concept, and those that focus on how personality affects responses to advertising.

Perception

Perception is a key focus for hospitality marketers, the reason being that marketing stimuli only exist at the external level. They must be perceived by consumers in order to impact upon them. Thus it is critical for marketers to understand how hospitality consumers perceive. The activities associated with the consumption of hospitality products all require individuals to interact with the external environment. As a result perception plays a big part in our understanding of those activities. Wilkie (1994: 205) defines perception as, 'the process of sensing, selecting, and interpreting consumer stimuli in the external world . . . the translation from the external, physical world to the internal, mental world that each of us actually experiences'. These stimuli are transmitted through our senses so that we can process the information they contain, prior to assessing and acting on them.

As individuals we use our senses to receive stimuli from the environment, that is to say sight, hearing, taste, smell and touch, and as consumers we use all of these senses when interpreting our environment. Marketers understand the value of researching our sensory processes and have conducted extensive research within this area. Wilkie, for example, cites the case of an Atlantic City casino that paid a significant sum of money to an interior design firm for remodelling the casino in order to create an environment that relaxed the morality of its customers, in order that they would gamble more. Among the changes it made were:

- the replacing of lobby windows with sheets of marble, thus reducing the likelihood of customers using daylight cues as a reason for stopping
- the false introduction of amplified gambling noise, as the noise increased excitement and thus gambling revenues
- designing the lighting at the tables to ensure that gamblers were in the light while spectators were in the dark, which increased the gamblers' sense of security
- designing the hotel rooms to be bright, noisy and uncomfortable, thus gamblers were not enticed to spend much time in their rooms.

Similar research has found, for example, that shoppers spend less time shopping in noisy environments than in quiet ones, but average spend is unaffected; that shoppers spend more when music with a slow beat is played, than when the beat is fast; and that consumers spend more if they are able to relate to the type of music being played (Statt, 1997).

In order to become aware of stimuli these have to be strong enough for our sensory receptors to pick them up, and the level at which these are achieved is known as the threshold. The level at which an effect begins to occur, and the minimum level at which a particular sensory receptor can discriminate senses, is known as the absolute sensory threshold. Thus, in a bar, menus that are too distant cannot be seen, music which is below our sensory threshold cannot be heard, etc. However, these sensory thresholds are not fixed, they vary among individuals, and they also vary for individuals dependent on physiological issues in play at any time. For example, we all know how our sense of taste is affected by alcohol. Thresholds are important to marketers, as they want their products to be instantly recognizable in a consumer's environment. If we are in a bar, for example, the marketers want us to be able to distinguish their products from those of their competitors, regardless of the levels of noise, lighting, etc.

An important element of sensory thresholds is a factor known as the just noticeable difference (JND), the minimum amount of difference that a consumer can detect. If you are able to notice the difference between two stimuli, it is because you have crossed the sensory threshold. However, again our ability to sense the JND varies. For example, if McDonald's increases the price of its burgers by £1.00 we would notice the difference; it would have risen by something like 50 per cent. However, if a Holiday Inn Hotel increased its room rate by £1.00 we would be unlikely to notice as the threshold difference is much less. The routine manipulation of the consumer's difference threshold is a common technique within hospitality marketing. For example, reducing the size of portions can save hospitality companies significant costs, and as long as it does not go beyond the consumer's difference threshold they are unlikely to be aware of the change. Conversely, knowing at what point a discount becomes significant to a consumer is important as discounts reduce margins. Therefore, hospitality companies do not want to go beyond what is absolutely necessary. It is common in hospitality to suggest that an effective JND is around 15 per cent of the first quoted price.

The way in which we perceive our external environment is dependent upon a number of factors, a key one of which is our ability to focus our perceptions – the way in which our environment gets our attention. Imagine sitting in a bar with friends. Why is it that we are aware of some of the songs playing on the jukebox, but completely unaware of others? The music is playing at the same volume, but some songs get our attention and others do not. The answer would appear to be that we are capable of focusing at any time on stimuli that are important to us; we filter them out from the background, ignoring the rest. This focusing or attention, 'the momentary focusing of our information processing capacity on a particular stimuli' (Wilkie, 1994: 217) is a result of many factors, and these have been extensively used in advertising and promoting hospitality goods and services. They include aspects such as position or placement (where messages are put), contrast (a change in the environment which stimulates attention), novelty, complexity, curiosity, etc. and are a key focus of much contemporary hospitality consumer behaviour.

A sub-area of perceptual attention that has gained significant exposure is that of marketing using subliminal perception – the presenting of messages below the threshold of conscious awareness. Subliminal stimuli are those that cannot be discriminated at the conscious level, but which are capable of being sensed. They form two types: visual messages that are presented so briefly that we cannot consciously detect them, or audio messages which are presented below our sensory threshold. Research within this area is mixed. No conclusive evidence has been presented that subliminal messaging affects behaviour. Indeed, the original research, which was for cola drinks in a cinema in the USA in the 1950s, has never been successfully replicated. However, most consumers believe that subliminal messaging occurs (Wilkie, 1994), and a number of research studies have suggested some linkage between subliminal messages and consumer behaviour.

Perception is important to our understanding of hospitality consumption as it is a feature of our self-image, as discussed earlier. The view we have of ourselves incorporates images of the goods and services we believe to be appropriate for us to buy, if we are to maintain our self-image. The result is that in a number of cases research has suggested that people are capable of defining the character or image of, for example, a bar or restaurant, and will only frequent those that correspond to their own self-image (Lazer and Wykham, 1961). As a result companies seek to influence hospitality consumer behaviour by suggesting that associations exist between them and desirable product images.

Risk and perception

A second area of perception is also important when we consider hospitality consumption – the issue of perceived risk. As consumers we make many decisions about hospitality goods and services and, as we have discussed previously, very many of these include an element of risk. We have no way of knowing the outcome. As a result when we are aware of this uncertainty we perceive a risk in our decision. Thus, when we enter a new bar for the first time, when we book a holiday or when we book a restaurant for an important occasion, we are aware of the risks involved in our decisions. Statt (1997) suggests that this risk can de defined in a number of ways, including:

1 *Performance*: will it perform in the way it is supposed to perform? For example, will the holiday live up to the promise of the brochures?

2 *Financial*: will it be value for money? For example, is the meal worth what we are paying for it?

3 *Physical*: is it safe? For example, is this nightclub a safe venue for me to attend?

4 *Time*: will this experience be time-consuming? For example, how long will I have to wait for my meal?

5 *Social*: does this experience reflect positively on my social status? For example, what will frequenting this bar say about me to others?

6 *Psychological*: what does this behaviour say about me? For example, how does opting for this holiday make me feel?

Risk is not perceived by everyone in the same way; we have various thresholds. Thus some people are seen as more risk averse than others. Conversely, some people are more willing to accept risk than others; look at behaviour on theme park rides, for example. These individuals are often deliberately targeted by companies with messages emphasizing the risk and exoticism of the experience. Long-haul holidays are often sold in this way, as are new bars and nightclubs.

Risk leads to anxiety, so in order to avoid it we seek to find methods of coping with risk, and in hospitality an increasingly significant means of reducing risk is the consumption of brands. As Statt (1997: 59) suggests, 'research has found that, generally speaking, relying on brand loyalty is the most popular strategy for reducing perceived risk'. Brand loyalty is demonstrated when hospitality consumers show a favourable attitude towards a brand, thus consistently consuming that brand over time. It is important in our understanding of consumer behaviour, as branding is a means of influencing or biasing the consumer's decision processes. On the positive side it can lead to savings in time and effort for consumers. However, it may not be the most efficient means of decision-making, and can lead consumers to pay premium prices or even to accept inferior quality. Hospitality consumers are clearly influenced by brands and brand images, and many research studies have consistently demonstrated the value of brands to hospitality companies.

As we have seen, investigating how our cognitive processes, such as perception, influence our consumption behaviour is a complex undertaking. However, the value of investigating these processes is that they are argued to be the building blocks of consumer behaviour. As such, investigating aspects like perception (how the external world gets translated into the world as we perceive it) will help us to better understand hospitality consumer behaviour, and this is demonstrated in Case Study 4.1.

Case study 4.1

Female-friendly bars: a case study of Six Continents' All-Bar-One brand

The purpose of this illustration is to examine how the licensed retail companies began to consider perception and issues of gender and servicescape in marketing the UK public house to women consumers, using Six Continents' All-Bar-One concept as an example.

Substantial research has been undertaken, which demonstrates that the characteristics women perceive to be important in their desired public house experience are diametrically opposite to that traditionally provided in male-dominated pubs (Schmidt and Sapsford, 1995; Clarke et al., 1998). As Schmidt and Sapsford (1995: 34) state: 'in the latter, barriers to enjoyment arise from the dynamic interplay between the physical environment and the behaviour of staff, which can act as reinforcement of the behaviour of established male customers, whose actions have the effect of signalling to women that they are unwelcome'. As a result public houses have had problems in creating customer loyalty among women, as they tend to be, at best, medium users of pubs and indifferent to distinctions between drinking in the public house and home.

As a result of the need to identify new markets and to encourage greater use of public houses by women, the public house companies began to consider the perceived benefits that could be achieved as a result of more careful management of the servicescape of public houses, in particular the design and management of the physical elements of the service and the interplay between the customer, the environment, employees and other customers, generated by customer perception of the symbolic nature of the environmental cues on offer. The environment of a public house can be used to establish or reinforce customers' perceptions of its image and thus influence satisfaction.

Research which was undertaken by Schmidt et al. (1995) identified a series of avoidance cues used by women public house users including a gloomy, smoky atmosphere, distinctively male, getting looked at, bare floorboards, having to stand, and black, and approach behaviour cues including a focus not just on alcohol, not just a drinking public house, sociable, big open fires and clean, warm colours.

Six Continents developed the All-Bar-One brand as a specific response to female criticisms of traditional male-dominated public house design, as suggested above, launching the first one in Sutton, Surrey, in 1984. All-Bar-Ones are designed to be classic cosmopolitan bars, which offer smart, social informality in a contemporary environment, with an emphasis on quality. They have a modern, open, airy design with soft furnishings including leather sofas, internal planting and natural colours, all of which are intended to offer women a perception of safety and security. Care has been taken in the selection and training of staff to ensure that they are knowledgeable and friendly, which encourages a buzzing contemporary feel in the bars. In addition, the style of food and drink is a central feature of All-Bar-One, with food freshly prepared, constantly evolving and decoratively presented, and an extensive wine list is available, most of which can be purchased by the glass.

The brand has been highly successful since its inception, having won the *Retailer* magazine, Retailer of the Year Award for Best Concept in 1999. It is now available throughout the UK, and is expanding into continental Europe.

Summary

Within this chapter we have focused on how hospitality consumption is influenced by an individual consumer's cognitive processes. We have investigated the role of such diverse factors as perception, personality, learning, memory, motivation and need, in terms of how they impact upon the consumer of hospitality goods and services. We have considered how hospitality consumers acquire, organize and interpret the messages that hospitality companies send out through their advertising, pricing structures and visual and other forms of stimulus. Many of the factors we have outlined in this chapter can be interpreted as the building blocks of consumer behaviour; internal processes that, it is argued, guide us in our actions as hospitality consumers. The research that has been described seeks to answer the questions: why do hospitality consumers behave in the ways that they do? How do hospitality consumers interpret the world of hospitality? How do we learn and retain our understanding of hospitality consumption? And it seeks to do this through an exploration of the internal factors that are seen to drive our behaviour. Investigating aspects like motivation (why hospitality consumers behave as they do) or perception (how the external world gets translated into the world as we perceive it) helps us to better understand hospitality consumer behaviour. However, as we see in the next chapter, it only supplies a part of the answer.

CHAPTER 5

Social and cultural influences on hospitality consumer behaviour

Key themes

- This chapter considers the main influences on hospitality consumers in their everyday consumption behaviour, through investigating the main factors in the consumers' environment.

- It seeks to explain how concepts such as culture, social class, ethnicity and status impact on hospitality consumption.

- Hospitality consumption always occurs within a context or situation and those contexts and situations are major influences upon that hospitality encounter. This chapter investigates a number of these contexts and the influences inherent within them.

- The environmental influences that affect hospitality consumers fall into two broad categories: cultural influences and group influences. The first of these is considered in some detail within this chapter.

Introduction to environmental aspects of hospitality consumption

The focus of this chapter is the impact of society and culture upon us as members of that society/culture, considered in the context of the consumption of hospitality goods and services. Our values and beliefs, generated by the society and culture to which we belong and assimilated as a result of socialization (Allen and Anderson, 1994), influence the decisions we make as consumers. Thus, in order to understand how we consume hospitality goods and services it is necessary to develop an understanding of the influence of such factors as the cultural context of consumption, ethnicity, social class, status, family and other reference groups. As Chisnall (1995: 103) states: 'The study of environmental factors such as cultural and social influences will help to construct what may be termed the mosaic of behaviour; from these many variables – personal and environmental – the intricate pattern of human behaviour will become apparent.'

Despite the preceding chapter focusing on our consumption activities through an individual perspective, it is clear that as consumers we are influenced by our environment, and indeed that at the same time our behaviour alters that environment. However, as Sivadas, Mathew and Currey (1997: 463) state, 'research in consumer behaviour has been dominated by studies of the individual'. For example, Leong (1989) reported that only 4.1 per cent of references in articles published in the *Journal of Consumer Research* between 1974 and 1988 were from sociology. This chapter considers some of the factors within the environment that influence our behaviour as hospitality consumers. However, this is a difficult undertaking as many authors have commented upon the problems involved in studying culture and its impact (Wright, Nancarrow and Kwok, 2001). For example Usunier (2000: xiii) states he has 'no wish to describe cultures, either from an insider's point of view or exhaustively ... provision [for readers of his book] is a method for dealing with intercultural situations in international marketing'. Culture has been studied extensively from a more general business perspective, in particular how organizational culture operates (Jeannet and Hennessey, 1998; Johansson, 2000; Venkatesh, 1995). However, due to the complexities involved, the influence of culture on marketing and consumer behaviour is not so widely investigated (Wright, Nancarrow and Kwok, 2001). For example Craig and Douglas (2000: 210) argue: the most significant problems in drawing up questions in multi-country research are likely to occur in relation to attitudinal, psychographic and lifestyle data ... it is not always clear whether certain attitudinal or personality constructs are equally relevant or equivalent in all countries and cultures ... even where similar constructs are mentioned in different countries, the specific items making up these constructs may not always be identical. While it would be possible, and indeed in some ways preferable, to consider environmental factors under the two broad headings of social and cultural perspectives, in other ways the synergy between these two areas is such that there are benefits in considering them together, as I have chosen to do here. Figure 5.1, adapted from Engel, Blackwell and Miniard (1995: 606) represents the external influences on consumption; this chapter will consider a number of these, with the remainder investigated in Chapter 6. This chapter begins by considering how contemporary studies of consumer behaviour have developed a sociological stance, in opposition to the more psychological and cognitive perspectives highlighted in the previous chapter. The chapter then investigates the role

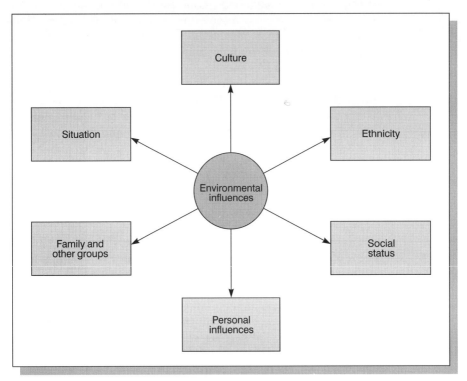

Figure 5.1 Environmental influences on consumer behaviour
Source: adapted from Engel, Blackwell and Miniard (1995)

played by culture in forming hospitality consumer behaviour, before moving on to consider the social influences on consumption.

The development of a sociological perspective in consumer behaviour

As we have discussed previously, from the 1980s onwards there has been a shift in the dominant perspectives within consumer research, with Belk (1995) suggesting that a major cause for this shift has been the move towards multidisciplinary research in the area. This, it is suggested, has led to marketing departments broadening their membership to include anthropologists and sociologists among other disciplines. As membership of these departments widened, the appeal of laboratory and anonymous scaled attitude measures declined. The result was a move away from a perception of the consumer as an automaton, receiving inputs and through a transformation process, producing outputs. As Belk (1995: 62) states: 'the new consumer behaviour precipitates the unavoidable conclusion that consumers are not mere automatons who receive information inputs and produce brand outputs that maximize satisfaction. Rather they are socially connected human beings participating in multiple interacting cultures'. The new consumer was perceived as a socially construing individual participating in a multitude of interactions and contexts. Within such a perspective the family is not a decision-making consumption unit, but a consumption reality involving hegemonic control, core and peripheral cultures and subcultures and relationships. Similarly, if we consider hospitality goods and services within the paradigm of new consumption studies a product such as a hotel is not simply a system of food, beverage and accommodation, but can be seen to be a vehicle for fun, status, prestige, power, sex, achievement, alienation, etc.

The use of the term 'consumer culture' is now widely expressed in a range of aspects of everyday life, and this focus on a consumer society is taken to suggest that not only is the economy structured around the promotion and selling of goods and services rather than their production, but also that members of such a society will treat high levels of consumption as indicative of social success, with the result that consumption is seen as a life goal for members of such a society. Within the sociology of hospitality consumption, there are a range of factors that will impact on behaviour and thus need to be investigated, including aspects such as social class, culture, reference groups, the influence of the household, ethnicity, ritual, symbolism and the consumption situation and setting. The remainder of this chapter will consider a number of these aspects in detail.

The impact of culture on hospitality consumption

'Culture' is one of the most widely used and yet misunderstood terms in our vocabulary. We use it in our everyday language to describe a wide range of experiences. For example, we describe someone as cultured if they frequent the theatre and read classic literature. Similarly, often when we think of culture we associate it with the opera, ballet or other arts. In aiding our understanding of hospitality consumer behaviour, however, 'culture' has a very different meaning, as Blythe (1997: 90) defines it: 'Culture is a set of beliefs and values that are shared by most people within a group . . . it is passed on from one group member to another . . . it is learned and is therefore both subjective and arbitrary.' Such a definition is supported by Bareham (1995: 63) who defines culture as 'the accepted values and ways of behaving which shape the society in which we live'. As such cultural beliefs and values profoundly influence the consumption decisions we make. Culture is seen to affect motives, intentions and attitudes and is an all-encompassing feature of our existence. Culture should be seen not as something we have, but as everything we are. Thus in the way we are using culture here it is the complete way in which society operates, not simply those parts which some elements of society consider desirable, such as the arts. As Chisnall (1995: 104) states: 'Culture is not a narrow view of human activities . . . it extends to include all the activities that characterize the behaviour of particular communities of people.' The cultures that societies develop are hugely important in the way that we understand behaviour; they are dynamic, they are complex and they affect every aspect of our behaviour. As McCraken (1981: 114) argues, 'Each culture establishes its own special version of the world . . . incorporating understandings and rules that have particular significance for its members'. Cultural values and beliefs are so deep seated that members of particular cultures are in many ways unaware of them. They are developed within societies and formulated by a wide range of language and symbolism that embeds them in society. As Assael (1998: 459) argues, 'Culture is a set of socially acquired values that society accepts as a whole and transmits to its members through language and symbols. As a result, culture reflects society's shared meanings and traditions'.

As the concept of culture is such a complex one Engel, Blackwell and Miniard (1995: 611), defining culture as 'a set of values, ideas, artefacts, and other meaningful symbols that help individuals communicate, interpret, and evaluate as members of society', listed the more important attitudes and behaviours influenced by culture as:

- a sense of self and space
- communication and language
- dress and appearance
- food and feeding habits
- time and time consciousness
- relationships
- values and norms
- beliefs and attitudes
- mental processes and learning
- work habits and practices.

As can be seen, many of the above impact upon the consumption of hospitality goods and services. Culture affects the consumption of hospitality as the ways in which we consume are deeply connected to the cultures within which we operate. People consume hospitality goods and services not only to experience their physiological benefits, but also as a way of expressing their cultures, that is, though socializing, participating in ritual, expressing symbolism, etc. As Bareham (1995: 65) suggests, 'eating and drinking are cultural events falling within the remit of anthropology ... the study of knowledge, skills, beliefs, values and activities which are passed from one generation to another'. Food and drink has always been strongly linked to culture (Holt, 1998; Wright, Nancarrow and Kwok, 2001). Consider issues such as the religious requirement on Jews to abstain from shellfish such as lobster, products which elsewhere are often seen to symbolize luxury and, indeed, gluttony (see Case Study 5.1). Similarly, cheese is considered a delicacy in most of Europe, with countries such as France offering a huge range of varieties, whereas in Japan, for example, cheese is rarely encountered. Very many similar examples exist: the practice of eating horsemeat, common in France, is considered barbaric in England, less than 25 miles away; cows are religious animals in India, yet are the staple ingredient in the beefburger; and many cultures shun alcohol, whereas for others outlets for alcohol consumption are a defining feature of their culture – consider the role of the English 'pub' in society, for example. The 2002 football World Cup, in Korea and Japan, provided a classic example of the role of culture in consumption, when Sepp Blatter, the President of FIFA, the sport's governing body, (and of European descent), made a public appeal for citizens of Korea to stop eating dog meat, fearful of the bad publicity it was engendering in much of the western press (*The Times*, 6 November 2001). It is clear that these differences are not a result of physiological factors such as taste but are explained by cultural differences, the behaviours shared by people from a particular society.

Case study 5.1

Kosher: the fitness of food for ritual purposes

The Kashruth, meaning fitness or kosher state, are the Jewish religious regulations that prohibit the eating of certain foods and the requirements that other foods be prepared in a specified manner. The term also denotes the state of being kosher according to Jewish law.

Known in Yiddish as *Kosher* and in Hebrew as *Kasher* this refers to the fitness of an object for ritual purposes and, while it is more generally applied to foods that meet the requirements of the *kashruth* dietary laws, kosher is also used to describe, for example, such objects as a Torah scroll, water for ritual bathing (*mikvah*), and the ritual ram's horn (*shofar*). When applied to food, kosher is the opposite of *terefah* (forbidden); when applied to other things, it is the opposite of *pasul* (unfit). In connection with the dietary laws, kosher is taken to imply a set of religious rules that must be followed, and these include:

1 That the food is not derived from the animals, birds, or fish prohibited in Leviticus 11 or Deuteronomy 14, that is to say, Jews observing Kashruth may eat only those fish that have both fins and scales (that is, not shellfish), certain birds, and mammals that chew the cud and have cloven feet.

2 That the animals or birds have been slaughtered by the ritual method of *shehitah* (which is described in detail below)

3 Because animal blood may not be eaten, meat must undergo a ritual process of pre-soaking and salting to draw off any blood that may remain within the meat after the ritual slaughter, after the carcass has been critically examined for physical blemishes and the ischiatic nerve removed from the hindquarters.

4 That meat and milk have not been cooked together and that separate utensils have been employed throughout the process. Strict separation of meat and dairy products is enjoined, both in eating and in preparation. This restriction not only forbids the eating of these two types of food at the same meal, but also requires that distinct sets of dishes, cutlery, utensils and table linen be used for meat and dairy products during the time of preparation. Some foods are neutral and are eaten freely with meat or milk; for example, no restrictions apply to the use of vegetables and fruit. In addition to the above, during the festival of Passover, special dietary laws exclude the use of leaven in bread and other baked goods.

Hospitality, Leisure & Tourism Series

In consequence of the second point above the term *terefah* (that which has been torn by beasts; Genesis 31:39) is extended to all food violating the law. Kosher wine is prepared under observation, to prevent libations to idols and to avoid handling by non-Jews, although this last regulation is presently observed only by the ultra-Orthodox.

The special method of slaughtering animals, known as *shehitah*, consists of an incision made across the neck of the animal by a qualified person trained for ritual slaughter, using a special knife that is razor sharp and has a smooth edge with no damage to the blade. The cutting is made by moving the knife in a single swift and uninterrupted sweep, which must not use pressure or stabbing movements, which severs the main arteries, rendering the animal unconscious and permitting the blood to drain from the body. The slaughterer (*shohet*) recites a prayer before the act of *shehitah*. Objections have been raised to this method of slaughter on the grounds of cruelty. For example, the sight of animals struggling during the slaughter aroused the concern of humane societies, and in some European countries this resulted in legislation forbidding ritual slaughter. In Orthodox Judaism the dietary laws are considered implications of the divine command to 'be holy', however, in Reform Judaism their observance has been declared to be unnecessary to the life of piety.

The regulations that prohibit the eating of certain foods and require that other foods be prepared in a specified manner, the Kashruth, are found in the Bible, primarily in Leviticus, Deuteronomy, Genesis and Exodus. Efforts have been made to establish a direct relationship between the kashruth and health, however, for Jews no other motive is required than that God has so ordained them.

Source: *Encyclopaedia Britannica* (2002)

Characteristics of culture

Extensive research has been undertaken into the role of culture and in particular the cultural values and characteristics that particular societies demonstrate. Cultural value has been defined as 'beliefs that a general state of existence is personally and socially worth striving for' (Rokeach, 1968: 548) and their relative importance to cultures are defined through a society's value systems, which can be seen to alter between cultures and over time within cultures. Thus in the 1980s the predominant culture of much of western society was seen as represented by the 'me first mentality' of individualism, summed up by films such as *Wall Street* and *Working Girl*. This was (arguably) replaced during the 1990s by a more 'caring/sharing' culture with an emphasis on green issues, the family, etc., as represented by the huge increase in television programmes about the garden and home. In a similar manner many eastern cultures are seen to be represented by a focus on inner harmony, for example Yoga, Feng Shui, meditation, etc., whereas western culture is represented by accomplishment and, increasingly, consumption.

While culture varies greatly, it is considered that a number of characteristics are generally true for all aspects of cultural value, and these are seen to include the following:

1 Cultural values are learned by individuals from childhood, a process known as enculturation, and can be formal, technical or informal learning. Enculturation occurs as a result of the values of a culture being instilled in its members, primarily through that culture's key institutions, such as religion, the family and education practices. Thus it is enculturation that is responsible for our understanding of what forms of behaviour are acceptable in various hospitality settings. Behaviour considered acceptable in a fast-food restaurant such as Burger King, for example holding your food in your hand, adult males using straws to drink with, sitting with your outdoor coat and hat on, the encouraging of child participation, etc., would not be tolerated in most hotel restaurants, where guests are often expected to wear a jacket and tie to dinner, diners are confronted with table settings containing specialist cutlery for each course, only females have decoration (such as fancy umbrellas and bits of fruit) in their drinks and children must be out of the dining room before eight o'clock in the evening in case they disturb the ambience for other diners.

2 Cultural values act as guides to our behaviour through the establishment of cultural norms, which identify appropriate ways of acting. If we deviate from these norms, then society penalizes that behaviour. Cultural norms suggest, for example, that by tradition the male pays for dinner on a date, regardless of who has the higher disposable income. In many restaurants it is still common for females to be given menus which have no prices on them, to avoid upsetting the sensibilities of the fairer sex! Similarly, males tend to be given the task of tasting/evaluating the wine in restaurants, regardless of who is hosting the party. Thankfully, patronizing norms such as these are gradually dying out.

3 Cultural values are very difficult to change; they tend towards permanence, due to the way in which they are passed from generation to generation. The British 'pub' is a unique product which in many ways has not changed in the recent past. As a result the current radical changes to the product, brought about largely as a result of governmental intercedence, are viewed by many as an attack on the very culture of Britain itself. Thus the Welsh Assembly has passed legislation to require licensed

retail companies to seek planning permission to change the names of public houses. This as a result of a perception that traditional names are under attack, despite the fact that the vast majority of Britain's 70 000 or so pubs still retain links with an increasingly irrelevant royalty, that is, being named after a piece of the anatomy of the royal family (Kings Head, etc.) animals with royal connections (Golden Lion, Unicorn, etc.) or famous royal escapades (the Royal Oak, etc.).

4 Contrary to what is stated above, culture is also seen as dynamic, with values changing to reflect the contemporary society. The reduction in Sunday observance laws, for example, mean that it is common for families to shop on Sundays, thus the 'traditional' Sunday lunch for an increasing number of families is taken in the cafeteria in Asda's or the nearest fast-food outlet. The dynamic nature of the culture of hospitality can also be seen in the increasing informality of many hospitality encounters. The growth of the budget hotel sector can in many ways be argued to be in rebellion to the set schemata and inflexible formality of traditional hotels.

5 Cultural values are widely held by individual societies and cultures, and are used to differentiate them from other cultures. Bars and clubs build up their own cultures; individuals within the culture understand it and replicate it, those outside of the culture have little or no understanding of how it operates.

As culture is about these widely shared values and beliefs, researchers have suggested it is possible to identify a range of national cultural beliefs. For example, Hofstede (1984) suggested that there were four nationally based dimensions to culture, namely:

1 *Individualism versus collectivism.* Hofstede suggested that some cultures value the freedom of the individual more highly than collectivism and group responsibility. Individualism is strongly associated with highly industrialized countries, such as the USA and the UK, while collectivism is most often seen to be associated with Far Eastern societies.

2 *Uncertainty avoidance.* This is seen as referring to the degree to which a country's culture encourages the acceptance of rules and customs, in order to avoid uncertainty. High levels of uncertainty avoidance are seen to be associated with cultures that encourage tradition, for example the Middle East etc., whereas cultures that encourage innovation and change are seen as demonstrating low levels of uncertainty avoidance, such as, again, the USA.

3 *Power distance.* This refers to the extent to which cultures favour centralization of power, and the distance (in terms of contact) between various hierarchies of power. Again western countries such as the USA and the UK are seen as having low power distances, while those of the Far East, etc. are seen as having high power distance.

4 *Masculinity/femininity.* Hofstede suggested that it was possible to identify the extent to which cultures exhibit characteristics traditionally associated with masculinity (for example, assertiveness, achievement, acquisition) or femininity (for example, concern, community, nurturing). Once again western cultures such as the USA and UK are seen as masculine, while the Far East, for example, is seen as feminine.

While Hofstede's work focuses on generalizations about culture, it would be wrong to take it on board too strongly. Within cultures, as we see later, differences can be greater than between cultures. Thus there are clearly very many entrepreneurs, with Far Eastern cultures, operating highly successfully in the hospitality industry, and similarly there are few cultures where power distance is more apparent than traditional UK and USA hotel companies.

Culture and hospitality consumer behaviour

From what we have said so far, if culture reflects the norms and values of a group or society it is clear that it will have an impact on the hospitality consumption of that group. As we have stated, consumers purchase hospitality goods and services both for physiological reasons and for cultural reasons, often expressed in the form of symbolism. As Engel, Blackwell and Miniard (1995: 615) state: 'culture has a profound effect on why people consume. Culture affects the specific products people buy as well as the structure of consumption, individual decision making, and communication in a society'. When consumers choose hospitality products they expect to gain three things: products that have function, products that have form and products that have meaning. For example, consumers choosing to spend their annual holiday on a cruise ship in the Caribbean expect their holiday to perform a function: to refresh them, to offer them experiences they do not normally have, etc. They will also have expectations about the form of the holiday; cruising is associated with numerous meals, lively evening entertainment, programmed activities, etc. However, consumers will also be seeking meaning through their holiday; cruising represents symbolism traditionally associated with aspects such as luxury, social class,

Hospitality, Leisure & Tourism Series

perfection, etc. As we see in later chapters, marketers recognize the need for such symbolism and use numerous tricks to ensure it is available. Tharp and Scott (1990) identified five symbolic roles of products that they suggested reflected cultural values:

1 *Products as a means of communicating social status.* Hospitality products often symbolize a consumer's status in society, and as a result marketers seek to establish their products as symbols of prestige. For example, health farms such as Forest Mere emphasize that their luxurious products are for the type of people who need to unwind and be pampered, but can afford to pay premium prices for the experience

2 *Products are a means of self-expression.* Hospitality marketers seek to reflect the values that are most important to consumers, by trying to associate their products with the symbolism of achievement, individualism, personal development, etc. Many hospitality services can be seen to be linked to elements of self-expression, for example the growth of speciality bars such as The Revolution vodka bars, or the trend towards boutique hotels in which the décor, furniture and fittings are stylized and designer led.

3 *Products are a means of sharing experiences.* Hospitality products provide the opportunity for sharing experiences such as social occasions and events, with the nature of the product itself having a key symbolic role. A restaurant dinner party with friends where champagne is served, for example, is usually interpreted in a different manner to one during which other forms of wine are served.

4 *Products are hedonistic.* Hospitality services are often hedonistic in nature, and the emphasis on this hedonism, as opposed to the utilitarian, reflects consumers' values. Again if we consider the example of health farms, such as Forest Mere, we can identify the hedonistic nature of typical hospitality services.

5 *Products are experiential.* Hospitality goods and services remind consumers of previous experiences. Thus a glass of Pernod will often remind the consumer of past episodes and situations where the product was drunk and will rekindle either positive or (in my own case) negative associations.

Culture is important to our understanding of hospitality consumer behaviour as, according to Statt (1997: 179), 'to the extent that members of a culture share common values and are guided by them, they can be expected to behave in similar ways when they are in similar situations, including buying and consuming. This kind of predictability is crucial to a marketing strategy'. In the global hospitality industry it is seen as important for companies to be aware of national culture, at least in broad terms, in order to understand the attitudinal differences that exist between cultures.

Hospitality consumption as ritual

As we have already discussed, culture influences the way in which hospitality products are consumed, in particular, culture is important in defining the ritual role of much hospitality consumption. It is suggested that it is possibly aspects of social rituals involving consumption that go most beyond the narrow focus of the consumer as an individual behaving alone. Such rituals involve aspects of family, society and culture, that is, the focus is on rituals as forums for social and cultural activity. Research which has been conducted on occasions such as Christmas, Thanksgiving, Halloween, theme park visits, etc., has shown the involvement of issues of gender, materialism, the family, sex role socialization and commercial appropriation (Fischer and Arnold, 1990; O'Guin and Belk, 1989; Wallendorf and Arnould, 1992). Recent research has focused on the role of shared brand choices and consumption loyalties, and the contention that consumers gain a sense of community through such loyalty (Freidman, Abeele and De Vos, 1993).

Rituals are defined as 'the symbolic behaviours that occur in sequence and are repeated frequently' Rook (1985: 255), and they are frequently associated with hospitality goods and services, in particular through the scripts that rituals often involve. These scripts prescribe how, when and by whom certain ritual artefacts will be used. So, for example, the traditional table setting in a restaurant, with its numerous sets of cutlery and its wide range of glasses for different drinks, are examples of hospitality ritual. In my first bar job I was asked for a glass of sherry, which I duly poured, only to be met with howls of scorn and derision as it was explained to me that sherry is not served in a wine glass, and certainly not a white wine glass; it is served in a special glass known as a schooner, which is used for no other drink that a bar serves! Indeed, in the British culture sherry deserves a category of ritual all its own as it is also the only drink which seems to be reserved for consuming at occasions such as weddings and christenings, when more often than not people hold on to it for the toast before depositing it somewhere, untouched, and then heading to the bar for a 'proper' drink. The manner and order in which we consume food is also ritualized, for example, in the UK we have a starter, fish course, entrée, dessert and cheese. This is in stark contrast to many other countries where a more informal grazing style is adopted with limited separation of courses. In Greece, for example, *meze* is delivered to the table and everyone is invited to partake, no one has their own meal and very little in the way of structure exists.

When such cultures intermingle it can cause dissonance to consumers. For example, in Spain, *tapas* is in effect a form of elaborate bar snack. However, when *tapas* was introduced to the UK the informality and lack of structure caused problems for consumers used to courses, menus and plated meals. The result is that many *tapas* bars in the UK bear no resemblance to their originals in Spain. A curious result of the global hospitality industry, however, is that in many areas of Spain popular with UK tourists, the *tapas* bars are now modelled on those that the tourists are used to in the UK; thus again they bear little resemblance to traditional Spanish *tapas*. Spanish *tapas* is just one of many similar ritualized food offers, including the Scandinavian smorgasbord, Greek *meze*, Egyptian *mazza* and Russian *zakuska*, which are all elaborate food displays offering many dishes, with traditional beverage counterpoints, for example, vodka or sherry. Many cuisines offer a mixed hors d'oeuvre, of which the Italian antipasto is one of the best known, made up of such foods as olives, nuts, cheese, sausage, peppers, fish, raw vegetables and eggs.

There are very many examples of rituals associated with food and drink. For example, the clambake is a seafood picnic traditional in the New England region of the USA, having been adopted from the coastal native Americans. Clambakes, undertaken on a large scale in the region, have long been a feature of civic celebration in areas where clams, lobsters, and fish are abundant. Preparations for a clambake begin with the digging of a deep pit on the beach. The pit is lined with stones upon which a wood fire burns for several hours to heat the stones thoroughly. Clams, lobsters, fish, chicken, ears of sweet corn, onions, and potatoes are placed on top of the stones and finally the food is covered with a thick layer of seaweed, which furnishes the aromatic steam in which the food cooks.

In a similar way the luau is a modern Hawaiian banquet, referring to dishes prepared with the leaves of the taro plant, the term nowadays designates the modern, informal feast, as distinct from the ancient ceremonial banquets that were highly ritualized and attended only by men. The standard luau is eaten at a low table that is covered with taro leaves and decorated with fruits and flowers. It traditionally includes dishes such as poi (pig baked whole in an underground oven), lau lau (luau leaves and pork wrapped in a ti leaf and steamed), lomi lomi salmon (marinated raw fish), baked sweet potatoes, fish or chicken cooked in coconut milk, shellfish and sweets. Dancing and music accompany the feast. Today, hotels and restaurants in Hawaii offer sanitized versions of the luau, to tourists visiting the island. One of the most ritualized food and beverage experiences is that of the Japanese tea ceremony, a description of which is included as Case Study 5.2.

The influence of subcultures on hospitality consumption

Subcultures are cultures within cultures, that is to say, they share many of the features of the dominant, for example national, culture while offering a range of additional characteristics. As Chisnall (1995: 123) states: 'A national culture is made up of several sub-cultures that have their own distinctive character-istics, some of which may be very different from the total pattern of culture.' Subcultures originate from a variety of sources. For example, they may be based on ethnicity, religion, age, geog-raphy, etc., and allow individuals to develop group and personal relationships, within which a set of common values emerge. They are important to our understanding of hospitality consumer behaviour as it is suggested that members of subcultures regularly consume the same goods and services.

Case study 5.2

Ritualized experiences of food and drink: the example of the Japanese tea ceremony

The Japanese tea ceremony, or *cha-no-yu*, is a ritual dating back to the thirteenth century, wherein tea is meticulously prepared and accompanied by a variety of delicate seasonal dishes. Every aspect of the ceremony – the setting, the flavours and textures of foods, the colours and shapes of the containers – is calculated to achieve harmony and effect.

The Japanese *chado*, or *sado*, which translates 'as the way of tea', also known as the *cha-no-yu*, the 'hot-water tea', is one of the most time-honoured institutions in Japan. It is derived from the principles of Zen Buddhism and founded upon the adoration of beauty in the everyday routines of life, being a ritualized way of entertaining guests, in which everything is done according to an established order.

The ceremony takes place in a *cha-shitsu* (tea house), for which great care is taken in the choice of materials and construction, so as to give it a sense of rustic, refined simplicity. The room is usually about 3 metres square with a *toko-no-ma* (alcove) at one end, in which is typically displayed a hanging scroll or flower arrangement. In addition the room usually contains a *ro* (small sunken fireplace) that is used in the winter months for heating the tea kettle. The *cha-shitsu* is entered through a small, low door, which is designed to suggest

Hospitality, Leisure & Tourism Series

humility to the guests. The tea ceremony consists of the host first bringing the tea utensils into the room, offering the guests special desserts, and then preparing and serving them tea made of tea leaves stirred in hot water, which is usually thin and frothy with a mildly astringent flavour. After the tea has been consumed guests inquire about the various tea implements, which are then carried from the room and the ceremony is concluded.

Ritualized tea drinking, originated in China, and has been practised in Japan from the end of the twelfth century, having been introduced by Zen monks, as an aid to meditation. It later became an integral part of Zen ritual, designed to honour the patriarch, Bodhidharma. It later came to be a gathering of friends in an isolated atmosphere to drink tea and discuss the merits of art, calligraphy, and flower arrangements displayed in the *toko-no-ma* or indeed the tea utensils themselves. The tea ceremony is seen as emphasizing four qualities: first, harmony between the guests and the implements used; second, respect, not only among the participants but also for the utensils; third, cleanliness, derived from Shinto practices and requiring participants to wash their hands and rinse their mouths as symbolic gestures of cleansing before entering the *cha-shitsu*; and, finally, tranquillity, imparted through long and caring use of each article of the tea ceremony.

The *kaiseki*, the highest form of cuisine and dining in Japan, has developed from the tea ceremony, coming as close to dining as an art form as any in the gastronomic world. The food served in *kaiseki* is selected according to the season and presented as a series of small dishes. The key to the composition of the *kaiseki* lies in *aishoh* (compatibility). Nowhere has more attention and imagination been given to the presentation of food than in Japan, where the delicacy and exquisiteness of Japanese table arrangements are matched only by the art displayed in the food itself.

Source: *Encyclopaedia Britannica* (2002)

As Assael (1998: 509) suggests, 'The individual who identifies closely with a certain religious, ethnic or national sub-culture will accept the norms and values of that group. As a result, members of a sub-culture frequently buy the same brands and products . . . and shop in the same stores'. Assael goes on to suggest that in terms of consumer behaviour the influence of subcultures is dependent on as number of factors, which he identified as:

1 *The distinctiveness of the subculture*, suggesting that the more distinctive a subculture is, the greater is its potential influence on consumer behaviour, as we see later within hospitality consumption. For example, the youth market is a very distinctive subculture within hospitality and has a profound influence on consumer behaviour.

2 *The homogeneity of the subculture*. Subcultures that demonstrate higher levels of homogeneity are seen as more likely to

influence its members. Thus, for example, religious subculture, due to the homogeneity of its members, will influence hospitality consumption in a significant manner.

3 *Subcultural exclusion.* Exclusion tends to increase a subculture's influence over its members, by isolating them from society and thus encouraging the development of subcultural norms and values. As many students are in effect excluded from the 'real' world, they develop behaviours that are acceptable to them but are unlikely to be replicated by society at large. This may include 'grazing' rather than eating at formal meal times, going to clubs until the early hours of the morning during the working week, drinking during the day, etc.

The distinctiveness, homogeneity and exclusion characteristics of subcultures act to replicate subcultural identity as distinct from that of the general culture, often leading to some elements of dissonance within the individuals who make up the group and conflict with the wider environment.

As we have stated earlier, subcultures are often characterized by factors such as age, geography, religion, lifestyle or ethnicity, and we will consider the implications of each of these for the consumption of hospitality goods and services. However, it should be remembered that while some subcultures are easily identifiable, their value to the members of the group might be questionable. As Statt (1997: 188) argues, 'a black woman may be put into the categories of skin and sex by a marketing observer but what might be important to her are her membership of the medical profession and her humanist beliefs, two quite different subcultures'.

Age subcultures

Age has commonly been identified as a subcultural character-istic within marketing, despite continuing debate as to the extent to which age groups are really homogeneous. The US department of health in 1996, for example, was categorizing the population as mature (those born before 1945), the 'baby boomers' (those born between 1946 and 1964), generation X (those born between 1965 and 1976), the teens (those born between1978 and 1984) and the pre-teens (those born between 1985 and 1989) (Wilkie, 1994). It is clear that these groupings are too large to be categorized as subcultures in any meaningful way; for example, the generation X category would have contained 47 million US citizens in 1996, which is only slightly smaller than the population of the UK. As generation X are described as 'more cynical and alienated than other age groups, with income levels well below their expectations . . . resentful of having to pay the future bill for an unbalanced budget and pollution' (Assael, 1998: 511), this adds up to a lot of depressed citizens. Despite this, intuitively most people would accept that the youth market, for example, consumes differently from other sectors of the culture it is part of. Hospitality companies have long recognized these differences and provided goods and services to match; for example, clubs and bars that provide more stimulus and external entertainment than traditional venues.

Many lifestyle models have been developed to try to identify subcultures characterized by age. Typical models describe subcultures by evocative names which then become part of mainstream vocabulary, and have included: YUPPIES (young urban professionals) defined as professionals between the ages of twenty-five and thirty-nine who earned at least £30 000 per annum; this was later subverted to GUPPIES (gay urban professionals) and BUPPIES (black urban professionals); Sloans (derived from Sloan Ranger), those who inhabit the shops and wine bars of the Sloane Square region of London, and taken to refer to upper and upper-middle class girls in general; DINKIES (dual income, no kids); and OPALS (older people with active lifestyles). While these models are evocative and thus generate considerable media interest, their real value in defining consumption habits is questionable, as is discussed in detail in later chapters.

Geographic subcultures

Geography as a characteristic of subculture can be seen to have the same difficulty as age – the designations may be too large to identify specific groups – but, despite this, marketers have continued to attempt to cluster consumers according to where they live. The growth of geography-based models of subculture reached its peak in the early 1990s when geodemographic analysis was a cornerstone of most marketing activity. Companies such as Bass and Whitbread, for example, made extensive use of research such as ACORN and MOSAIC, which are both geodemographic mapping tools, in order to aid in the decisions they made about public house investment, purchase and retention. However, as we discuss in Chapter 7, the value of such models has been heavily criticized, with authors such as Jon Epstein (quoted in Evans and Moutinho, 1999: 33) arguing that 'Marketers have become ignorant or lazy. They think they have to buy data from databases, I challenge the idea that if they buy data and overlay it they'll understand their customers better'.

Religion as subculture

Religion can be seen to be a subcultural factor as it is so closely tied to tradition and custom, and thus significant consumer behaviour may arise from religious beliefs. As we have already discussed, religion is reflected in the things that groups are allowed to consume, for example. However, religion again suffers as a means of considering groups of consumers due to the size of the resultant groups, and in addition Chisnall (1995: 128) suggests that 'it may be hypothesized that the importance of religion as a sub-culture group affecting the consumption of products is likely to be subservient to that of socio-economic groups'. In terms of hospitality consumption, however, some interesting research was undertaken by Hirschman (1981), who found that religious affiliation could influence the ways in which consumers evaluate brands.

The subculture of ethnicity

Within large communities subcultures based on ethnicity often develop and, as a result, as Chisnall (1995: 126) suggests, 'some ethnic cultural differences may be reflected in the brands and types of products consumed . . . in some cases ethnic influences form distinctive behavioural patterns'. Ethnicity is the process by which people use labels to define themselves and others, and is important in consumer behaviour dependent upon the strength or weakness that people have in their associations with their ethnic group. As Hirschman (1982: 86) states: 'to the degree that people in an ethnic group share common perceptions and cognitions that are different from those of other ethnic groups or the larger society, they constitute a distinct ethnic group'. It is clear that some evidence of specialized provision for ethnic subcultures is apparent; one has only to consider the range of specialist shops that appear wherever a predominantly ethnic population develops, in order to meet the cultural needs of that specific section of the population. However, it is also clear that extensive crossing of cultures is evident, with examples ranging from music, through fashion to entertainment and food. Where such crossing occurs research suggests that the new subculture is more than a fusion of the two existing cultures, a unique subcultural style emerges (Chisnall, 1995). Within hospitality one of the best examples of this process of fusion is the case of the Indian-style Balti restaurant: customers readily consume the product (which is cooked in a large wok-like bowl) in the belief that it is a traditional form of curry, despite it having been developed as a form of cooking by the families of migrant

Indians in Birmingham in the mid-1980s. Cultural diversity, resulting from the fusion of various ethnic groups, is often valued in multicultural societies. However, the values and norms of ethnic subcultures may also cause conflict with those of the overall culture.

Summarizing the role of culture in hospitality consumer behaviour

In order to understand the consumption of hospitality goods and services we must seek to understand the role of culture, as Chisnall (1995: 129) states: 'Culture gives people an identity and social cohesion, it may also profoundly affect consumption behaviour.' Such a view is supported by Wright, Nancarrow and Kwok (2001: 355) who state: 'what drives preference? Preference reflects in part the consumer's social and cultural origins, social ambitions and the cultural capital acquired, either as part of their upbringing or more deliberately'. The meaning given to hospitality goods and services is significantly affected by aspects of culture. For example, gender differences in hotel provision might be small but the critical question is, what do those differences mean for women as compared to men? Where a business-class hotel room, for example, contains expensive trouser presses but inadequate security and lighting, what message does this relay to women executives? Attempts to understand hospitality services in terms of their symbolic meanings for their users continually flounder on the tensions between those services' cultural meanings and their primary functions.

Basic cultural values are enduring, as culture is so deeply ingrained; it is not something we have, it is everything we are. Despite this, culture is not static or unchanging. The reverse is actually true, cultures are in a constant process of change. However, that process is so long term that it appears to be static. The branded fast-food restaurants which are so prevalent a part of the contemporary high street are, in fact, a relatively recent introduction to our culture, dating back only to the mid-1970s, despite this for many people the 'Big Mac' and the 'Whopper' are 'traditional' Sunday lunches. In a similar vein, the Indian restaurants, which play such a significant role in introducing people to the restaurant experience, have only been a major feature of the UK hospitality industry since the 1960s. In order to aid our understanding of the role culture plays in hospitality consumption, we have included the introduction of Disney theme parks to Europe, in the early 1990s (see Case Study 5.3).

Case study 5.3

EuroDisney: cultural Chernobyl

The purpose of this case study is to examine how the EuroDisney debacle came about, albeit that today Disneyland Paris, as it was rebranded, is the single most popular visitor attraction in Europe.

EuroDisney was conceived of as a pure transplant from the Disney parks of the USA, exporting the character themes evident in the rides, infrastructure, employees, food and entertainment, a process which proved to be highly successful when the concept was exported to its first overseas culture, that of Tokyo, in 1983. The success of the Tokyo park convinced the Disney management that the theme park concept could be readily exported to 'alien' cultures. Europe was seen by many Disney executives as being an easier option than Japan had been, after all the market was familiar with the Disney product and Europeans were some of the major customers of the existing parks in the USA.

After considering a number of location options, including England and Spain, Disney agreed a deal with the French government in 1985, for a site 32 kilometres east of Paris. The deal was sweetened for Disney by the French government offering plentiful cheap land, road and rail links, tax breaks and other financial incentives, in return for putting a prestigious development on a site of high unemployment.

During the construction phase optimism prevailed. However, soon after its opening in April 1992, this optimism was increasingly replaced by cynicism as queues formed for rides that refused to function, service in the restaurants was heavily criticized and many of the European employees seemed to struggle with the need to conform to Disney codes of behaviour.

Exactly what went wrong at EuroDisney is a matter of opinion. However, it is clear that it was beset by a number of problems, some external and others of its own making. In 1992 Europe was in the middle of a major recession and, as a result, the value of the franc fell against many currencies, not least the British pound and the Italian lira. In addition, partly as a result of very high interest rates, the French property market collapsed, leaving EuroDisney in possession of its own hotels, which were not generating sufficient income to service their borrowings. Finally, Disney were unsure about the future of the park and were refusing to sanction the planned second phase of development, which was necessary in order to encourage long-stay guests, and thus fill hotel rooms.

Despite this, it is clear that recession was not wholly to blame for the park's misfortunes, as EuroDisney admitted in its 1993 financial report. Disney simply did not understand the cultural aspects of the proposed developments and failed adequately to plan for them. Little attempt was made to understand why Europeans were so enthused about the Disney parks in the USA, and they failed to understand that the theme park concept per se was only one part of the equation. Equally important, for example, were the weather, especially to UK visitors for whom sunshine is at a premium, the comparatively low cost of accommodation in the USA and easy access to a number of other activities, in particular the film studio and water parks of Orlando, Florida, that were an integral part of a USA 'Disney' holiday. The developers failed to address the very simple question, why would consumers choose to go to the 'faux' EuroDisney, rather than the 'real' park in Orlando. If Disney had been aware of some of the cultural issues it would surely have chosen England, which has a more closely shared language and culture, or Spain, which has a better climate. Instead it chose northern France, which has weather similar to England, and a culture snobbishly famous for artists and philosophers, a group of people who came out firmly against the development, arguing that Mickey Mouse was not an appropriate cultural icon for France and terming EuroDisney 'cultural Chernobyl'.

As a result of the characteristics outlined above, attendance figures for EuroDisney proved to be wildly optimistic, and in particular the French failed to participate in any significant numbers. Visitors chose to stay in Paris and only visited the park for one day, which resulted in low average spends, and they also refused to take on board the Disney intent that visitors were not able to bring in their own food, but had to eat at one of the restaurants provided, with the result that food 'smuggling' was rife.

There were also employee-related cultural problems as the French employees, unused to the strict Disney regime common in much of the USA, refused to style their hair as dictated, to wear uniforms they were allocated, unadorned or unaltered, and most importantly to smile and be 'nice' to the customers, a concept alien in most French hospitality scenarios. The result was very high labour turnover, and the need to maintain a labour ratio to customers far in excess of the USA norm.

Today, the rebranded Disneyland Paris is a success. It attracts more visitors than any other attraction in Europe, new attractions have opened, a new park is coming on line and others are in the pipeline, and attendance and occupancy rates are much healthier. However, it does provide a salutary lesson to what happens when organizations believe they have all the answers, are unrivalled in their expertise and thus lose sight of the importance of appropriate research into customer behaviour. It also demonstrates the effect that misinterpreting culture can have on the fortunes of even the most sophisticated organizations.

Sources: Curwen (1995); Ritzer (1999); www.DisneylandParis.com

The influence of social class and status on hospitality consumption

Despite class being one of the central foci of sociology, it is still an ill-defined and often ambiguous term. Anecdotally we understand what we mean when we say someone is middle class, but understanding how this affects their consumption of hospitality goods and services is quite another thing. Engel, Blackwell and

Miniard (1995: 126) define social class as 'relatively permanent and homogeneous divisions in a society into which individuals or families sharing similar values, lifestyles, interests and behaviours can be categorized'. However, despite suggesting that it encompasses a wide range of factors, they conclude that social class is largely a factor of economic performance. Statt (1997) suggests that the concept of class is Roman in origin, dating back to the use of wealth as a system of classification for administrative purposes; however, today 'social class is predominantly defined by the occupation of the individual' (Blythe, 1997: 94). There is, however, more to class than simple classifications of occupation. Class implies power, hierarchy, life chances, education and status, while simultaneously impacting on such issues as gender and ethnicity, among others. As Statt (1997: 161) states: 'a stratified society, like a stratified cliff face, implies the existence of a hierarchy between the top and bottom strata . . . in society this denotes social groups that are more or less highly valued . . . [it also] implies the existence of a fundamental inequality in the way the resources of a society are distributed'. Within marketing aspects of social stratification have become a major focus of research activity, to the extent that Miller (1991) suggests that some 30 per cent of all research in major sociological journals is devoted to the nature and effect of social stratification. Despite this research, however, Sivadas, Mathew and Currey (1997) suggest that a number of factors have impeded our understanding of the role of social class on consumer behaviour, citing changing demographics, the problems of empirical research in investigating contemporary society and ill-fitting research tools, among others.

The influence of social class or social stratification is that people within stratum largely interact with others from the same stratum. This is a result of living in the same area, having a similar education, working in similar occupations and often having the same circle of friends. Social groups are not physically separated; however, as a result of group values and norms they tend to behave as if they are. Weber (1946), for example, discussed class in terms of life chances, concluding that class is determined by the opportunities available to an individual in terms of earnings and, thus, resulting possessions. If we consider social class in this way, it suggests that consumption is both a result of social class and a factor in its determination, as Statt (1997: 163) states: 'a person's future socio-economic status is therefore dependent to a considerable extent on the social hand he or she is dealt at birth'.

Social class, while largely a feature of economic performance, is also demonstrated by a range of other factors, identified by

Economic variables	Interaction variables	Political variables
Occupation	Personal prestige	Power
Income	Association	Class-consciousness
Wealth	Socialization	Mobility

Source: adapted from Engel, Blackwell and Miniard (1995)

Table 5.1 Variables of social class

Engel, Blackwell and Miniard (1995) as listed in Table 5.1, and we will consider some of these in terms of their effect on consumption of hospitality products.

Occupation

Occupation is often seen as the best indicator of social class by consumer researchers, as the work we do greatly affects our lifestyles, and is an important factor in the way in which prestige and respect are awarded. Unfortunately for us, hospitality is not seen in the UK as a profession which demands the same respect as other occupations such as accountancy, for example, despite the requisite levels of ability and skills required successfully to operate a bar, restaurant or hotel.

Socialization

Research tends to suggest that people are most comfortable when they are with others who share similar values and behaviours. Thus our social interactions tend to be limited to our immediate social class. For example, the likelihood of marriage within social class is much greater than between social class. Public house retailers have long recognized this factor and have traditionally developed public houses around very simple social categorization schemes such as estate public housess for social class D/E, taverns for the middle classes and trendy urban bars for the professionals.

Possessions and symbols

As Engel, Blackwell and Miniard (1995: 685) state: 'possessions are symbols of class membership, not only the number of possessions but also the nature of the choices made'. In terms of consumption, social class in effect operates as a series of subcultures, based on education, occupation and the economic power of its members. However, as it is such an ephemeral subject, it tends to be the symbols associated with class and status that are important. The exclusivity of goods and services denote status. Thus, if everyone can own a Mercedes or a Maurice Lacroix watch it cannot be used as a status symbol. Similarly, in hospitality if everyone can stay at the Savoy, dine at the Ivy or holiday at the Sandy Lane they cannot be used to denote prestige. It is the exclusivity of a symbol that is its attraction; as such it symbolizes a wide range of other characteristics. Statt (1997: 163) suggests that in order to denote status or prestige products have to demonstrate one of five factors:

1 *Exclusivity*: only a few people should be eligible to acquire it; the status of corporate hospitality at events such as Henley, Ascot and Wimbledon is largely a result of such exclusivity.
2 *Expensive*: one of the ways, but not the only one, in which status symbols retain their exclusivity; thus for most of us holidays at the Sandy Lane are beyond our means.
3 *Quality*: there is an assumption that status is reflected in the quality of goods and services; thus advertisements for facilities such as Forest Mere Health Club focus largely upon the quality of the experience, confirming that this is more than simply a spa.
4 *Limited*: as we have already suggested if everyone can eat at restaurants such as the Ivy, it does not offer scope for prestige. In truth, those with status do not have to make reservations.
5 *Respect*: status symbols only operate as long as people respect the symbolism; thus designers such as Dior lost their power to denote status through franchising the name to a huge range of merchandise, much of which was of inferior quality. In hospitality many of the restaurants owned and operated by 'celebrity' chefs such as Worrell-Thompson came under fire when it became clear that the involvement of the celebrity was often nothing more than name alone, with a resultant decline in quality and thus status.

All societies have a system of social class and status; the questions from a hospitality consumption viewpoint are, how many classes are there? How identifiable are they? How does their existence impact on their consumption behaviour? In the UK the standard British classification uses six categories designated by the letters A to E. However, for marketing purposes companies often combine A, B and C_1 (a total of almost 40 per cent of the population) and C_2, D and E (the remaining 60 per cent of the population).

Class-consciousness and social mobility

Class-consciousness refers to the extent to which people are aware of their social class and the characteristics that define it, and thus are aware of themselves as a distinct group with shared consumption patterns. Social mobility refers to two aspects: first, that people move between strata, largely as a result of the related factors of income and education; and, second, the argument that stratification itself is undergoing significant changes, not least due to movements such as postmodernism which indicates a blurring at the edges of social stratification. In western ideology it has always been a source of achievement for individuals to seek upward mobility within society, with the result that countries such as the UK and the USA have both seen a bulging of the population classified as middle class.

The impact of social class on hospitality consumption

Social class affects the consumption of hospitality products in a number of ways, for example, the type of leisure preferred, the food and drink we consume, the holidays we take, etc. These choices are made based on the activities of others within the same or closely adjacent social levels. For example, much to their surprise, towns such as Rock and Newquay in Cornwall have become a focus for end of school-year activities for predominantly middle and upper-middle class girls and boys in recent years. The bars, clubs and restaurants of the area have responded by redirecting their activities to this high-spending segment of the market. However, these towns need to be aware that fads such as this will end as quickly as they began. In a similar manner we can see the influence of class in the holiday destinations we choose – the Spanish mainland and islands are closely associated with lower-middle and working class holidays, areas such as inland Italy and Brittany with the middle classes and the Caribbean with the upper-middle classes. Similarly, forms of recreation are often seen as class based – polo is upper class (with tournaments sponsored by companies such as Cartier), tennis is middle class (with tournaments sponsored by companies such as Stella Artois) and bingo is lower class (and is subsequently funded by the participants themselves with limited opportunities for sponsorship). Social class values give direction to hospitality marketers. For example, it is suggested that social class impacts upon advertising (Assael, 1998) with the upper classes being more open to symbolism and individualism; thus advertisements for hotels are often linked to status and/or power. Social class is also seen to be linked to the distribution of hospitality services.

For example, lower classes tend to consume in their neighbourhood, where they are most comfortable; thus if this is the market a product is aimed at it makes little sense to locate it on an out-of-town retail park (Prasad, 1975). Research also suggests that social class is a feature of design (Roscoe, LeClaire and Schiffman, 1997) with the upper classes emphasizing style and colour, whereas working-class consumers emphasize fitness for purpose, that is, does it work. This of course might be a self-fulfilling prophecy, the working-classes often do not have the luxury of replacing items on aesthetic grounds. This feature can be seen in many hospitality venues; boutique hotels, for example, feature designer fabrics and furnishings, in a minimalist manner. Compare this to the Travel Inn where rooms are stuffed with items, all of which are necessary if the hotel is to work for its customers. The Malmaison hotel brand, which is designed to look like an upmarket French *pension*, is a good example of this feature of social class, being aimed squarely at upper-middle, upper class and professional customers, the exclusivity being ensured by price among other mechanisms. However, it does not offer concierge services, room service, leisure facilities, crèches or any of the other features that one would associate with this standard of hotel, and certainly features that customers of other social classes would consider essential. Malmaison suggests that if you are the kind of person who needs to haul lots of luggage around this is not your sort of hotel, its customers have limited, but frequently laundered, clothing.

It is clear that the world of hospitality is full of symbols associated with class and status, ranging from exclusive hotels (indeed, Forte once had a brand of hotels known as the Exclusive Hotels of the World), to celebrity restaurants and designer bars. Bars like the 'Met' in London signify status and class to their customers, and when they are no longer fashionable those seeking the attached status quickly move on. In any given society status and prestige is available to very few. However, many people will aspire to higher status and the consumption of hospitality goods and services are often associated with status, and thus may confer this on the consumer. In addition, it is increasingly argued that the value and appropriateness of using social classification as a mechanism for investigating consumer behaviour is changing. While clearly we have not achieved the much trumpeted classless society (look at the undue deference still given to a few people of limited ability or qualification on account of their parents being lucky enough to live in Buckingham Palace), it is clear that society is much more fragmented than was previously the case. The increasing presence of mass media, higher disposable incomes, a period of political stability and economic prosperity, and a wider, though still inequitable, distribution of economic and political power, have all contributed to the decline in fixed social stratification. Due to the role that the above play in contemporary hospitality consumption we discuss them in greater detail in later chapters, as Wells (1993: 303) states: 'with more acute awareness of sociological models and methods, consumer researchers would see new approaches to old problems'.

CHAPTER 6

The influence of reference groups on hospitality consumers

Key themes

- This chapter considers the influence of reference groups on hospitality consumers and the various roles played by group members.

- It seeks to examine the variety of methods that have been used to measure the relative influence of reference groups.

- It considers the nature and types of conflict that reference groups engender and the ways in which hospitality consumers resolve such conflicts.

- The chapter considers the ways in which people are influenced by others around them, including family, friends, peers and other reference groups with whom individuals interact in the act of consuming hospitality goods and services.

An introduction to the influence of groups on hospitality consumption

As we saw in the previous chapter, consumers are influenced by other people with whom they interact, and the effect of that influence can be extremely important, for example, the role of institutions in structuring the culture within which we are immersed. When we consider hospitality consumption the influence of others becomes even more significant, because in general we consume hospitality as part of a social group – even if we go to a bar or restaurant by ourselves it is likely that we will soon be interacting with other consumers. As Dubois (2000: 256) argues: 'for everyday products it is often true that the buyer and the consumer are the same person, on the other hand, for many products such an assumption is inaccurate as many people intervene in the purchase and consumption process ... in such cases one can talk about collective decision-making and the notion of the consumer as an individual must be abandoned in favour of that of a decision-making unit'.

It is for this reason that we need to consider the role that groups take in the consumption of hospitality products. Groups can be formed for a number of reasons, and thus there are numerous definitions of what constitutes a group, dependent upon the context for the groups' development, as Bareham (1995: 119) states: 'it could be said that someone standing in a queue at a supermarket checkout was in a group'. In the social sciences the term 'group' has a relatively precise meaning, being defined as 'two or more people who share some common goals or objectives and who interact to achieve these' (Bareham, 1995: 119), or 'a social entity that allows individuals to interact with one another in relation to particular phenomena' (Chisnall, 1995: 157). In consumer behaviour this is taken a stage further and groups are defined as 'two or more people who share a set of norms and whose relationship makes their behaviour independent' (Blythe, 1997: 98). When we are considering groups in consumer behaviour the focus is on reference groups and these are further defined as 'a person or group of people that significantly influences an individual's behaviour' (Beardon and Etzel, 1982: 184), that influence being generated by providing standards and norms by which consumers judge their attitudes and behaviour. The concept of a reference group was originated more that fifty years ago, and has now largely been assimilated into social scientific theory, as Chisnall (1995: 158) suggests: 'on the common-sense level, the concept says in effect that behaviour is influenced in different ways and to different degrees by other people – reference group influence represents an unrealistic truism which has long been recognized'.

There is a wide range of possible types into which we can put reference groups, with Blythe (1997) suggesting the following categories:

1 *Primary groups*. Primary groups are the people with whom we are most closely associated, in particular family, but also close friends and colleagues, those with whom we share hobbies, etc. The primary group tends to be small as the interactions required with the group are labour intensive, for example, visiting, meeting, regular communications, etc. However, the result is cohesion and mutual participation, generally over an extended period of time. The cohesive nature of primary groups results in, and results from, shared beliefs and values and similar consumption behaviour, as its members tend to identify with goods and services in similar ways.

2 *Secondary groups*. Secondary groups are those people we only see on occasions, and with whom we have shared interests, for example, members of the same sports clubs would constitute a secondary group. Secondary groups are less influential on our behaviour, with most influence being felt through the subject of joint interest, that is, the sport in question.

3 *Aspirational groups*. These are groups that individuals aspire to belong to, and for that reason can be very powerful motivators of behaviour, with individuals adopting the characteristics of the group and behaving in ways that are seen as more likely to result in membership. Aspirational groups are important, as marketers often use aspiration as a means of influencing consumer behaviour, through the implication that buying certain products will result in membership of the aspirational group. Timeshare sales, for example, are often marketed as offering the aspiration of owning your own property overseas. Cruising originally had similar aspirational overtones, although as the market has become more universal these have reduced. Fisher and Price (1992) suggest that purchasing products linked to aspirational groups was a means consumers used to establish a connection to the group, and that an important condition for the influence was that the product had to be visually obvious. Companies such as Planet Hollywood and Hard Rock Café have maximized this feature of groups in their merchandising to the extent that it likely that in many of their stores these companies make as great a turnover from merchandising as they do from sales of food and drink.

4 *Dissociative groups*. These are the reverse of aspirational groups; they are those groups that individuals seek to avoid being associated with, and again these groups impact on consumer behaviour, with individuals actively avoiding certain products

associated with their dissociative groups. Bars and restaurants often result in dissociative groups as individuals consider them not to be 'their kind of bar'. During the 1980s sales of Guinness were in serious decline as drinkers sought to disassociate themselves from the kind of people assumed to drink the product (old men who nursed a drink all evening). However, a highly successful advertising campaign during the 1990s which used stylish images, a cult actor of the period and music which went on to become a number one hit in the charts, combined with a social change which idealized everything Celtic, revitalized the product and moved it to become seen as aspirational by drinkers. Aspirational and dissociative groups are highly subjective; what is aspirational to one person will indeed be dissociative to another, and vice versa. Similarly, groups that were once viewed as aspirational by an individual can very soon become dissociative as individuals become cynical about their behaviour.

5 *Formal groups*. These groups have a known membership who is required to comply with certain rules and whose behaviour is constrained by the group, such as trade associations, formal clubs, etc. Within the hospitality sector a number of formal clubs exist, within which structures and rules dictate the customers behaviour, for example, the days in which members may invite guests, the dress code of the club, etc. Golf clubs, for example, often have the most overelaborate rules, considering that at the end of the day they are large park-like venues for hitting small balls around. Typically, rules dictate the days in which 'the ladies' can play (never at weekends!) in case they slow up play for the men (most of whom are so overweight they cannot even bend over to address the ball), the clothes that can be worn, for example, long socks which reach the knee worn with shorts are considered the very height of sartorial elegance by golfers, who can buy drinks in the bar (often clubs do not allow women or guests to address the bar, only the members), and the handicap level of visitors to the club (usually set very high despite the fact that most of their own members could not hit the side of a barn from the tee).

6 *Informal groups*. These are unstructured groups and are formed from the circle of people that surround individuals. However, their effect on behaviour can often be the equal of formal groups, as individuals strive to adopt group norms. It would take a brave man on a boys' night out to be the one ordering the white wine spritzer among the ten pints of bitter, or to order the korma in the Indian restaurant as they do not like spicy food.

7 *Automatic groups*. These are the groups that individuals belong to by virtue of the categories into which they fall, for example,

age, gender, cultural, social class or educational. In many ways, as they are involuntary groups, it can be assumed that they would not exert much influence on our consumer behaviour, but group norms pressure people to behave in acceptable ways. It is still a relative rarity to see females drinking pints in bars, with the exception of many student venues perhaps, and most customers of health clubs belong to a certain age, gender and social category.

It should be noted that these groups are not mutually exclusive, for example, secondary groups could be either formal, such as membership of a golf club, or informal, such as the group of friends you go out with for drinks on a Friday night. In such cases the context determines the formality. As Chisnall (1995: 161) argues, 'it would be as well to bear in mind that people generally belong to several different groups, just as their activities during the day will also vary'.

Reference groups influence hospitality consumer behaviour in a number of ways, however, the most important of these has been suggested above, that of normative compliance. Where individuals seek to belong to groups they will behave in ways that make acceptance more likely, and where membership is indicated by observable consumption, they will ensure their consumption reflects the norm of the group to which they belong, or aspire to belong. As Bareham (1995: 120) suggests, 'reference groups influence behaviour in several ways, first, they influence aspiration levels and thus play a part in producing satisfaction or frustration ... second, reference groups influence kinds of behaviour ... they produce conformity'. The level to which reference groups determine consumer behaviour is a feature of the characteristics of those groups, and were identified by Blythe (1997: 103) as:

1 *Judgement standards.* The criteria used by individuals to evaluate the need to conform to the group norms, some of which may be very evident, such as the rules within a golf club, others less so, such as the dress code in a middle-ranking hotel restaurant.
2 *Product characteristics.* The features of the product which are important to the group, usually that the products are visible in order to denote group membership, and that the products are to an extent exclusive, again to denote group membership. In theme restaurants, such as Planet Hollywood and Hard Rock Café, the importance of merchandising is largely to denote to others that customers are part of the group that frequent such places.

3 *Member characteristics*. The characteristics of the individual which determines their level of susceptibility to group pressure to conform. Research (Park and Lessig, 1977) suggests that factors such as personality, status, security, age, etc. impact on the conformity of individuals.

4 *Group memberships*. The characteristics of the group that influence the level of conformity are seen to include such aspects as the size of the group, group cohesiveness, leadership, etc. If four friends are dining in a restaurant, it is more likely that if the majority want starters everyone will partake, even if they had not intended to. However, this group conformity is less likely when the group is bigger and individuals feel under less scrutiny.

5 *Role model*. Role models are people we respect or admire and wish to imitate, leading us to consumer behaviour that replicates that of our role models. Marketers have used role models to sell us products for many years. Thus if we see our role model drinking whisky, that becomes our drink of choice, similarly when Delia Smith used cranberries in one of her recipes the effect was to clear the supermarket shelves of cranberries.

It is suggested that reference groups influence consumer choice in three ways, *informational influence*, *comparative influence* and *normative influence*, and this is indicated in Table 6.1.

Informational influence operates through the value consumers place on those that they consider credible sources of information or expertise, which may be personal sources such as friends and family or commercial sources such as suppliers. There are two conditions wherein informational influence is likely to be considered important by hospitality consumers: first, where there

Nature of influence	Objectives	Perceived characteristics of source	Type of power	Behaviour
Informational	Knowledge	Credibility	Expert	Acceptance
Comparative	Self-maintenance and enrichment	Similarity	Referent	Identification
Normative	Reward	Power	Reward	Conformity

Source: adapted from Assael (1997)

Table 6.1 Types of influence exerted by reference groups

is a risk in buying a product; and, second, where those buying have limited product knowledge. When we are choosing our annual holiday we often ask friends and family for recommendations, and in addition we seek the advice of expert travel agents. This is in part because our annual holiday is a significant purchase and also because most of us we have limited knowledge of the opportunities available. The importance of personal sources of information verses sales and marketing influences has been extensively researched. For example, Robertson (1971) found that personal sources were more important than commercial resources for many purchases, with consumers allotting expertise to friends and family.

Comparative influence is indicated when consumers compare themselves with reference groups which they consider important; thus they align themselves with groups with similar attitudes and behaviour and disassociate themselves from groups that do not. As Assael (1997: 547) argues, 'the basis for comparative influence is in the process of comparing oneself to other members of the group and judging whether the group would be supportive'. Thus, when we are looking for a holiday, we try to identify resorts which suggest customers similar to ourselves, as these are more likely to reinforce our own attitudes and behaviours. This is why resorts tend to be made up of people with similar socioeconomic profiles. For this reason comparative influence is largely self-maintaining; the objective is to support our own attitudes and behaviours through associating with groups that reinforce them. Within the marketing environment companies have used comparative influence through the use of celebrities and sales people that consumers perceive as having similar attitudes to their own, as Wright, Nancarrow and Kwok (2001: 354) suggest, 'competitiveness in fighting for market share has added fuel to the constant battle of each brand, consumers are fed the endorsements of celebrities'. Within hospitality many bars and restaurants seek to employ staff that share the same characteristics as the customers, thus encouraging elements of comparative influence.

Normative influence refers to the extent a reference group exerts its norms and values on its members, and is a characteristic of commitment to the group, the significance of the referent group rewards and punishments, and the extent to which conformance behaviour is visible to members of the reference group. Within nightclub culture, for example, individuals are aware of appropriate clothing, drinks and dance etiquette; those who do not conform are soon excluded. Hospitality marketers aim for group conformity as it means consumers will buy the products that the group approves of, thus bypassing the decision process. This makes the marketing activity simpler as the focus can simply be switched to those who act as the models for the group. The value of conformity to hospitality marketers cannot be understated as many individuals are unable or unwilling to reject group pressures. The extent to which individuals are willing to withstand group pressures depends on a number of factors, including:

1 *The individual's value system.* If the proposed behaviour is in conflict with deep-held norms and values, individuals are more likely to reject it. In the past the use of drugs was such an example. However, in contemporary society drug use is more common and, indeed, is seen as a cornerstone of much of youth hospitality consumption, including the nightclub scene.
2 *The intensity to conform.* Research suggests that consumers will conform to group pressure only up to a certain point, beyond which they reject the pressure and cease to conform.
3 *Commitment to the group.* The greater the commitment to the group, the more likely individuals are to conform. Thus, if we consider the nightclub scene, individuals are more likely to participate in drug taking if they are highly committed to the reference group.
4 *The value of individuality.* Many people place value on individuality and do not wish to be seen as conforming. Again marketing companies recognize such individuality and seek to exploit it through their advertising campaigns.

The family as reference group

In general the family is one of the key influences on consumer behaviour, as Dubois (2000: 256) states: 'in the world of consumption ... the most prevalent decision-making unit is undoubtedly the family unit'. This is supported by Chisnall (1995: 166) who states: 'the family occupies a unique place in society: it is the fundamental social unit ... the effects on its members are pervasive; the effects of its attitudes, interests and motivations not only will be felt in the formative years but are likely to extend throughout life'. Families are characterized by factors such as extensive intimate contact, which allows families to interact and behave as advisers, information providers and decision-making groups. Families also share much of their consumption. For example, a parent making a purchase of a dishwasher will be making that purchase on behalf of all family members and, thus, their needs may form part of the decision process. As a result of this shared consumption families tend to have one member who is active in purchasing most of their goods and services, and this clearly has an impact in terms of who marketers are targeting. Finally, families are seen to subordinate their individual needs to the needs of the family and, as a result, many purchases are seen not to act as satisfiers for individuals, but to satisfice the overall needs of the family.

The definition of the family is a flexible concept, as Blythe (1997: 104) suggests 'within the UK, a family is usually defined in narrow terms – the parents and their offspring, however, in most families there will be other family influences'. The most common definition of the family is that of Statt (1997: 115) 'a group of two or more people living together who may be related by blood, marriage, or adoption'. Studies (Euostat, 1996) have argued that the traditional family (man and woman with children) is still predominant in Europe, representing about 72 per cent of the population, though other arrangements are becoming more popular. As a result within consumer behaviour it is becoming more common to talk about households, which are usually defined as 'shared residence and common house-keeping arrangements', thus it is more inclusive than the term 'family', covering almost all of the population. Despite this, the value of the family is underlined when it is considered that in a survey 90 per cent of participants stated that family life was one of the most important things to them (Eurostat, 1996). As Dubois (2000: 257) states, 'as far as consumption is concerned, the family purchase remains the rule rather than the exception', and this can be confirmed when we consider that one of the prime family consumption periods, the Christmas season, accounts for more than half of all purchases in the USA (Belk, 1987).

The complexity of understanding family consumer decision behaviour is summed up by Wilkie (1994: 396) when he states: 'although most of us easily relate to the issues that are involved, this [family] remains one of the most formidable research areas in the entire field of consumer research'. The question of why this should be can be answered by considering some of the characteristics that are common to much family consumer behaviour, and which were identified by Wilkie as:

1 *Family consumption decisions are regular and continuous*. As a result, the number of decisions made is too numerous to generalize about them with any confidence. Typically families will make hospitality-related decisions such as whether to eat out, where to eat, whether to go to the cinema or bowling, where to go on holiday, etc., on a regular basis. The nature, extent and regularity of these decisions do not allow adequate investigation.

2 *Family decisions are made in private.* Many of the types of hospitality decisions described above are made intimately, within the social group. They are therefore difficult to observe and may depend on past activities to which researchers are not privy.

3 *Family consumption decisions are not made independently of each other.* This means that such decisions are difficult to study, as they are often the result of trade-offs for other previous or future decisions. The decision of whether and/or where to go on holiday requires families to consider the opportunity cost of such a decision. This has to be traded-off against other alternative uses for the money involved, for example a new washing machine.

4 *Families have multiple decision-makers.* The range of choices that families make means that sometimes decisions are made by a single individual, while others can involve many members of the family. Understanding the processes when numerous decision-makers are involved is complex and challenging.

5 *Family decision-making is dependent on the type of service involved.* The decisions families make about products differ dependent on the type of product, thus, decisions about where to eat a burger are likely to be significantly different in format to those regarding choice of holiday.

6 *Families differ from each other.* Characteristics such as personality, income, age, social classification and lifestyle combine to ensure that no two families are alike. These differences are compounded by the way in which families make decisions, for example the level of democracy, and by the fact that the families' approach to decision-making will alter over time.

All the characteristics listed above, when taken in conjunction, suggest that meaningful research into family consumer behaviour is an extremely complex undertaking, however, the topic is of such significance to our understanding of hospitality consumption that it cannot simply be ignored.

Due to the sheer number of purchases that families make, role specialization becomes important in family decision-making, with individual members of the family becoming responsible for various purchases. This means that the person responsible for activities on behalf of the family tend to be responsible for the purchases associated with it. Thus, someone interested in gardening tends to purchase gardening products, while the person responsible for childcare purchases those related products. Traditionally, roles such as childcare and car care have been associated with females and males respectively, but in contemporary society, as traditional roles decline, this can no longer be assumed. As a result marketers need to identify those individuals within families responsible for the purchases of particular goods and services or, alternatively, to ensure that the messages they are seeking to communicate are understood and valued by a wide range of potential customers. For consumer decisions within families Dubois (2000) suggests it is possible to identify up to five roles linked to any decision. If we consider the case of a family going out for dinner, these roles may include the *initiator*, the person responsible for originating the idea, for example the person who suggests going out for something to eat. Following this we have the *influencer(s)*, all those who either directly or indirectly play a part in directing the decision process; in our case this may include the children, the parent(s) etc., however, in our case characters such as Ronald McDonald can also be seen as influences, as they indirectly seek to direct the purchase behaviour of the children in favour of McDonald's restaurants. The third role is that of *decision maker(s)*, the people who make the evaluation and choose from among the range of products on offer. Our decision-makers have to evaluate all of the various restaurant brands on offer, when to consume and where, etc. The *buyer* makes the actual transaction, by taking possession of the goods or services in exchange for currency. Finally, the *user* consumes the product, that is, the family eat their meal. Dubois (2000) suggested that heads of families act in the same way that large corporations do, and identified six functions of family decision-making, which arose from an INSEE study, see Figure 6.1. The first zone is that of major decisions, such as the choice of friends, where to live, where to holiday, etc. These decisions, which he terms *syncratic* decisions, are usually made jointly, as are those of the second zone, the *investment* decisions, that is, those relating to major items such as televisions, washing machines, cars, etc. For items such as provisions, Dubois suggests that these are operational or tactical aspects, which culminate in the *household* purchases such as food. *Administrative* decisions, such as budgeting are seen as the responsibility of either the man or the woman, but rarely both, while *maintenance* tasks such as taxation matters are largely male.

The type of product being consumed affects consumers in making decisions. For example, if a family is going out to eat it is likely most of the members of the group will be involved in some element of the location decision. It is for this reason that McDonald's emphasizes the child element of the product offer, that is, the cartoon characters such as Ronald McDonald and the fun element of the 'Happy Meal'. McDonald's is aware of the influence of children on the family decision of where to eat; it know the value of the adage that if the children are happy the

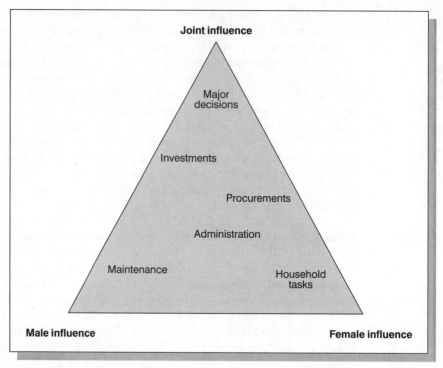

Figure 6.1 Functions of household decision-making
Source: adapted from Dubois (2000)

parents are likely to be happy too. This characteristic of family consumer behaviour is further explored in Case Study 6.1, which looks at the role of the Happy Meal in McDonalds.

Case study 6.1

McDonald's Happy Meals and collectables

To understand the implications of families, and in particular children, on consumers of hospitality services we have chosen to look at how McDonald's uses the Happy Meal to influence families' choice of restaurant.

In 1937 Dick and Mac McDonald opened a carhop (fast-food drive through) in Pasadena, California, in which service was based primarily on speed, an innovation which allowed them to gain a significant competitive advantage. The drive-ins were franchised during the late 1940s and early 1950s, one of which was taken up by a former supplier, Ray Kroc, who formed a company titled McDonalds System Incorporated, which changed in 1960 to its current name McDonald's Corporation. Kroc was so successful that in 1961 the McDonald brothers sold their entire business and rights to him for US$2.7 million dollars. Today McDonald's has more than 30 000 stores worldwide.

Kroc, in association with a second franchiser, Goldstein, had a vision of using children to help sell his products and began to advertise on television, by sponsoring a programme called Bozo Circus, and by promoting Bozo, to become a major television star. When the programme was axed in 1963, Goldstein asked an agency to find something to replace Bozo the clown, who had become McDonald's spokesman for the increasingly important children's market. The agency decided the best option was to establish McDonald's own clown and produce its own adverts, instead of sponsoring a show. Originally the clown was called Archie McDonald, in reference to the Golden Arches found outside McDonald's restaurants, but this was found to infringe another character's copyright, so he was renamed Ronald McDonald by Willard Scott (the original Bozo the clown) who played the character. He made his debut in late 1963, with a costume that consisted of a hat in the shape of a tray containing a burger, fries and milk shake; boots in the shape of burger buns; a nose made out of a drinks cup; and a belt buckle made from a burger, out of which he magically pulled hamburgers. His appearance marked the first occasion a 'character' was used in a commercial in the USA. By 1965 Ronald McDonald had become the national spokesman for the McDonald's restaurant chain, a position it retains today.

In the 1960s McDonald's began to run meal combinations, beginning with the All-American Meal, aimed primarily at adults, and at around the same time their agency introduced children's advertising, with an advert featuring a number of employees dancing and singing around a restaurant, but which did not feature any food. The agency created a theatrical land, called McDonald-land, which it filled with characters including Hamburgler, Mayor McCheese, Grimace and Officer Big Mac. In 1975, a Mayor McCheese bag promotion was designed for children, featuring Mayor McCheese graphics and advertised as 'the Honorary Meal of McDonaldland'. It contained a cheeseburger, fries, cookies and a McDonaldland Citizenship certificate, what has now become known as a premium and is generally a toy of some sort.

In 1978 McDonald's introduced the Happy Meal, in a promotion called Circus Wagon, which featured a burger, fries, cookies, a drink and a premium, in a toy box, and they have been so successful they have become McDonald's most important promotional tool, with several themes each year. In 1980 the Happy Meal promotion made its international debut with a number of generic toys, and in 1985 it was introduced to the UK with 'Fast Macs' which used the McDonaldland characters along with Ronald in a self-propelled vehicle. Each year in Europe several promotions are introduced, all of which have up to eight collectables (in the USA sets have up to twenty-one collectables), one of which is themed, for example, World Cup Football, etc.

Today the promotions are available globally, and many of the premiums are the same, but are contained in different packages with multilingual graphics and colour variations, and they are developed in association with other major corporations such as Walt Disney (Aladdin); Warner Bros (Batman Forever); Mattel (Barbie); Jim Henson Productions (Muppet Babies); Universal Studios (the Flintstones); Paramount (Star Trek) and Nintendo (Super Mario).

As a bizarre result of the success of the McDonald's Happy Meals promotions, a whole industry has spawned for collecting the premiums, with opportunities and web sites dedicated to allow devotees to swop premiums to seek a complete set. As a result, in 1995, McDonald's collectables were advocated by reputable auction houses to be the most collectable toys anywhere in the world.

The consumer behaviour of families is also affected by elements of culture and, as we have previously stated, religion, ethnicity and national culture will, to a greater or lesser extent, affect the way in which decisions are made. In those cultures which are male-dominated, consumer decisions are likely to be made by males; similarly, in cultures where traditional roles have not been subsumed, males and females will still be responsible for the purchases with which they are traditionally associated. For example, research by Green (1983) suggests that consumer behaviour within African cultures tends to be male dominated, whereas that of European and North American cultures demonstrates more egalitarian forms of decision-making. Alongside culture, the social class of the family is also seen to affect its decision-making, with research suggesting that where incomes are lower, decisions tend to be more matriarchal. Thus where decisions are about whether families can afford to eat out, rather than where they should eat, decisions tend to be female dominated.

Gender roles are also seen as important in family decision-making, with the role of women having changed dramatically in recent years, largely as a result of the number of women in employment. This change has led to a situation where major purchasing decisions are most likely to be made jointly, and that those decisions traditionally associated with one gender or another being blurred at the edges. However, gender role orientation has an impact here. For example, in most families with traditional views about gender roles, or where the male is the sole earner, decisions tend to be made by males. In addition, some categories of products tend to be dominated by gender. For example, computers and hi-fi sales are predominantly made by males, hence the number of superfluous but colourful buttons on such items.

The family life cycle

As families evolve over time the notion of a family life cycle has emerged which seeks to structure this evolution into a number of characteristic stages. The earliest life cycle models were developed in the mid-1960s by Wells and Guber (1966), and should be considered with some caution given the huge social changes that have occurred since this time. However, as Blythe (1997, 109) suggests, 'the family life cycle is a useful rule-of-thumb (if we remember) it is unlikely that many families would pass through all of the stages quite as neatly as the model suggests'. Various life cycle models exist, but they are mainly based on the original work of Wells and Guber, such as the typical example indicated below:

1 *Young singles no longer living with parents*: limited income but latitude to use it as they choose; discretionary spending is largely used for fashion and entertainment.
2 *Young married with no children*: increasing incomes with both partners working; spending tends to be homemaking and leisure.
3 *Married couple with children under six*: reduced incomes as one parent gives up paid employment, coupled with increased spend due to need for larger property, car, household durable goods, items for the children, etc.
4 *Married couple with children over six*: financial situation improves as both parents are able to return to work; needs of children are significant but are focused around school and outdoor activities.
5 *Older couples with children*: financially at ease, families move to larger house and buy second car; health and education needs tend to dominate spending.
6 *Older couples without children, head of household working*: financial situation at its peak with the level of resources enabling the purchase of luxury products and allowing the couple to devote resources to travel, leisure and saving.
7 *Older couples without children, head of household retired*: incomes decline while health spending often increases; houses exchanged for smaller properties in non-metropolitan areas.
8 *Older single working person*: income relatively high; spending tends to be on travel, leisure and health.
9 *Older single retired person*: income in decline; spending on affection and security.

Extensive research has been undertaken into the value of the life cycle concept, not all of which supports conclusions drawn on the concept, as we see in Chapter 7. However, it has been argued that the life cycle suggests a number of useful characteristics of family decision-making relative to hospitality. For example, it is argued that as we get older we are less susceptible to the effectiveness of advertising, that the introduction of children to the family results in fewer joint decisions, that the longer people are married the less likely they are to engage in joint decision-making, and that life cycle is an indicator of sport participation and is a better indicator of leisure spending than age or social class.

Contemporary characteristics of the family

Demographic and social changes have had a profound impact on the shape of the traditional family in contemporary society, and in particular on the size of the typical household. Household size has fallen in most of the western world, and the trend is increasingly being seen in other parts of the world, and as household size has decreased the number of households has increased. Decreases in household size are the result of many factors, including:

1 The birth rate in many countries, including all of Europe, has fallen, to the point where many countries have a falling population. In Europe the average birth rate is 1.45 children per woman, in order to remain a constant population a rate of 2.1 children per woman is required.

2 A decline in the number of marriages is noticeable, with the result that many more single-person households are generated.

3 Where people are marrying this is happening at a later stage in life. Within Europe, for example, the average age for marriage is now twenty-nine for men and twenty-seven for women, up from twenty-four and twenty-two respectively only thirty years ago.

4 Divorce is an increasing feature of society, especially in countries such as the USA, where the divorce rate is five per 1000 citizens. Only countries such as Ireland, where divorce is largely prohibited, have avoided this trend.

Theses characteristics of contemporary society have huge impacts on consumer behaviour, and particularly that of hospitality. For example, it is estimated that almost 50 per cent of Club Med customers are single people holidaying alone. Services such as bars and restaurants have had to alter to take into account that markets exist for single people and for groups of single-sex customers, throughout the age range. Thus companies such as Bass Taverns have developed concepts like All-Bar-One, which they market as female friendly, and target at slightly older females than would normally be the target for city centre bars.

The original life cycle models have undergone extensive redesign in order to try to incorporate some of the characteristics of contemporary family life. For example, models have been introduced which make distinctions on the basis of income against a group mean (Schaninger and Danko, 1993). Other models have more categories (Wilkes, 1995), while yet others have fewer (Roberts, 1992). However, as Statt (1997: 125) suggests, 'there are many ways of categorizing life-cycle, the most elaborate of these has 18 stages, although the authors concede that their long list has no more predictive value than the shorter ones from an earlier generation'. While, as we discuss in Chapter 7, some of the evidence for the value of life cycle models can be questioned, authors such as Dubois (2000: 268) state: 'whatever the model adopted, the family life-cycle is a very fruitful notion since it enables the identification of homogeneous groups which can be reached with the help of specifically adopted commercial policies'.

The influence of children on hospitality consumption

Marketers are interested in understanding the consumer behaviour of children and adolescents because of their influence in one of the most important decision-making and consumption units, the family. Kelly (1998) suggests, for example, that adolescents are responsible for between US$82 billion and US$108 billion of direct spend each year in the USA alone, and that, if we also consider consumption activities over which they have a significant influence, this rises to more than US$300 billion per year. It is clear that children influence consumer decision-making, both through direct and indirect mechanisms, but current research on their actual influence is limited in nature. According to Dubois (2000) children influence purchases made on their behalf in only 5 per cent of cases when they are less than six years old, however, this increases as they get older, moving to 30 per cent for six- to eight-year-olds, 55 per cent for eight- to ten-year-olds and more than 70 per cent for those over ten. In addition, it is suggested that children are increasingly influential in the family purchases of items such as environmentally friendly products (Carlson, 1994) and branded items they have seen advertised (Peracchio, 1992).

Children are increasingly important in hospitality consumer behaviour, a trend that it is argued originated in the USA before moving into other similar consumer cultures, with children seen to apply pressure to the family in order to sway decisions their way. This pressure, increasingly termed 'pester power', can be very intense and research suggests that parents are increasingly swayed in their decision-making as a result (Ekstrom, Tansuhaj and Foxman, 1987), especially as in an age of increased satellite television as children are among the population's heaviest television viewers.

Consumption behaviour of children occurs as a result of a process known as consumer socialization, 'the process by which young people acquire skills, knowledge, and attitudes relevant to their functioning in the marketplace' (Ward, 1990: 416), and the role of the family in this process cannot be understated. As Moschis (1985: 910) suggests, while other factors may have a persuasive influence on what children see and how they react to certain products 'the family is instrumental in teaching young people rational aspects of consumption, including basic consumer needs'. In terms of hospitality consumption, research suggests that the family is responsible for teaching children to be effective consumers through teaching issues of price-quality, teaching children how to compare products, influencing their brand preferences and encouraging them to distinguish between fact and fiction in advertising.

Despite the pre-eminence of the family, however, children are also socialized as a result of their direct interactions with a wide range of other institutions and media. For example, television and schools are also important sources of socialization, as children learn to make connections between consumer behaviour and advertising, and as companies such as Tesco and McDonald's sponsor activities, and even equipment, for schools.

McNeal (1991) studied the consumer socialization of children and suggests that they go through five stages as they develop to become full-blown consumers:

1 *Observing*. At the age of six months children construct images of products and brand symbols, and begin to recognize, for example, that the 'golden arches' represent sources of things they wish to consume.
2 *Making requests*. At around the age of two years children begin to make specific requests for products that they want, partly as a response to stimuli from media images. At this stage they are unable to carry the representations with them so only make requests in the presence of things that remind them, for example, logos, brands, etc.
3 *Making selections*. As they reach the age of around three children begin to develop the capacity to remember store layouts and locations, and thus find products for themselves. It is at this age that children remind parents of a favourite fast-food outlet or public house play area in the locale.
4 *Making assisted purchases*. By the age of five children seek permission to obtain products in stores and restaurants. In

addition, as many children of this age have money of their own, they are developing the ability to spend it for themselves.

5 *Making independent purchases.* After the age of eight many children are mature enough to buy without parental assistance, they have a good understanding of money and are able to convince parents that they can make responsible purchases on their own. Thus, for example, they are likely to choose their own meals in restaurants, and have increasing influence on decisions such as choice of holiday.

The discussion so far suggests that intergenerational influence is one-directional, that is, it passes from parents to children. However, as any parent will confirm, nothing could be further from the truth. Children, and in particular adolescents, are likely to influence the consumption behaviour of parents for a wide range of products. This influence is largely shaped by the nature of the product itself. A study by Yankelovich, Clancy and Shulman (1990) listed the types of products that children bought or influenced the purchase of. While the highest categories of goods that were bought were items such as chocolate (50 per cent of children purchased for themselves) and toys (30 per cent purchased for themselves and 70 per cent influenced the purchase of them), fast food scored highly in the survey. Almost 20 per cent of children under twelve years of age buy fast-food products for themselves and almost 40 per cent have a significant influence on the brand of fast food chosen.

Hospitality companies have long recognized the role that children play in influencing decisions for their products, and have developed promotional material specifically to encourage children to favour their brands. McDonald's and Burger King are constantly under pressure from children to ensure that the latest fad toy is the one that their brand of 'kid's meal' incorporates as a 'give-away' or premium. These toys, which are often linked to the latest children's movie release, are a prime motive for children opting for one brand over the other and, given the value of the 'kid's meal' to the respective brands, especially in the UK, successful premiums are a vital part of the brand's profitability.

One of the most innovative schemes was introduced by Forte hotels in the summer of 2000, and involved a tie-up between the Posthouse brand and the children's television channel, Cartoon Network. The initiative involved a large marquee being built in the hotel grounds within which a range of activities linked to the cartoons on Cartoon Network were undertaken, and the distribution of give-away bags containing merchandise from both the hotel and the Cartoon Network. The activities ranged from films, video games, colouring competitions, soft play areas, etc. through to exercise equipment, appearances by cartoon characters and face painting, all of which were supervised by staff linked to the programme, leaving parents free to enjoy the other hotel amenities. After the stay children received reminders of their visit in the form of additional competitions and pictures, presumably with the intention of encouraging them to influence any future hotel stay decisions.

The issue of whether it is ethical or appropriate for companies to target children in the ways that McDonald's, Burger King, Forte and many other companies have done is a continuing one within marketing. Critics claim that it encourages materialism, the consumption of inappropriate products such as fast food and a lack of consideration in how to consume appropriately, while marketers claim that consumer socialization is a parental responsibility not theirs. As Armstrong and Brucks (1988: 110) argue, 'parents can best monitor their children's television viewing, get children to think about advertising claims, evaluate children's purchase requests, and help children compare advertising claims against product performance'. However, such consumer socialization requires greater skill than most parents are able to offer and, as a parent who swore when his first child was born that the house would not be full of Disney videos and 'girly' things, I have to admit my failings. My three daughters 'enjoy' a choice of all the films Disney ever made, and their bedrooms are a shrine to all things Barbie!

Resolving consumption conflict within the family

Whenever two or more people have to make choices there is always the potential for conflict. Think about deciding among your friends whether to go out to the cinema, your 'local', the latest bar in town, etc., Families are no different. Decisions, such as where to go on holiday, which films to see, where to eat out, whether to go bowling or to the cinema, are often causes of conflict for families. As Wilkie (1994: 403) suggests, 'when household members disagree about goals, decisions are much more difficult to reach without bringing out the inherent conflict in the situation'. This is supported by Lee and Collins (2000: 1182) who state: 'although serious conflict in family purchase decisions are rare, some form of conflict is highly probable, because forming a joint preference requires a combining of individual preferences of family members'. Conflict resolution within family consumer decision-making has long been a key topic for researchers; however, few studies have come up with any empirically supported evidence, and researchers continue to be interested because, as Lee and Collins (2000: 1181) argue, 'researchers and practitioners are interested in conflict, and conflict resolution in the family decision-making process because of its impact upon the outcome of the decision'.

A number of models have been developed in order to investigate conflict resolution within the family, including those by Spiro (1983), Nelson (1988) and Quall and Jaffe (1992), however, most are built on the original work of Sheth (1974). A useful model which summarizes much of the earlier work is that developed by Zaichkowsky (1985), who suggests that families use a range of techniques to resolve consumer conflict, namely:

1 *Coercion*: including behaviour such as assumed expertise, authority, threats, reward and punishment. Coercion strategies usually involve a more detailed information search and often employ the expertise of members outside the family. For example, when choosing a holiday one parent might assume an authoritative role having undertaken a search of available literature on the choices and having consulted a travel agent.

2 *Persuasion*: the use of reasoned arguments presented in a reasonable manner, or the coalition of a number of family members who collude to influence the outcome, such as the children colluding to influence a choice of restaurant to one that offers play areas and promotional material. Vuchinich, Emery and Cassody (1988) suggests that more than 50 per cent of family decisions are made as a result of coalition forming, while Scanzoni and Szinovacz (1980), undertaking research into holiday plans, found that children tend to be coalition members used by one parent against another.

3 *Bargaining and negotiation*: strategies of give and take, which often end up resembling bribery, wherein members of the family seek to gain influence by exchanging a decision now for one later.

4 *Manipulation*: a psychological strategy that can include withdrawal, sulking, silence, etc., all in an effort to pressure others into agreement. These emotive forms of persuasion are often linked to criticism and intuition, but rarely to more rational decision-making, such as gaining additional information.

However, despite these strategies, Wilkie (1994: 404) suggests that 'in general, research has found that underlying decision conflict is common in many household decisions, but that most households work hard to minimize its appearance and effects'.

Research by authors such as Spiro (1983) confirms Wilkie's opinion, Spiro's own work, for example, suggesting that 88 per cent of households encounter regular disagreements in terms of consumer behaviour and have to undertake a range of resolution strategies. While, as we have seen, there are a number of pieces of research which have sought to investigate family conflict, few have proven very much in empirical terms and investigations in the field of hospitality consumption are very rare indeed. More research is clearly needed if we are to understand this aspect of family decision-making. As Lee and Collins (2000: 1196) argue, present studies focus on decision strategies used by the whole family, 'future research should consider determining the dominant decision strategies used by each family member and relate this to the amount of influence exerted by each member in the decision-making process'.

Summarizing the role of reference groups within hospitality consumption

As we have seen, the importance of reference groups to consumer behaviour within hospitality cannot be underestimated. Consumers are inspired to behave in certain ways as a result of such aspects as family norms, aspiration and conformity, and because of the value which we attach to the opinions of the groups that act as our references. Thus the bars we frequent, the holidays we take, the restaurants we dine in, etc. are all in some ways influenced by reference groups, and this influence can be extreme. For example, research suggests that more than 70 per cent of individuals choose the bank of their parents as their own first bank. Hospitality marketers need to identify the extent to which consumers identify with the behaviour patterns of group members and the extent to which they seek individuality, for a wide range of hospitality goods and services. As Chisnall (1995: 159) argues, 'marketing managers should carefully consider how much variety within their product range is necessary in order to satisfy consumers' needs for self-expression'. Society is a complex mix of interrelated groups, many of which impact upon the way in which we act as consumers, some in a negative manner and others as forms of reference for our consumer behaviour. One of the most important, but least understood, of these reference groups is the family, a unique subcultural grouping with profound psychological, social, cultural and economic influences upon us. However, other groups also impact upon the ways in which we consume hospitality; for example, friends, neighbours, work colleagues, heroes and celebrities.

Hospitality, Leisure & Tourism Series

In considering the practical value of reference groups to hospitality marketers Bourne (1989) poses a series of questions:

- How relevant is the influence of the reference group to the particular marketing situation in question?
- How are we assessing the influence of the reference group?
- How are particular reference groups or referent others identified in the marketing situation in question?
- Once we have identified the specific reference groups, how is effective communication with those groups achieved?

As we have seen, the complexities which underlie much of reference group theory suggest that it is not easy to answer these questions, and thus it is not a simple matter to evaluate the contribution made by reference group influence to hospitality consumer behaviour.

PART 3

Understanding the Hospitality Consumer in Contemporary Society and Beyond

CHAPTER 7

The end of the marketing concept

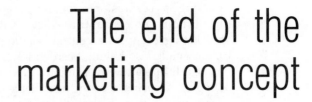

Key themes

- Hospitality businesses have increasingly adopted a marketing focus, based on the marketing concept advocated by Kotler and others since the mid-1950s.

- In essence, the marketing concept holds that the key task of an organization is to determine the needs and wants of target markets and to adapt the organization to deliver the desired satisfaction more effectively and efficiently than can its competitors.

- A key element of the marketing concept is that of market segmentation, primarily based on an understanding of the social, economic and, to a limited extent, psychological location of the consumer.

- In recent years a groundswell of criticism has been attributed to the marketing concept, and in particular its cornerstone theories of segmentation and positioning, with mounting evidence suggesting that systematic violations of the concept by consumers are the norm rather than the exception.

Introduction

In the increasingly complex and dynamic business environment of the late twentieth century the discipline of marketing is seen as offering a cornerstone for business strategy by companies, institutions and countries. Few authors would argue that marketing occupies a central position in the business environment, while also having been widely applied to fields as diverse as health care and government. As Robson and Rowe (1997: 655) suggest, 'It seems to be the case that leading marketing academics are currently viewing both themselves and their discipline as the critical factors in business success'. Within hospitality education the proliferation of publications and the centrality of marketing on all undergraduate and postgraduate degree programmes clearly demonstrates that marketing is in the ascendancy. Numerous hospitality textbooks attest to the belief that marketing is the key to the long-term success of any business, as Teare, Mazanec and Crawford-Welch (1994: viii) argue: 'The marketing function plays a pro-active part in the creation of a realistic service vision to which every part of the organization can contribute.'

This begs the question, why have companies so readily adopted marketing to the extent that for some organizations it seems to have become a panacea for all organizational ills? As Kotler (1980) asks, what leads companies to discover marketing? This chapter seeks to answer this question by, first, discussing the development of the marketing concept, and subsequently by considering its role in the contemporary hospitality industry. The development of the marketing concept through a production and sales orientation to the marketing orientation of the mid-1950s onwards is explored and the pervasive nature of the marketing concept in the hospitality industry is considered. Subsequent criticisms of the role of the marketing concept when applied to hospitality are identified and its value in considering contemporary hospitality consumption is evaluated. The chapter concludes by arguing that marketing in hospitality has to begin to consider alternative approaches to consumers if it is to develop and succeed in the new millennium.

The evolution of the marketing concept

In order to answer the question 'why have companies so readily adopted marketing?' we first need to define what we mean when we refer to marketing. Marketing has been defined as, 'The conception, pricing, promotion and distribution of ideas, goods and services in order that exchanges may be created that are able to satisfy both individual and organisational objectives' (Evans and Moutinho, 1999). The Chartered Institute of Marketing in the UK focuses on the issue of matching the requirements of both the company and the consumer, suggesting marketing is a management process that identifies, anticipates and supplies customer requirements efficiently and profitably. A general definition of hospitality marketing, and one which is appropriate for use within this chapter, is that marketing is communicating to and giving the target market customers what they want, when they want it, where they want it, at a price they are willing to pay (Lewis and Chambers, 1989).

The issues this raises are how do firms determine who are their target markets? Where are their markets? What price are they willing to pay for goods and services? As Foxall and Goldsmith (1994: 7) argue, 'in a competitive economic system, the survival and growth of firms requires accurate knowledge about consumers, how they buy, why they buy, and where they buy ... nowadays successful management depends more than ever on matching every aspect of the business to the satisfaction of the customer'.

A simple, but useful, way of visualizing the development of the marketing concept is that of the 'three eras' approach advocated by Keith (1960) and Baker (1995) among others, highlighted in Figure 7.1. This, while being an oversimplification of a complex process, does seek to highlight the change of emphasis in the relationship between supply and demand over time.

Baker (1995) identifies the earliest forms of marketing as being seen in terms of marketing = exchange, whereby exchange came

Early forms of marketing	▪ Marketing = exchange
Production orientation	▪ Increase in productivity ▪ Industrial revolution ▪ Sophisticated institutions for facilitating exchange ▪ Specialization
Sales orientation	▪ Sell what we can make ▪ Products and services seen as a solution to generalized consumer needs
Marketing concept	▪ Process starts with market research ▪ Marketing seen as integral to all aspects of the business process ▪ Make what we can sell

Figure 7.1 The evolution of the marketing concept

about due to surplus in excess of the immediate needs of a producer. Assuming that two producers of different products are brought into contact, each having a surplus and desiring the others' surplus, it is logical to assume that a mutually beneficial exchange can take place. The evolution of a money-based economy encouraged greater specialization and has led to the development of sophisticated institutions for facilitating exchange both nationally and internationally. The Industrial Revolution led to increased productivity, which in turn led to the need for more sophisticated institutions for marketing. As a result this era has become characterized as production orientated.

King (1965: 37) summarized the period of production orientation as 'an era of managerial concern with problems of capacity creation, work methods and volume production'. He goes on to argue that during this period, problems related to production assumed greater significance than those related to identifying and developing markets. The emphasis during this period was on volume rather than differentiation or choice, and is exemplified by the model-T motor car produced by Henry Ford. As Baker (1995: 4) argues, 'Ford made his model-T available to vast segments of the market that otherwise would never have had the opportunity to own the basic product, which they sought, the colour of which was irrelevant'.

It is argued that the situation that brought the production orientation to an end was the creation of excess production. Excess occurs when markets cease to absorb all of a firm's supply and the economic model of reducing prices to stimulate demand is unacceptable due to the low prices that would be required. Faced with such a situation the response of managers was to maintain volume of sales through non-price competitive mechanisms, that is, through product differentiation, promotion and sales activities. This led marketing from a production-orientated approach through to a sales-orientated one, defined as 'selling what we can make'. With a sales-orientated approach products or services are taken as a given and people are encouraged to view them as the solution to generalized consumption needs. The sales orientation within organizations came to an end as a result of mass industrialization and the rapid growth in technological innovation. This was coupled with a slowing down in population growth in those markets where consumption was traditionally a key feature. As a result most markets became buyers' markets as production outstripped consumption, leading to intense competition among companies.

From the 1950s onwards a new philosophy was seen in the market, one that moved from a position of 'selling what we can make' to 'making what we can sell'. The difference is seen as one in which customers themselves led production and marketers organized the supply of consumer-desired objects or services. King (1965: 35) argues that the fundamental differences between selling and marketing are: 'Under the traditional sales concept, engineering designed a product, manufacturing produced it and then the sales people were expected to sell it. Under the modern marketing concept, the whole process starts with marketing research and sales forecasting to provide a sound, factual, customer-orientated basis for planning all business operations, and the business function that has sales responsibility now participates in all the stages of the business planning process.' As such, the marketing concept introduces marketing at the beginning of the process rather than at the end and integrates marketing into all phases of the business. In essence, the marketing concept says find wants and fill them, rather than create products and sell them. Thus the marketing concept, as defined by Kotler (1980: 31) is 'a management orientation that holds that the key task of the organization is to determine the needs and wants of target markets and to adapt the organization to delivering the desired satisfaction more effectively and efficiently than its competitors'. The marketing concept as outlined by Kotler has been taken up by most of the literature within marketing to the extent that as Foxall and Goldsmith (1994: 7) suggest 'the essence of marketing success stems from the adoption and implementation of the marketing concept'.

Market segmentation

Central to the use of the marketing concept is market segmentation, the disaggregation of markets into clusters of buyers with similar preferences (Kotler, 1980; Littler, 1995). As Jenkins and McDonald (1997: 19) stated: 'If an organization is to enjoy any level of marketing success, this is through an ability to match its own capabilities to the requirements of the marketplace; central to this matching process is the segmentation of the market.'

As already discussed, since the 1960s organizations have moved away from the single brand that was mass produced, mass distributed and mass communicated; a scenario that had been developed to ensure lowest costs and greatest market potential. However, it was recognized that as competition intensified prices fell and earnings declined, owing to the fact that companies could not control the price of their products due to the lack of product differentiation. The response to this scenario has been the development and use of market segmentation techniques. These seek to guide marketing strategies through distinguishing customer groupings and relating them to perceived needs.

Organizations that seek to operate in a market are encouraged to recognize that they are not able to serve all of the customers in that market. Customers, it is suggested, are too numerous, widely scattered or heterogeneous in their demands to be effectively served by a single organization. As a result firms are encouraged to identify those parts of a market that are most attractive to it. This, it is suggested, can be achieved by two steps – market segmentation and target marketing. These two aspects have increasingly come to be seen as the cornerstones of the marketing concept, as Firat and Shultz (1997: 204) suggest, 'Segmentation and positioning [are] two of the most central and strategic concepts in marketing'.

The criticisms contained within this chapter incorporate discussions of many aspects related to the marketing concept and its associated theories, including aspects such as the product life cycle (PLC), the Boston matrix (BCG), the 4 Ps (or any number of Ps depending whose work one uses), marketing warfare, relationship marketing, etc. However, as we have seen, the basic building blocks of the marketing concept are segmentation and positioning. If these foundations are seen to be at fault, this leads us to question the stability of subsequent developments. For this reason, while we discuss a number of the aspects outlined above, we will focus on segmentation and positioning.

Segmentation and positioning have been singled out as, despite being the cornerstones of marketing management, emerging criticisms suggest that traditional concepts of either may not be as meaningful or satisfactory as once imagined. As Firat and Shultz (1997: 203) suggest, 'An articulation of postmodern insights for marketing and the consumers of a postmodern era may suggest that some of the most central tenets and/or principles of the marketing concept be rethought and modified extensively ... especially as it pertains to segmentation and positioning, two of the most central and strategic concepts in marketing'. Market segmentation works on the basis that at the most detailed level every buyer's requirements are probably distinct in some way. However, on the basis of similarities and differences, such unique requirements can be grouped into subclasses. The result is that within a subclass the requirements are more related to each other than are the requirements between subclasses. Market segmentation has been defined by Kotler (1980: 195) as 'The subdividing of a market into distinct sub-sets of customers, where any sub-set may conceivably be selected as a target market, to be reached with a distinct marketing mix'.

The argument for such an approach is that in periods of intense competition organizations can prosper through the development of offers for specific market segments. It is argued that the process of segmenting and selecting markets makes the allocation of resources more effective, because resources can be directed at specific and identifiable groups, and efficient, as resources are allocated to smaller groups of consumers (Foxall and Goldsmith, 1994). As Green, Tull and Albaum (1988: 113) suggest, 'Market segmentation deals with determining which preferences, charac-teristics or other aspects of consumer choice might differ across buyer groups'. The presumption is that, if these differences exist, can be identified, are reasonably stable over time and can be efficiently reached, the organization might increase sales, and thus profitability, beyond those that would be achieved through assessing market homogeneity. Market segmentation is based on an understanding of the social, economic and, to a limited extent, psychological position of the consumer. Social location being determined by such aspects as status, class, family and other group memberships, and cultural observances, while economic location is determined by such aspects as income, access to credit, savings and other financial commitments. Finally psychological location includes such attributes as attitude, personality, prior learning, etc.

The advantages segmentation claims to offer to hospitality organizations are numerous and include:

- allowing an organization to exploit services by better selecting compatible market niches
- separating two or more brands of the same company in order to minimize cannibalism
- identifying gaps in the market which may represent new market opportunities
- encouraging more sharply focused strategies
- encouraging customer loyalty as a company's offering is more closely geared to those in a market segment.

The key questions that have to be addressed in segmentation, however, are what are being grouped together to form segments? What process is used to group segments? As Oliver (1986: 92) suggests, 'Operation of a segmentation strategy can offer con-siderable competitive advantage. It also has the capacity to generate considerable disillusionment'. A potentially bewilder-ing range of possibilities exists by which to segment markets, each supported by a wide body of evidence and literature. The nature of this problem becomes clearer through a consideration of some of the bases that have been utilized. As discussed earlier, the main approaches to specifying segments have been to classify customers by their socioeconomic, demographic or other similar characteristic, for example, age, gender, life cycle stage, etc. In general, segmentation is based on identifying a relationship between a number of variables. Contemporary market segmentation literature suggests that there are four basic approaches available:

- the traditional *a priori* approach, using product-specific variables or general consumer characteristics as the basis for segmentation
- the clustering or *post hoc* approach which segments markets *post hoc* through the clustering of respondents
- the flexible approach which is a hybrid version of the first two approaches
- the componential approach, which seeks to identify attributes and characteristics of individuals and links these to particular product features (Greene and Kreigner, 1991).

Frank, Massey and Wind (1972) offer a matrix that separates segmentation approaches on the basis of whether the criteria are intuitive or observable and cross-references this in terms of whether the segmentation is general or situation specific. The outcome is a matrix, which, while not being all encompassing, does offer some indication of the various segmentation approaches possible. This is reproduced in Figure 7.2.

	INTUITIVE	OBSERVABLE
GENERAL	Personality Lifestyle	Demographic Economic
SITUATION	Attitudes Perception and preferences	Usage Purchasing behaviour

Figure 7.2 General approaches to market segmentation
Source: adapted from Frank, Massey and Wind (1972)

The most popular approaches to segmentation, based on Frank, Massey and Wind's general approaches, are briefly considered next.

Geographic segmentation

Geographic segmentation divides the market into a series of locations such as nations, regions, cities or neighbourhoods. This is the simplest approach to segmentation, being dependent upon there being regional disparities in taste or usage. While it is argued that historically this was the case, accounting for marked variations in perishable products such as foodstuffs, these were more likely a result of issues of media, transportation and production, than real market segments. More generally today market segmentation on the basis of geography is a matter of administrative ease, rather than the fact that consumers in regions represent unique segments. However, geographic descriptors are often incorporated into other kinds of segmentation strategies. An example of this would be the development of the ACORN (A Classification Of Residential Neighbourhoods) system, a UK-based model developed by Richard Webber in 1979 in association with the US company CACI. This model depended on there being a discernible difference in consumption patterns based on the kind of housing a person lives in. The model, which purported to identify fifty-four neighbourhood types, used a database amalgamating residential postcodes and census information. This has since been linked to more detailed information gathered through market research. The apparent success of ACORN led to the development of a number of similar competitor systems, including MOSAIC (which analyses census data, credit card information and county court bad debts) developed by Richard Webber after leaving CACI. Public house retailers have long utilized tools such as MOSAIC as key variables in attempts to segment their estates, usually combined with other socioeconomic data. Figure 7.3 highlights a typical segmentation model of this type, used by a leading public house retail company during the 1990s.

Problems have been expressed with the validity of this process for segmenting markets as it should be noted that these methods are based on clustering consumers primarily on geographic location and, therefore, may be simplistic and as such lack real value.

In addition, it is argued that strategies based in geographic segmentation may be too static and involve responses to situations as they exist rather than encouraging the development of approaches aimed at operating in a dynamic environment.

Pub type	Main purpose	Location	Core custom	Facilities	Food and drink
General local	Social drinking	City, town on through road	B, C_1, C_2 (male)	Games, teams, music	Standard beers, lunchtime food only
Community local	Social drinking	Large post-1920s estates	C_2, D	Pool, amusements, teams, gardens	Standard beers, limited food only snacks
Circuit public house	Music, socializing, business	Town centre	B, C_1, C_2 (young)	Sound systems	Premium beers, bottled.
Town boozer	Serious drinking	Town/city centre	C_2, D (male)	Amusements and television	Keg beer and lagers, no food
Quality traditional	Eat or drink	Village or rural	A, B, C_1	none	Cask beers and wine, simple food
Destination public house	Eat or drink	15 minutes from large population	C_1, C_2	For children	Standard beers, wine. Mainly frozen food

Figure 7.3 A typical public house segmentation model

Demographic segmentation

Demographic segmentation divides the market on the basis of such factors as age, gender, religion, social grade, family composition or ethnicity. Kotler (1980: 200), for example, suggests 'these have long been the most popular bases for distinguishing significant groupings in the marketplace ... one reason is that ... demographic variables are easier to measure than most other types of variables'. It is fair to argue that until recently demographics provided the only form of market profiling that hospitality organizations relied on and, in many cases, this is still a valid contention. Demographic variables have been used by hospitality organizations over several decades and it does offer a basic profile with which marketers are familiar. Some aspects of demographics are valid as segmentation tools within hospitality, for example age (young adult segments do appear to demand their own products and seek their own identities through consumption). Similarly, it would be fair to assume that some services are gender specific, and again hospitality retailers have recognized this, developing concepts such as Six Continents' All-Bar-One as a response. Other categories, however, are more problematic, it is fairly simple to deduce the difficulties in defining consumption patterns as a result of ethnicity, for example.

As with geographic segmentation, it is difficult to determine that a significant difference in consumption patterns is discernible on the basis of demographics. It is clear that evidence exists which suggests that consumers do not operate in the manner expected, and as a result they are more often used as additional material to support other strategies. Criticisms of demographic segmentation are largely to do with the extent to which such approaches are sufficiently refined so as to embrace a diverse range of subgroups. As we see in later chapters, trends in society can be argued to be blurring traditional social class distinctions, with the result that in many cases intra-class differences can far exceed intra-class similarities, making demographics a very blunt tool.

Socioeconomic segments

These models are based on segmenting markets on the basis of economic performance. The difficulty is that generalizations based on income are often unhelpful. While some partial explanations of variables in consumption can be seen to be related to income, to simply apply it to all products and services cannot be taken as valid. Despite the difficulties of using such models as social class in segmentation, it is still a key strategy for many hospitality organizations. Hospitality businesses have adhered to a basic principle of social stratification, but have tended to avoid researching possible segments on the basis of social class in any true sociological sense (Evans, Moutinho and Van Raaij, 1996). This is because such a scenario would involve complicated assessments of income, wealth, power, etc. As a result where social grading is used it is simply based on the family's chief income earner. This has led to the situation wherein occupation-based systems of classification remain the standard for both market and social research. One of the reasons for this is that the now familiar $AB/C_1/C_2/DE$ model, first identified by JICNARS for advertising media, and listed overleaf, has become dominant in this area.

Since the early 1980s a number of significant criticisms have been made of segmentation based on social grade, focused around the number of anomalies being identified. For example, in research conducted by O'Brien and Ford (1988) it was demonstrated that of 400 respondents allocated to groups, 70 per cent were found by subsequent interview to have been wrongly allocated.

Social grade	Social status	Head of household's occupation
A	Upper-middle class	High managerial, administrative or professional
B	Middle class	Intermediate managerial, administrative or professional
C_1	Lower-middle class	Supervisory, clerical, junior managerial
C_2	Skilled working class	Skilled manual workers
D	Working class	Semi-skilled and unskilled workers
E	Lowest levels of subsistence	State pensioners, widows, casual or lowest grade workers

A strategy that has developed, which uses demographics combined with socioeconomic factors as a basis, as discussed in Chapter 6, is that of family life cycle (largely based on the marketing tool, PLC) . This assumes that it is possible to identify, within families, stages of life cycle based on a combination of age, marital status, gender and number of children A typical example is included in Figure 7.4. Family life cycle models suggest that the family unit's interests and buying behaviour changes over time.

Life cycle stage	Percentage of households
Bachelor	1.7
Newly married couples	3.8
Full nest 1 (pre-school children)	14.6
Full nest 1 (lone parent)	1.5
Middle age, no children	1.5
Full nest 2 (school-age children)	2.1
Full nest 2 (lone parents)	2.4
Launching families (non-dependent children)	7.8
Launching families (lone parent)	1.8
Empty nest 1 (childless age 45–60)	11.6
Empty nest 2 (retired)	11.7
Solitary survivor (under 65)	3.3
Solitary survivor (retired)	17.4
Total	100

Figure 7.4 UK modernized family life cycle
Source: adapted from Evans, Moutinho and Van Raaij (1996)

Models such as SAGACITY, a model which extends the use of life cycle through adding twelve classifications cross-referenced through income and social class, demonstrates how marketers are constantly developing more and more sophisticated computer-based models, albeit on somewhat tenuous bases. As Jon Epstein (quoted in Evans and Moutinho, 1999: 33) argues: 'Marketers have become ignorant or lazy. They think they have to send all their customers a questionnaire, or buy data from lifestyle databases. I challenge the idea that if they buy data and overlay it they'll understand their customers better ... most companies still can't tell you who has responded to a particular campaign and they usually have no idea how they acquired the customers they do have.'

The key criticism of socio-demographics as a model for segmenting hospitality markets is that it merely offers a profile of consumers; any relationship with actual buying behaviour would appear to be based on inference rather than causality. In addition, as Evans and Moutinho argue, the demographic profiles reported in commercial market reports are usually based on very few characteristics, for example, age, gender and occupation. The value of socio-demographic profiling is not proven, to the extent that even advocates of such models accept there is a difficulty facing marketers in assessing the incremental value added by lifestyle data.

Psychographic segmentation

Psychographic segmentation is based on personality inventories of attitudes expressed by consumers when discussing products, brands or services. In psychographic segmentation buyers are divided on the basis of personality differences. Typical models within this area would include those based on attitudes, lifestyle or situation. Lifestyle approaches are usually based on the presentation to individuals of a series of response statements, with the resultant data then grouped to identify respondents who are relatively homogeneous within a group.

Lifestyle models refer to perceived distinctive modes of orientation, inferred from questions regarding activities, interests and opinions. The segmentation is based on clustering these conclusions and focusing them on particular brands or products/ services. An example of this would be that of Carat Research's Media Graphics classification of consumers by the types of newspapers and magazines they read. The Managing Director of Carat Research, Phil Gullen (quoted in Evans and Moutinho, 1999: 33) argues that, 'Media graphics works not only because

Hospitality, Leisure & Tourism Series

people choose their media to fit in with their attitudes and lifestyles but also because what they read and watch helps develop these attitudes and gives ideas on how to live their lives'. Within psychographic segmentation, personality has been used as a form of segmentation using models based on the self-concept, with marketers endowing their products with brand personalities designed to appeal to corresponding consumer personalities. Such models are based on the premise that we as consumers buy those brands that extend the personality characteristics that we think we possess, or would like to possess or that we want others to think we possess. A perceptual map is developed which is used to investigate differences caused by different social norms. As a result it is argued that it is possible to identify certain brands as displaying certain values, while others display different values. However, the limited empirical testing that has taken place has failed to confirm that consumers of different products demonstrated the personalities perceived by the marketers.

Many studies have been undertaken into the value of psychographic segmentation; however, in most cases the results are not conclusive. Many models have been developed, for example, VALS (Values and Lifestyles), which are evocative, for example describing consumers as belongers or emulators, but empirical evidence to support the value of such schemes is very limited. It can be seen that there are a number of potential problems with psychographic profiling, not least of which is that it is often based on a self-selected sample. As typologies are often developed on the basis of self-completed questionnaires in magazines or surveys, it is open to bias in that not all respondent interests are identified, and participants may make false claims in order to be rewarded by the firms organizing the sample. In addition to the above, the application of psychographic segmentation may pose difficulties, not least because it may be problematic clearly to identify buyer types according to criteria, which are intuitive in nature. As a result, empirical research has failed to identify causal relationships between lifestyles, personality and purchase choices (Littler, 1995).

Benefit segmentation

This model was proposed by Haley (1968) as a means of identifying causal segments. Based on segmenting markets on the basis of what the consumer signals that they want to use the product or service for, benefit segmentation segments essentially by different reasons (for example, goals, beliefs, wants, etc.) for consumption. It is argued that, as individuals identify different benefits from products, the same product or service might serve different segments or markets.

The difficulty with this model is that while benefit segmentation may appear to be the most customer orientated, benefits may not be easily identifiable. For example choosing a benefit group to market to is difficult as it may not be possible to estimate the size of the different benefit groups in the total population. In addition, it is suggested (Kotler, 1980) that in some cases consumers may be choosing on the basis of a benefit bundle rather than an individual benefit, and this would require marketers to identify benefit bundle groups, which may cloud the issue.

Volume segmentation

A relatively recent development in segmentation models, volume segmentation is based on the premise of differentially targeting customers according to their levels of buying and their relative contribution to sales and profit. This model of segmentation is heavily linked to issues of loyalty and reward, and is concerned primarily with identifying the top X percentage of a firm's customer spending and targeting these with offers. It is generally accepted by proponents of volume segmentation that a relatively small proportion of customers contribute the lion's share of company sales and profit. In addition, volume segmentation is linked to the arguments regarding the cost of attracting new customers as opposed to keeping existing ones, the latter having been identified as substantially cheaper than the former (Evans and Moutinho, 1999; Lashley, 2000).

It is clear from Frank, Massey and Wind's (1972) model, and the descriptions above, that there are many ways to segment any given market. As Kotler (1980: 194) suggests, 'Any market with two or more buyers in it can be segmented'. However, the issue that has to be considered is to what extent are the resulting segments meaningful from a marketing perspective. Kotler suggests that, to be useful, market segments must exhibit three characteristics. First, Kotler says they must be *measurable*, defined as the degree to which the size and purchasing power of the resultant segments can be measured. It is clear that certain characteristics consumers of hospitality services display are difficult to measure. Intangible aspects of a product, good or service such as atmosphere, style or performance are hard to define accurately and, therefore, to measure. Second, Kotler says segments must be *accessible*, defined as the degree to which segments can be reached and served. There would be little point in identifying a market segment that it was not possible to communicate with. Finally, Kotler argues, segments must be *substantial* enough to be worth identifying and targeting with specific offers. Segments, it is argued, should be the smallest unit for which it is practical to tailor a specific marketing programme.

Segmenting hospitality markets

Hospitality researchers have used a variety of techniques and methods to investigate hospitality market segments, a number of which were identified by Bowen (1998). However, as Bowen (1998: 294) argues, 'Research to test if segments are statistically different is called for in the hospitality industry. Hospitality products usually attract a large number of segments. Identifying segments that on the surface may appear to be different, but are really not significantly different ... is a valuable technique'. Bowen identifies one of the major problems within contemporary segmentation theory, that is, the argument that due to issues in respect of measurability, accessibility and substance, contemporary hospitality firms are facing a problem Kotler (1980: 210) identified early in his research: 'The problem facing all firms that segment their market is how to estimate the value of operating in each segment'.

Identifying potential segments using any one of the plethora of segmentation models available is one thing. Identifying the value of the resultant segment, in any meaningful way is quite another. Typical hospitality segmentation research has used models such as stages of change, used by MacKay and Fesenmaier (1998) to investigate travel behaviour. This is based on socioeconomic factors overlaid with more psychological ones such as motive. Grazin and Olsen (1997), on the other hand, used a form of volume segmentation when investigating consumers of fast-food restaurants, segmenting consumers into three categories: non-users, light users and heavy users. Using a form of cluster analysis Oh and Jeong (1996) segmented restaurant customers into four lifestyle categories: neat service seekers, convenience seekers, classic diners and indifferent diners. Also using a form of psychological profiling Williams, Demicco and Kotschevar (1997) segmented restaurant consumers using age as the main criteria. Among their findings were that older consumers preferred cream and liver to fruit and vegetables!

Bowen (1998) identifies some twenty-eight pieces of hospitality segmentation research, ranging from the needs of Japanese business travellers (Ahmed and Krohn, 1992) through to the positioning of destination resorts (Alford, 1998), before concluding: 'Marketing segmentation is one of the most important strategic concepts contributed by the marketing discipline to business. Researchers and practitioners need to keep up with the advances in marketing segmentation techniques.'

However, as we have seen, each of the models proposed has criticisms associated with it. Geographic segmentation, while offering a simple framework, can in many ways be seen as too simplistic; it lacks any detailed analysis of hospitality consumer behaviour. Similarly, demographic profiling is not refined enough to embrace the diversity of subgroups that we find in hospitality consumption. The practice of combining geographic and demographic information, rather than making the data more valid, simply compounds the problems identified in each. Socioeconomic profiling, which is widely used throughout the hospitality industry due largely to its quasi-scientific nature, is also flawed. First, the models used do not investigate class in any true sociological manner and, second, we would have to question their worth in an era of blurring social class distinction. Psychographic profiling, again popular due to its quasi-scientific flavour, is not proven empirically; no hospitality research has demonstrated a clear causal relationship between lifestyle and purchase behaviour. Finally, the benefit model can be seen as too complicated for segmenting hospitality services, as it is clear that hospitality consumers do not seek an identifiable, individual benefit from the services offered. Hospitality consumers seek bundles of benefits from hospitality services, requiring marketers to identify benefit-bundles, an impossibly complex undertaking.

The pervasive nature of the marketing concept

In the 1980s hospitality organizations became focused on customers, terms such as *customer focused*, *market focused* or *market driven* dominated the hospitality literature (Carpenter, Glazer and Nakamoto, 1997). During this period market segmentation became the buzzword in the hospitality industry, with practitioners and researchers directing increasing resources to the issue (Crawford-Welch, 1994). As Crawford-Welch argues, within the hotel market, for example, the single-brand company that proliferated in the 1960s had all but disappeared in the 1990s.

In addition it is anticipated that segmentation will continue to be a major strategy for hospitality firms in the future as it is conventional wisdom that segmentation allows firms to develop a range of product offerings within their portfolio, in order to balance earnings' streams. Segmentation is also seen to offer hospitality firms the opportunity to grow in saturated markets. The importance placed on the marketing concept in hospitality is highlighted by Teare, Mazanec and Crawford-Welch (1994: vii) when they suggest, 'To succeed in hospitality and tourism markets ... firms must be able to interpret the needs of their customers [and] identify appropriate ways of segmenting the markets in which they wish to compete'.

This is supported by Calver (1994: 285) who suggests that 'In recent years, many hospitality organizations, especially in the United Kingdom and the rest of Europe have grasped the terminology and professed their conversion to the cause of the marketing concept'. As a demonstration of this he points to the enhanced sales forces involved and the expenditure of hospitality firms on advertising.

The use of segmentation in hospitality has been aided by developments in computer-generated market information. Tools such as ACORN and MOSAIC have encouraged marketing departments in their attempts to introduce sophisticated segmentation profiles. The result is that it now appears to be an accepted belief that segmentation of hospitality markets is an invaluable tool in aiding operators to gain competitive advantage. As the leading UK trade magazine, *Caterer and Hotelkeeper* (27 July 1995: 54) suggests, 'Segmentation has meant proper targeting of promotional activity, increased effectiveness and helped to eliminate waste'. When the marketing concept was introduced in the mid-1960s it was intended to provide a focus for changing a producer orientation of unthinking control and dominance, to one perceived as more sophisticated where customers' wants dictate production patterns. We have now arrived at a position whereby market segmentation is seen as an absolute must by the bulk of marketing academics and practitioners, a centre point for all marketing activities and indeed if some authorities are to be believed a panacea for all organizational ills.

If we consider a range of typical statements, we can see the pervasive influence of market segmentation and the way in which it is unquestioningly accepted within hospitality. For example, Baron and Harris (1995: 129) state: 'By grouping together customers with certain similarities, for example those of the same age, employment, ambitions etc. the service provider is in a better position to design an appropriate service package.' This is supported by Mazanec (1994: 108) who argues, 'Market segmentation rests on a very simple and plausible assumption, subgroups in the consumer population may be homogeneous in terms of motives, attitudes or activities. Therefore they may be expected to react to product offerings and promotional efforts in a similar manner', Foxall and Goldsmith (1994: 9), 'the practice of segmentation makes the design of marketing strategy more effective as the manager has the sense of directing resources at specific and identifiable groups of people, rather than diverse collections of individuals' and Green and Kreigner (1991: 28), 'It [segmentation] is one of the most talked about and acted upon concepts in marketing'. Finally, Wearne and Morrison (1996: 35) state, 'There are many ways of segmenting a market to form a complete picture for planning purposes', and the leading UK hospitality trade magazine concluded: 'Pubs should be grouped by type and most owners now use this (segmentation based on location and socio-demographic information) system in some form' (*Caterer and Hotelkeeper*, 27 July 1995: 54).

The collapse of the marketing concept

In recent years a discernible shift has been recognized by a number of marketing researchers leading to a groundswell of criticism being attributed to the marketing concept. As Robson and Rowe (1997: 655) argue, 'It seems to be the case that leading marketing academics are currently viewing both themselves and their discipline as the critical factors in business success. Hundreds of marketing academics and so-called marketing professionals demonstrate an unfailing allegiance to a concept, which has failed to deliver a cogent, defensible general theory in over 40 years of development'. They go on to conclude that a core concept for the discipline of marketing has not been developed which makes consistent sense, arguing that the marketing concept does not provide a starting point for the development of a general theory as the underpinnings of the discipline have been misappropriated from other disciplines. As they suggest, 'The laws of marketing are derived from economic theory and the behavioural sciences. These laws have been misappropriated to the point where they are barely visible in the marketing textbooks. For example we see concepts such as utility, and supply and demand, expressed simplistically as laws of the marketplace' (Robson and Rowe, 1997: 658). This is supported by Thomas (1997: 55) who suggests, 'Consumers (and hence consumer behaviour) has never been so unpredictable, hence traditional consumer research is incapable of providing the insights required by marketing decision makers'.

Littler (1995) identifies a number of the criticisms that, he argues, can be levelled at segmentation typologies, including: buyers may not be consistent in their purchase behaviour; segments may be unstable; it is difficult to conclude with certainty that a particular segmentation measure leads to a specific form of action; and it is difficult to satisfy the criteria Kotler (1980) laid down for segmentation, that is, accessibility, measurability and substance. In dealing with the issue of the process used to segment markets many authors (Piercy and Morgan, 1993; Reynolds, 1965; Saunders, 1987) argue that the difficulties in meaningfully applying segmentation strategies are underestimated, with the result that it is more often talked about than practised. Such a belief is summed up by Sir Colin Marshall, Chairman of British Airways, who argued that 'As markets have become more complex, so has the essentially basic concept of market segmentation. It is the view of many that ... the art of defining target markets rarely progresses beyond the assembly of somewhat dull demographics. The logical conclusion is that, if everybody is doing the same, differential advantage is difficult to attain' (McDonald and Dunbar, 1998: 33).

Similar criticisms of the process of market segmentation have been expounded by Knight (1991) and Jenkins, Le Cerf and Cole (1994) and Jenkins and McDonald (1997) all of whom argue that while segmentation should simplify consumer behaviour, in truth it tends to reflect a company's internal issues and culture. As Jenkins and McDonald (1997: 25) suggest: 'Conventional segmentation theory has been founded on conceptual, rather than empirical evidence, based on how organizations should segment their markets. A counter view suggests that the market definition of many organizations is often a function of internal factors such as organizational culture and process. Empirical evidence (Jenkins et al., 1994) found that many managers defined and segmented their markets on the basis of internal products rather than external customer groupings.' Other criticisms of segmentation are largely to do with the extent to which such an approach is sufficiently refined so as to embrace a diverse range of subgroups. As a result it is argued that the value of segmentation is not proven, and there is a difficulty facing hospitality managers in assessing the incremental value added by such data. Hooley (1980) and Bonomo and Shapiro (1984) argue that too much emphasis is placed on the techniques associated with segmentation, with the result that implementation is ignored. In addition, it is argued that many segmentation strategies may be too static and involve responses to situations as they exist rather than encouraging the development of approaches aimed at developing in a dynamic environment.

Further criticism is offered by Crawford-Welch (1994) who suggests that there is considerable evidence that in hospitality, product development is not market orientated, but product orientated. As evidence, he offers the example that in a survey of lodging and restaurant organizations in the USA over 33 per cent of firms viewed conducting market research as unimportant. As Crawford-Welch (1994: 173) suggests, 'Many organizations are guilty of claiming to engage in a strategy of market segmentation when in fact they are practising a strategy of product differentiation'. All the above raise questions about the validity of market segmentation, and further questions as to the role of segmentation in the hospitality industry are indicated in Case Study 7.1, which, taking Crawford-Welch's argument, looks at whether Six Continents' hotel portfolio has developed as a result of market segmentation or simply the segmenting of product offers.

Case study 7.1

Market segmentation or product segmentation? The case of Six Continents Hotels

The purpose of this case study is to consider the extent to which the portfolio of major hospitality organizations are truly examples of offers developed with particular market segments in mind or, alternatively, if they demonstrate expansion through product segmentation and other strategies, using the hotel portfolio of Six Continents Hotels as an example.

Apart from a small chain of hotels acquired in 1987, Bass' (now renamed Six Continents) first significant move into the hotel sector came in 1989 when it purchased Holiday Inns International, at the time the leading hotel brand worldwide, and then Holiday Inns of America Inc. In 1991 it expanded its portfolio by introducing Holiday Inn Express, a limited service concept, and again in 1994, with the upscale Crowne Plaza. In March 1998, it spent £2 billion acquiring the Inter-Continental brand, again an upmarket offer, before finally, for now, acquiring the ex-Forte and Granada branded Posthouse chain for £810 million, which it set about converting to Holiday Inns.

Today Six Continents Hotels offers a wide range of accommodation through its portfolio of hotel brands, namely:

- *Inter-Continental Hotels and Resort*. A truly global brand, operating at the top end of the upscale market, Inter-Continental has been a major hotel brand for the world's business community for more than fifty years. Sited in prime city centre and resort locations in over seventy countries, each hotel seeks to reflect the local culture and customs, enabling travellers to experience the unique flavour of the country they are visiting.
- *Crowne Plaza Hotels and Resorts*. Again an international brand offering upscale accommodation with enhanced services and amenities to business and leisure travellers. Every Crowne Plaza property offers high-quality meeting facilities, a professional conference staff, extensive business services, quality health and fitness facilities, and upscale dining operations. Crowne

Plaza properties are located on major city centre sites and at significant business centres around the world.

- *Holiday Inn.* Holiday Inn is considered to be the world's most recognized hotel brand, and offers dependable, friendly service, modern facilities and excellent value to both the business and leisure traveller. There are currently more than 1500 Holiday Inn hotels in more than sixty countries, and this is growing daily.
- *Express by Holiday Inn.* Contemporary hotel styles for the value-conscious traveller, operating in the limited service sector worldwide, the Express hotels are perceived to be fresh, clean and uncomplicated, offering competitive rates for both business and leisure travellers. For example, guests are entitled to a free breakfast bar and free local phone calls.
- *Staybridge Suites by Holiday Inn.* A distinct hotel concept, designed to meet the needs of travellers around the world who require accommodation for overnight stays of five consecutive nights or more, whether they are leisure or business customers. Accommodation within the Staybridge Suites includes studios and one- and two-bedroom suites, with two queen-sized or one king-sized bed, a sofa-bed, interactive television, a large well-lit work area, kitchen facilities and many other residential design features.

The question that this wide range of provision raises, however, is the extent to which the offers are intended to meet the needs of significantly different market segments, as based on any of the criteria we have discussed within the main body of the text. An alternative perspective may be to view them, as many people do, simply as product segments that are not aimed in any significant way at different segments of the market, but depend upon context, purpose and purchase reason for their distinctiveness – behaviours of hospitality consumers that as we have seen are very difficult to interpret.

It is clear from the above that despite the perceived importance and value of the marketing concept a number of commentators are suggesting that the concept has flaws. Indeed, many (Cova and Svanfeldt, 1992; Marrion, 1993) suggest that the flaws in the concept are so fundamental that they render it invalid. Typical among this group of doubters are Piercy (1992: 15) who argues that the marketing concept 'Assumes and relies on the existence of a world which is alien and unrecognizable to many of the executives who manage marketing for real'. On a similar note McKenna (1991: 67) states, 'There is less and less reason to believe that the traditional approach can keep up with real customer wishes and demands or with the rigours of competition'. While Thomas (1993) one of the UK's foremost marketing academics has confirmed he has serious doubts about the continuing efficacy of the marketing concept. A number of similar commentators further support the crisis of confidence currently

Hospitality, Leisure & Tourism Series

advocated in respect of the marketing concept, including McGregor (1995: 41), 'The environment has changed so dramatically that marketers are simply not picking up the right signals any more', Jenkins and McDonald (1997: 21) 'There is a lack of research, which attempts to understand how organizations actually arrive at and sustain market segments', Gummerson (1996: 36), 'The present marketing concept . . . is unrealistic and needs to be replaced' and Buttle (1994: 8), 'The only thing we know with certainty is that we do not know very much at all. Not much of an outcome for 50 years' scientific endeavour'. Indeed, some contemporary commentators are very scathing about the role of the marketing concept in today's markets concluding 'large-scale surveys of consumer tastes, based on simplistic questionnaires, are outdated and methodologically mechanistic. Standardized inflexible questionnaires will not capture "tastes and meaning". But we knew that all along' (Thomas, 1997: 142), 'it is questionable whether the marketing concept as it has been propagated can provide the basis for successful business at the end of the 20th century' (Brownlie and Saren, 1992: 38) and, most critically, 'the secret history of marketing . . . is one of crisis, failure, confusion, misunderstanding, and occasional joyous, inexplicable, successful hitting of the jackpot' (Weir, 1996: 28).

In hospitality marketing Crawford-Welch (1994) offers the example of the development of all-suite hotels, which since their original introduction have been segmented into limited-service all-suites, full service all-suites and extended stay all-suites. What began as a straightforward idea – a limited service hotel product geared to business travellers, with the attraction being a home-like two-room suite – has grown into a multi-tiered segment encompassing a number of hotel classifications and markets. As Crawford-Welch (1994: 180) concludes: 'There are said to be at least thirty-five companies with hotels in the all-suite segment, including economy, moderate, upscale and luxury properties. It is questionable whether the plethora of market segments for which these products were designed really exists.'

It is not simply market segmentation and positioning that has come in for criticism, however. For example, Thomas (1997) questions the value of another theory, that of the Boston matrix, developed by the Boston Consulting Group, and now widely used in all manner of analysis. Within hospitality for example the Boston matrix is applied to analyses ranging in scale from an analyses of market sectors at the macro level through to an analysis of menu items at the micro level. The problem is, however, as Morrison and Wensley (1991: 65) suggest, 'It is a real worry that the original [Boston] matrix is seductively simple, and the temptations and risk of using it off the shelf are real . . . those who use it now may be boxed in terms of restrictive assumptions about both the nature of marketing and competitive dynamics . . . it is a badly taught, outmoded and discredited orthodoxy, which is seductive and dangerous for our young managers of tomorrow'. Similarly Denison and McDonald (1995: 55) concede that 'Classical 4 P's marketing . . . is not as relevant a framework . . . as we have become prepared to accept'. Cova and Badot (1995: 421) consider the implications of the mounting criticism for much of marketing theory, concluding: 'The PLC, SWOT analyses, Maslow's hierarchy, the Howard-Sheth model, the trickle down principle, the strategic matrices of Ansoff, Porter and the BCG, the typologies of retailing institutions, hierarchies of advertising effects, the wheel of retailing, and needless to say the 4P's . . . are basically modernist in orientation.'

A similar all-encompassing criticism of the marketing concept is offered by Brown (2000) who argues that despite forty years of marketing academia and practice the 'holy grail' of marketing as science has not been achieved. Brown concludes that the anticipated models of marketing science – rigour, objectivity, prediction, objectivity, theory-building and law-giving – have not transpired and are never likely to. A number of other authors have also focused on the extent to which marketing is based on fundamental laws in developing its theories. Robson and Rowe (1997: 657), for example, suggest: 'Broadly speaking theories are judged by their ability to describe, explain and predict the phenomena of interest. Marketing theory fails to convince many that these criteria are satisfied . . . little wonder that we come to criticize the conceptual frameworks that are marketing when we cannot see the logic which underpins such frameworks and where logic does exist it is almost entirely based on empiricism.'

Authors such as Robson and Rowe (1997), Brownlie and Saren (1992) and Brown (2000) argue that marketing does not provide a substantive theory in helping to explain, predict or model consumer behaviour. The reasons for this, it is argued, are that the laws of marketing have been adapted from the laws governing such disciplines as behavioural science and economics, but these 'laws' have been misused and applied so simplistically so that it is no longer possible to determine their base points. As Robson and Rowe (1997: 660) suggest: 'We can criticize theories such as the Boston Box, diffusion of innovation, PLC, segmentation. If such theory demonstrates no obvious linkage to abstract laws then what is its value. The theories of marketing are neither truly positivist nor truly interpretive.'

The question this raises is do these criticisms of the marketing concept actually matter when we consider the consumption of hospitality services? The answer appears to be that it does. Such is the preponderance of hospitality marketing texts and so central are they to most hospitality courses that it is a safe assumption that most managers within hospitality companies have been exposed to marketing's conceptual techniques. As a result it is argued (Brown, 1995; 2000) that hospitality practitioners are employing marketing concepts and acting on their predictions, even though the concepts themselves are far from proven. To support this view Brown offers the examples of sound products withdrawn because of the executives' belief in the proposed PLC, and the marketing world view of competition as warfare that has since been superseded by the rhetoric of relationships and strategic alliances. As Brown concludes, the implications of the centrality of marketing concepts in contemporary hospitality organizations is that they do not simply reflect events in the marketing environment; they directly affect marketing behaviour. As Brown (1995: 27) concludes: 'Theory is not neutral, it influences and alters the phenomena to which it pertains.'

The conclusion for hospitality consumption

While there have been many strands to the criticisms of the marketing concept as applied to contemporary hospitality markets, they can be seen to focus around the issues of fragmentation of markets and the predictive power of universal marketing models. If we consider the first of these issues, it is clear from a consideration of much of the current literature in hospitality marketing and consumer behaviour that markets are being analysed in increasingly sophisticated manners, leading to the identification and targeting of apparently well-defined markets. However, it is also clear that markets are themselves fragmenting, not least due to a perceived trend to individualism.

Increasingly sophisticated technology facilitates the segmentation process, as does the growth in media forms. However, the whole of the marketing concept as it relates to hospitality consumption is reliant on getting specific information at the purchase level and in such detail that household characteristics, buying behaviour and possessions can be readily identified. What is actually happening is that the lists and databases that have been developed during the 1980s and 1990s are being linked to provide consecutive overlaying of information as the basis for segmenting markets (Evans, Moutinho and Van Raaij, 1996). The lengths to which hospitality organizations are going in order to identify customers in terms of customizing services and advertising messages has led authors such as Hoyt (1991) to suggest that practitioners are increasingly dealing in segments of one and, as a consequence, are no longer involved in marketing.

As I have argued in this chapter, a dominant view of competitive advantage within the hospitality industry, and one that has grown in importance during the 1980s and early 1990s has been the marketing concept, as formalized by Kotler (1980). While the argument that we should listen to the customer and give them what they want seems correct, as we have demonstrated there are a number of problems with such a philosophy. First, it is based on assumptions of consumer behaviour that may not be valid. Second, the question has to be addressed if all hospitality organizations are operating in this way where is the competitive advantage? Finally, mounting evidence suggests that systematic violations of the marketing concept by consumers are the norm, rather than the exception. As Carpenter, Glazer and Nakamoto (1997: 121) argue, 'Buyer preferences are shown to be context dependent such that a buyer's preferences may depend on the context of choice created by a set of products available . . . buyers use a variety of decision making strategies to choose amongst alternatives, these strategies are context dependent. Buyers may use different rules for different occasions or choice situations'.

This argument presents a challenge to existing views of marketing for hospitality goods and services; if consumer choice is not static but varies with context and if consumers do use a range of decision strategies, the essence of the marketing concept, that is, to target segmented markets, becomes impossible as consumers will move through segments dependent on the context of the purchase. This brings to the forefront the question, how can competitive advantage be gained through marketing strategies that segment consumers into recognizable types if preferences and decision-making are context dependent?

Given some of the issues raised in this chapter, it is fair to argue that what is needed for the contemporary hospitality industry is an alternative way of looking at consumers and markets, a way that is truly consumer led. The result, as Foxall and Goldsmith (1994: 2) argues, is that 'An increased awareness of the more dynamic amorphous consumer behaviour patterns requires marketers to adopt approaches that concentrate on a willingness to listen to consumers and to accommodate marketing management to the emerging lifestyles of consumers. As such the approach of founding marketing strategies on traditional segmentation criteria is no longer appropriate'. Such an argument is supported by Firat and Venkatesh (1993), who argue that the marketing concept has previously been content to portray images of normality and stereotypicality. What is required, they suggest, is a greater awareness of the huge diversity and heterogeneity of consumers of hospitality services.

The key criticism of the marketing concept is encapsulated by Robson and Rowe (1997), who argue that theories are judged by their ability to describe, explain and predict phenomena. Marketing theory as we have seen fails to convince many that these criteria are satisfied. The result is as Robson and Rowe (1997: 662) conclude: 'It is the contention of the authors that marketing theory is not really theory at all, in terms of social theory; we ought to consider marketing theory as an empirical prepositional scheme'. Thus it can be argued that, as the marketing concept is difficult to justify either philosophically or empirically, marketing can best be described as no more than an ideology (Brown, 2000; Robson and Rowe, 1997).

What are the implications of this for individuals and companies involved in the hospitality industry? Elliot (1993) suggests that in contemporary society meanings are determined not by marketers but by consumers, with the result that inconsistent interpretations become the norm. This has serious implications for hospitality companies seeking to segment markets in order to determine investment and human resource and operational policies, based on such limiting criteria as social and economic location. As Brown (1995) suggests, such a proposition, positioned as it is with an emphasis on normality, is unlikely to be effective at refocusing on today's emphasis on diversity. As a result, suggests Brown, theories and concepts such as those surrounding marketing, grounded in economic rationality, can be seen to be flawed. As Firat and Shultz (1997: 203) argue: 'Marketing must no longer conceptualize any consumer unit as a point of conclusion but as a moment in the continual cycle of (re) production. And since this consumer is no longer representing a centred, unified, consistent, single self-image, but a fragmented and fluid set of self-images, conceptualizing the consumer as a member of a relatively homogeneous market segment is increasingly difficult'.

If companies are to be effective in the highly competitive marketing environment that comprises the contemporary hospitality industry, it is imperative that they understand contemporary consumers and consumer decision-making. As we have seen, it can be suggested that many of the approaches that are currently being advocated are based in the arguably flawed models of the marketing concept. Simply to continue in both hospitality theory and practice to expound the theories inherent in the marketing concept without question will not in the long term offer our industry the progressive marketing developments it needs to succeed in the new century. As we have identified, many leading authors are beginning to seriously question the value of the marketing concept in understanding contemporary markets. The hospitality industry with its perceived focus on the customer has not been immune to the pervasiveness of the marketing concept orientation. As Brown (1995: 178) concludes, however, 'The fundamental issue to which we should address ourselves is not marketing myopia, but the myopia of marketing'.

CHAPTER 8

Postmodern consumers of hospitality services

Key themes

- There is increasing evidence to support the argument that consumption of hospitality services in contemporary western society is fragmented in nature.

- A perceived breakdown in fixed social roles has left individuals free to adopt a wide range of identities in a postmodern society.

- Within hospitality, postmodern consumption is based around three central tenets: the breakdown of grand narratives, the centrality of communication technologies and the consumer culture of late capitalism.

- The transition from a modernist to a postmodernist approach to consumer behaviour has implications for all those involved in marketing hospitality services.

Postmodern marketing

According to Thomas (1997: 54) postmodernism has very serious implications for contemporary consumption studies. He suggests that this is because 'Marketing, real-time, real-world marketing is thoroughly postmodern ... because postmodern marketing openly challenges some of the major axioms of the conventional wisdom as reflected in the standard marketing textbooks'. Continuing, Thomas identifies a number of these axioms, including:

- consumer needs
- consumer sovereignty
- behavioural consistency
- customer orientation
- perceived value
- product image
- buyer–seller separation
- individual–organization distinction
- product–process separation
- consumption–production division.

If we accept the premise offered by authors such as Thomas (1997), Brown (2000), Firat and Shultz (1997) and others previously identified in this book, it is clear that we need to investigate postmodernism as it relates to contemporary hospitality consumption.

This chapter seeks to explore a number of the key themes within postmodernism and to investigate the ways in which they can be defined within the contemporary hospitality industry. It is not intended within this chapter to discuss in detail the development of postmodernism, nor to discuss its use in investigating contemporary society. We will limit ourselves to exploring postmodernism only as it pertains to features of hospitality consumption

An introduction to postmodernism

A common theme that runs through much of the current literature on consumption is that in contemporary western society consumption is fragmented in nature. It is argued (Ogilvy, 1990) that a shift has been recognized from values and beliefs based on industrial mass production and universal patterns of taste to one founded on personal tastes and preferences, as evidenced by eclectic patterns of purchase and consumption and a recognition of the ambiguities inherent in modern artefacts

(Foxall and Goldsmith, 1994). This transition from a modernist to a postmodernist approach to consumption has implications for all individuals involved in the marketing of hospitality goods and services.

With a perceived decline in fixed social roles, individuals are left to adopt a wide variety of identities in a postmodern society. Each of these identities has a given role within specific everyday situations that individuals subsequently encounter. As Foucault (1980) suggests, there is no real self; individuals are free to construct identities from a wide range which are available and are constantly in a process of change. Ogilvy (1990: 15) states: 'Where the modern consumer bought goods to adorn and express a more or less consistent and recognizable lifestyle, the post-modern consumer plays with an eclectic combination of goods and services to experience a series of tentative inconsistent identities'. Ogilvy goes on to argue that, whereas market research previously segmented the population into sets of recognizable consistent types of consumers, postmodern market research would have to be undertaken with a recognition that individuals do not remain true to type. Adapting Ogilvy's example: dependent on mood or situational context, the same individuals may behave as upscale achievers at one moment, for example, frequenting the likes of the Dorchester Hotel or the Ivy restaurant, and downscale consumers the next, for example, staying in budget accommodation and eating at local bars. Fragmentation and a lack of commitment have resulted in consumers who do not present a united, unified, coherent self, and therefore set of preferences, but a jigsaw of multiple representations (Firat and Shultz, 1997). It is for these reasons that we must consider the potential impact postmodernism may have on the consumption of hospitality services. At a time when a number of forms of academic discipline are examining the implications of the postmodern condition, it is clear that consideration of its implications for hospitality need to be investigated.

Defining postmodernism

It is not intended within this chapter to discuss at length the development and continued role of postmodernism in contemporary society; such arguments are available elsewhere, in particular through the work of authors such as Best and Kellner (1991), Baudrillard (1983), Lyotard (1984), Seidman and Wagner (1991) and Foucault (1977). What we are seeking to achieve is a consideration of some key aspects of postmodernism and the ways in which they can be seen to relate to a key feature of contemporary society, the role of consumption and, in particular, hospitality consumption. In order to achieve this, however, it is necessary to discuss the origins of postmodern thought and briefly to discuss the key elements of postmodernism. These elements will then be applied to aspects of the contemporary hospitality industry throughout the remainder of the book. The argument that the traditional modernist approach to consumer behaviour, as outlined in Part Two of this text, with its focus on objectivity, and quantitative analysis has been replaced by postmodern perspectives, with their focus on ritual, myth and symbolism, will be the focus of the third part of this book.

One of the major problems with investigating postmodernism and its application to the study of consumption within hospitality is that it is difficult to define exactly the concept we are considering. Postmodernism encompasses a broad range of developments, not only in philosophy and social science, but also in architecture, the arts, literature, fashion and much more. As such the term is used and subsequently defined in many different ways. These difficulties are summed up by Brown (1995: 10) when he says of postmodernism: 'It is essentially intangible; a mood, a moment, a perspective, a state of mind, rather than a body of theory or a conceptual framework.' A similar view is expounded by Gellner (1992: 22) who suggests that 'Postmodernism is a contemporary movement. It is strong and it is fashionable. Over and above this, it is not altogether clear what the devil it is ... there appears to be no postmodern manifesto which one could consult so as to assure oneself that one has identified its ideas properly'. Similarly Crotty (1998: 183) argues that 'Postmodernism is the most slippery of terms ... it is used, and defined, in a multitude of ways. So too is the "modernism" to which it is related by virtue of the preposition "post", which in its turn is understood in almost equally inconsistent fashion'. In addition, the problems of definition are exacerbated by the fact that postmodernism has come to mean different things within different areas of study (Featherstone, 1991). As Brown (1995: 11) suggests: 'The only discernible point of consensus among postmodernists is their lack of consensus on postmodernism.'

Problems with defining postmodernism are exacerbated by the fact that postmodernism has been incorporated into a wide range of disciplines: examples exist of postmodern design and décor, film plots, record constructions, television commercials, magazines, critical articles and videos (Hebdige, 1986). In addition, as the range of disciplines within which postmodernism is located expands, distortion of the concepts in which it is based are inevitable, simply being a reflection of its dispersion among this range of disciplines (Brown, 1995). The heterogeneous nature of postmodern thought also causes considerable confusion, as Rosenau (1992: 14) argues: 'The cut and paste character of postmodernism, its absence of unity is both a strength and a weakness. Everyone can find something with which to agree, but an infinite number of alternatives allow different and varying ways to put together the elements that constitute postmodernism ... Postmodernism is stimulating and fascinating, and at the same time it is always on the brink of collapsing into confusion.'

However, problems with defining the concepts of postmodernism are not sufficient reason to reject its use for a consideration of marketing and consumption in contemporary hospitality. Definitional problems are common in many disciplines. Postmodernism is a concept which is obscure and which, as a result, is difficult to use, however, it can also be argued to offer valuable insights into contemporary hospitality consumer behaviour. This becomes clear if we consider the extensive literature currently available regarding postmodernism, much of which, while not written with a hospitality marketing audience in mind, can be seen to have clear implications within the discipline. Such texts include those by Featherstone (1991), Brown (1995), Elliot (1993) and Firat (1991). In addition a range of texts, which seek to clarify postmodernism, have been published In particular, those by Harvey (1989) and Rosenau (1992) are seen as having value in aiding our understanding of a complex concept (Brown, 1995).

Towards an understanding of postmodernism

An understanding of postmodernism begins at the centre of western society, with the culture of the Enlightenment, a radical and permanent break with the perceived irrationality and superstition of the proceeding ages. It included such aspects as the unity of humanity, the individual as the creative force of society, the superiority of the West, the notion of science as truth and a belief in social progress (Seidman, 1994). These beliefs have until now been fundamental to Europe and the rest of the western world. However, it is argued by postmodernists that this perspective is under attack and that this attack is signified by such aspects as the resurgence of religious fundamentalism, the decline in the authority of key social institutions, crisis in western political ideologies and in criticism of literary and aesthetic cultural paradigms. It is suggested that a broad social and cultural shift has occurred in western society and that this is captured in part at least by the concepts of postmodernism. As such postmodernism could be argued to be 'A philosophical orientation that rejects the dominant foundational programme of the western tradition. There are no absolute truths and no objective values. As for reality itself . . . it does not tell us what is true or good or beautiful. The Universe is not itself any of these things, it does not interpret. Only we do, variously' (Rue, 1994: 272). Such a view is supported by Wolin (1992) who talks of postmodernism as a movement of unmaking. When considering some of the key phrases used within postmodern literature, such as deconstruction, decentring, demystification, discontinuity and dispersion, Wolin suggests that they express a rejection of the cogito of western philosophy.

Although within the literature there has never been a general consensus regarding the nature of modernism, it is suggested that it is possible to identify a dominant cultural understanding of the concept. Seidman (1990) suggests modernity includes such notions as an evolutionary notion of humanity; social progress evidenced by high art, science and a unitary notion of the individual; and a conception of human evolution that anticipates self-realization and an end of domination. Modernism embraces the idea of progress, reason, scientific discovery and techno-logical innovation. In addition it holds that, once we understand the fundamental laws of the physical and social world, we can analyse, plan and control them (Smart, 1992).

Crotty (1998) suggests that the 'modern' world is typified by rationality, following a Weberian model; as such the modern world is viewed as one in which instrumental reason holds sway. As described above, this rationality is embodied in the certainty and precision of science and the control and manipulation of nature that science is perceived as making possible. Modernism demonstrates great faith in the ability of reason to discover absolute forms of knowledge. As Horkheimer and Adorno (1972: 3) argue, modernism involved 'The disenchantment of the world, dissolution of myths and the substitution of knowledge for fancy . . . [it] has always aimed at liberating men from fear and establishing their sovereignty'. According to Seidman (1990) the debate about postmodernism can be precisely situated, with Seidman arguing that the first discussions regarding post-modernism took place in the late 1960s, and grew to become a major focus for sociology during the 1970s and 1980s, until in the 1990s postmodernism has become to be seen as a description of broad changes in our sensibilities, norms, values and beliefs.

The question postmodernism first raises is does 'post' moder-nism imply that modernism has now been replaced by post-modernism. However, within the literature this question is not easily answered, largely depending as it does on how we define the term 'modernism'. Some accounts of postmodernism see it as emerging out of, and in reaction to, modernism, with the continuity between the two maintained (Milner, 1991). Other authors, however, see postmodernism as a definite opposite to modernism, arguing that it calls into question all that modernism asserts as true. While it is clear that postmodernism arose out of the modern movement, if modernism is, as has previously been argued, founded on the beliefs of the Enlightenment – clarity and certitude, the abolishing of ambiguity and the individual as self-reliant and controlling – then postmodernism is clearly a rejection of modernism. Postmodernism refutes all concepts of a totalizing all-encompassing orientation. As Crotty (1998: 185) argues: 'Where modernism purports to base itself on generalized, indubitable truths about the way things really are, postmodern-ism abandons the entire epistemological basis for any such claims to truth. Instead of espousing clarity, certitude, wholeness and continuity, postmodernism commits itself to ambiguity, relativity, fragmentation, particularity and discontinuity ... delights in play, irony, pastiche, excess – even mess'.

This, it can be seen, is a clear-cut way of determining the difference between modernism and postmodernism; one is simply the converse of the other. However, it is not so simple. Many authors would argue that the problem of seeing the modern/postmodern debate in this way is that many of the characteristics, which are commonly associated with post-modernism, are not specific to postmodernism. In particular, as Crotty (1998) argues, many of the criticisms of modernist thought are espoused by constructionists such as Adorno (1977) and Giddens (1979), but as constructionists are not postmodernists per se, such an argument would suggest that serious anomalies appear if we simply see postmodernism as the antithesis of modernism. This debate continues in the postmodern literature and is likely to do so for the foreseeable future. For our purposes, however, I intend to use postmodernism in its sense of being post-'modernism', while remaining cognizant of the counter-arguments.

In addition to the above, I do not seek to argue that modernity has come to an end, as Crotty (1998: 184) suggests, 'Postmodern-ism certainly does not imply that once there was a modernism and now this has been replaced by postmodernism ... [anymore than] the emergence of post-positivism has meant the demise of positivism'. In the West the key symbols of modernity are still in place, for example, an industrial-based economy, politics orga-nized around key interest groups, economic argument fixed on a valuation of the comparative merits of the free market versus state regulation. These issues are all key to the concepts of modernity and, as such, it would be unwise to suggest that postmodernism has replaced modernism in western society. As

Seidman (1994: 1) suggests, 'Modernity has not exhausted itself; it may be in crisis but it continues to shape the contours of our lives'.

The relationship between modernism and postmodernism is described by Crotty (1998: 193) as 'With postmodernism, the adversarial relationship between modernist and mass culture is considered to have come to an end. In the context of a new world variously described by, or as, radical internationalism and transnationalism, post-industrialisation, mass communications, universal consumerism, hyperreality ... modernism has been unable to retain its elitist character'. The terms 'modern' and 'postmodern' should be seen as simply referring to broad social and cultural patterns that can be distinguished and analysed for the purpose of highlighting perceived social and cultural trends. Authors (Miller and Real, 1998; Seidman, 1994) suggest that these trends can be discerned in areas such as the collapse in the distinction between high art and popular art, the eclectic mixing of aesthetic codes in architecture, a nostalgia for tradition throughout art, the breakdown of traditional boundaries between social institutions and cultural spheres, and the de-territoralization of national economies and cultures. As Seidman (1994: 2) argues, 'Postmodern knowledge contests disciplinary boundaries, the separation of science, literature, and ideology, and the divisions between knowledge and power'. In essence, perhaps the main defining difference between modernism and post-modernism is the latter's rejection of the modernist notion that social experience has fundamental real bases; postmodernism argues that many of the modernist ideals are arbitrary and ephemeral, rather than fixed and essential (Firat and Venkatesh, 1995).

A common mechanism for investigating the differences between modernism and postmodernism has been the wide-spread use of indicative lists of modern/postmodern characteristics. While accepting the criticisms that such lists of decontextualized adjectives can be meaningless, differ widely from author to author and tend to give the impression of a systematic, integrated movement, it is fair to argue that they do give a feel for postmodern sensibilities and, as such, a typical listing is included here:

Modernist emphasis	Postmodern emphasis
Object	Image/symbol
Cartesian subject	Symbolic subject
Cognitive subject	Semiotic subject
Unified subject	Fragmented subject
Centred subject	Decentred subject

Signified	Signifier
Objectification	Symbolism
Representation	Signification
Truth (objective)	Truth (constructed)
Real	Hyperreal
Universalism	Localism
Society as structure	Society as spectacle
Logocentric reason	Hermeneutic reason
Knowing	Communicating
Economy	Culture
Capitalism	Late capitalism
Economic system	Symbolic system
Production	Consumption
Sciences	Humanities
Euro-American centrism	Globalism
Phallocentrism	Feminism/genderism
Colonialism	Multiculturism

Consuming hospitality: learning lessons from postmodernism

While competing definitions of postmodernism, drawing from architecture, design, history, literature, sociology, etc., have made the term 'postmodern' controversial and notoriously difficult to define, in terms of relating it to the consumption of hospitality products and services, it can be argued to comprise a number of recognizable principles.

These are highlighted by Miller and Real (1998) as:

- the breakdown of the grand narratives that we have previously used to aid comprehension
- the centrality of communication technologies
- the consumer culture of late capitalism.

The breakdown of grand narratives

This refers to the use of metanarratives to solve generalized problems where Lyotard (1984) is seen as being central to the debates over postmodernism, in particular those regarding knowledge. It was Lyotard who introduced one of the key themes of postmodernism, the decline of the legitimating power of metanarratives, referring to the foundational or grand theories of knowledge, for example the overarching philosophies of history such as the Enlightenment, and issues of class conflict and proletarian revolution as discussed by Marx (Fraser and Nicholson, 1990). Postmodernism suggests that such metanarra-

Hospitality, Leisure & Tourism Series

tives no longer justify contemporary social practice, as Lyotard (1984: 88) suggests, 'The postmodern condition ... is one of incredulity towards metanarratives, a refusal to accept there is one particular way of doing things and one way only', and again (Lyotard, 1990: 330), 'The narrative function is losing its functors, its great hero, its great dangers, its great voyages, its great goal'.

Postmodernism suggests that no single form of knowledge is privileged; no theories are ordinate or subordinate to others. To Lyotard it is no longer possible to believe in a metadiscourse capable of capturing the truth of every discourse. A meta-discourse is simply one more discourse among others. As Lyotard argues, in order to understand postmodernism we need to be sensitive to differences, embrace uncertainty and fragmented individuality, steer clear of totalizing systems of thought and avoid the suppression of heterogeneity through consensus. The value of postmodern knowledge is in making us aware of social differences, ambiguity and conflict, and in developing our tolerance to this. Lyotard's work focuses on one of the major themes within postmodernism – the decentring of the subject. Lyotard suggests that in postmodernism there is no centre, no coherence and little overall purpose. Postmodernism is, according to Lyotard, characterized by a lack of certainty and a decline in the belief of a unitary, coherent self. According to Lyotard the shift from metanarratives to local narratives and from general theories to pragmatic strategies suggests that we need to replace the concept of a universal, rational knowing subject, with one of individuals with multiple minds and knowledge which reflect social location and history (Seidman, 1994). In terms of our interest in the application of the concepts of postmodernism to an understanding of hospitality consumption, Lyotard suggests that, in addition to a shift in the way we think about knowledge, we should accept a parallel decentring in the social world, whether we are referring to politics or the self. As suggested earlier, Lyotard (1984) insists that there is no centre, no unifying theme, no coherence and no order, and this loss of certainty applies to the self equally as much as it does to the whole. Postmodernism is, according to Lyotard, primarily characterized by a lack of certainty and a decline in the belief of a unitary, coherent self.

The breakdown of grand narratives leads to a dissolution of difference and distinction, which in turn is seen to lead to fragmentation replacing totality, ambiguity replacing certainty, and irony, parody and pastiche replacing clear-cut distinctions (Crotty, 1998). As Crotty (1998: 194) argues, 'Owing to the extent and degree of the massification that has occurred, society is experiencing a state of implosion in which distinctions are obliterated and a postmodern condition of radical ambiguity, hyperreality, and simulation prevails'. In essence postmodernists reject attempts to impose order on the chaos and fragmentation of reality. Instead, they argue we should accept the limitations of our knowledge, question the value of generalizations and accept the impossibility of universal truths. As Firat and Shultz (1997: 199) argue: 'In an environment where there is increasingly less commitment to any one spectacle or brand, but only a momentary attachment, a continual reproduction, reformulation, repositioning and regeneration of images is necessitated. In a system of fragmented narratives where none has the power beyond the image that it represents, success is only possible through a marketing sensibility that recognizes the linguistic, symbolic and communicative aspects of signifiers to employ and re-signify them in ways that represent spectacular images.' If we relate this to our questioning of the value of the marketing concept within hospitality, we can see that this breakdown in grand narratives has a significant impact, given that, as we have discussed, much of contemporary hospitality marketing is based on the universal truths of the marketing concept. Postmodernism questions the value of such overarching theories, suggesting generalizations of this nature are limited. The marketing concept seeks to impose order on the chaos and fragmentation that characterizes the contemporary hospitality industry. Postmodernism rejects such attempts on two grounds: first, it ignores the limitations of our knowledge about the fragmentation of hospitality consumption and, second, little evidence is available to support such generalizations about hospitality consumption.

The centrality of communication technologies

This is relevant in postmodernism as it provides global access to a culture of mass reproduction and simulacra, that is, copies for which no original exists (Baudrillard, 1983). Baudrillard has been described as the first person to organize a postmodern social theory (Kellner, 1988), and argued that in its widest sense, postmodernism represents an altered mode of perception, one fostered in an era of instant communication, through an ever-widening range of media. As Solomon (1998: 36) suggests, 'Viewing the world as a television camera views it, the postmodern eye reduces the length and breadth of experience to a two-dimensional spectacle, a carnival of arresting images and seductive surface'. Saturation by technology is a key feature of the postmodern age, to the extent that it is argued that models, codes, simulacra, spectacle and the hyperrealism of simulation, have replaced the use-value of commodities. As a result, we live in a world of simulacra where the image or signifier of an event replaces the actual experience and knowledge of its referent or signified (Miller and Real, 1998), the postmodern experience is one of synchronicity; it investigates the past for its images and in using them denies their historical roots. In postmodern society, it is argued, people have become fascinated by signs and, as a result, they exist in a state of hyperreality where signs have become more important than what they stand for. The result, the argument continues, is that today's consumers consume imagery and do not focus on what the images represent or mean. As Miller and Real (1998: 30) argue, 'We live in a world of simulacra where the image or signifier of an event has replaced direct experience and knowledge of its referent or signified'.

Hyperreality refers to a blurring of distinction between the real and the unreal in which the prefix 'hyper' signifies more real than real. When the real, that is, the environment, is no longer a given but is reproduced by a simulated environment, it does not become unreal, but realer than real, to the extent that it becomes what Baudrillard (1993: 23) refers to as 'A hallucinatory resemblance of itself', for Baudrillard, with the advent of hyperreality, simulations come to constitute reality itself. Hyperreality is a situation wherein models replace the real and is exemplified throughout the hospitality industry, Baudrillard himself used the example of Disneyland, arguing that it is more real than the USA itself. When referring to Mickey Mouse, Baudrillard (1993: 139) argued that it is one of the best examples of 'A model of the real without origin or reality . . . this representational imaginary . . . is nuclear and generic and no longer secular and discursive'. Indeed, at his most extreme Baudrillard argues that Disneyland has been created in order to disguise the fact that the rest of America is no longer real, but a simulation. Such a proposition is at least partly supported by Venturi (1995: 67) when he suggests 'Disneyworld is nearer to what people want than what architects have ever given them. Disneyland is the symbolic American utopia'.

Appignanesi and Garratt (1995) describe another sort of Disneyland hyperreal tour of the past as offered at the Holocaust Memorial Museum in Washington, DC – a theme park representing genocide. On admission customers are issued with an identity (ID) card matching their age and gender to the name and photo of a real holocaust victim. As they progress through three floors of exhibitions they enter their ID into a monitor to see how their real-life subject is faring. All this occurs in rooms which run videos of the killing squads in action on huge video screens throughout the complex. Similar arguments are developed by Eco (1987), who suggests that the western world has become obsessed with realism, through the construction of perfect replicas, real copies or authentic representations. As Eco (1987: 6) suggests, 'The imagination increasingly resorts to simulations, which dissolve the boundaries between "true" and "false", "reality" and "reproduction". Brown (1995) highlights this tendency when referring to the heritage centres that have recently sprung up, for example, the Jorvik centre in York. These comprise a mixture of museum and theatre, where everything is meant to suggest authenticity, but being perfect simulacra, nothing is. Hyperreality is exemplified throughout the hospitality industry; indeed, it could be argued that contemporary hospitality and tourism is founded on aspects of hyperreality. Due to its pre-eminence within hospitality consumption, this feature of postmodernism and its application to the consumption of hospitality products and services is further investigated in Chapter 9.

The consumer culture of late capitalism

This refers to the ways in which the puritan ethic of consumption has been replaced by a commercial ethic of conspicuous consumption (Featherstone, 1991). Indeed, for many people it seems that postmodernism and consumption are largely one and the same, with consumption deeply woven into the threads of postmodernism (Featherstone, 1991; Jameson, 1985). As Brown (1993b: 50) argues, 'The urge to consume is a characteristic symptom, perhaps the characteristic symptom, of the postmodern condition'. It is argued (Jameson, 1991) that the characteristics of late capitalism have been a driving force in creating the world of postmodernism, and the period of postmodernism can be referred to as one of a multinational capitalism, spectacle or image society in which culture is no longer endowed with the autonomy it once had. It is argued that in contemporary society consumption has become all-important, thanks to a revolutionization of consciousness as a result of mass communications, media, advertising and publicity. The result is that we now live in an artificial world where even desire itself is manufactured. This view is supported by Bocock (1993: 4) who argues: 'Consumption has been seen as epitomizing the move into post-modernity, for it implies a move away from productive work roles being central to people's lives, to their sense of identity, of who they are. In place of work roles, it is roles in various kinds of family formations, in sexual partnerships of various kinds, in leisure time pursuits, in consumption in general, which have come to be seen as being more and more significant to people. These concerns have become reflected in sociology and social theory as a debate about whether or not western societies are moving towards becoming postmodern.' Moreover this consumption is characterized by disorder and unpredictability, with consumers doing as they please, contradicting the usual reference systems and failing to maintain the categories, which have been developed for them. As a result, consumers are seen as increasingly fickle and unreliable, making it difficult to pinpoint buying behaviour.

In addition to the above, in the postmodern era it is not seen that there is a natural distinction between production and consumption, every act of consumption is also an act of production and vice versa (Firat and Venkatesh, 1995). Within the hospitality industry such a view has been commonplace for many years; indeed, the lack of differentiation between production and consumption is seen as one of the key characteristics of the hospitality industry, as discussed in Chapter 2. This lack of differentiation between production and consumption has resulted in production losing its status at the centre of our culture, to be replaced by that of consumption. In modernity, consumption was viewed at best as a secondary event and trivialized by being determined as a private, feminine activity – part of the household duties. At worst it was portrayed as a moral evil (Mort, 1989). In postmodernism consumption takes on a greater significance, becoming the means by which individuals define their existence and themselves in relation to others. As Bocock (1993: 109) suggests: 'The question "who am I?" is as likely to be answered in terms of consumption patterns as it is in terms of an occupational role by many people in western capitalism.'

Applying postmodernism to the consumption of hospitality products

This chapter so far has dealt with postmodernism through an overview of the ideas of postmodernism's main theorists. While necessary as an aid to understanding, it is clear that such an approach can also be a difficult and inaccessible point of entry into postmodern thought. In order for us to apply postmodernism to the consumption of hospitality products and services, therefore, we need to identify frameworks, which simplify some of the more abstract aspects. In order to accomplish this we will investigate two frameworks, the first developed by Firat and Shultz (1997), the second by Brown (1995; 2000). These frameworks provide insights into the complexities of postmodern discourse, in particular with regard to marketing and consumer behaviour.

Firat and Shultz's postmodern conditions

This ten-aspect framework, outlined in Figure 8.1, with a brief descriptor added, was developed from original work by Firat and Venkatesh (1993) who identified the first six aspects. The framework was adapted by Van Raaij (1993) who added the seventh aspect, and further adapted by Brown (1993a) who completed the current framework by adding three further aspects, relating specifically to perceived tendencies of postmodern

POSTMODERN CONDITIONS	BRIEF DESCRIPTION
Openness/tolerance	Acceptance of difference without prejudice or evaluations of superiority and inferiority
Hyperreality	Constitution of social reality through hype or simulation that is powerfully signified and represented
Perpetual present	Cultural propensity to experience everything in the present 'here and now'
Paradoxical juxtapositions	Cultural propensity to juxtapose anything with anything else including oppositional, contradictory and essentially unrelated elements
Fragmentation	Omnipresence of disjointed and disconnected moments and experiences in life and sense of self – and the growing acceptance of the dynamism which leads to fragmentation
Loss of commitment	Growing cultural unwillingness to commit to any single idea, project or grand design
Decentring the subject	Removal of the human being from the central importance he or she held in modern culture
Reversing consumption	Cultural acknowledgement that value is created not in production but in consumption
Emphasizing form/style	Growing influence of form and style in determining meaning and life
Accepting disorder/chaos	Cultural acknowledgement that rather than order, crises and disequilibria are the common states of existence – and the subsequent acceptance and appreciation of this condition

Figure 8.1 Brief description of postmodern conditions
Source: adapted from Firat and Shultz (1997)

Fragmentation	Refers to the disintegration of social organization, mass-market economics and the unified self. Linked to this are the disconnected images generated by a fragmented media
De-differentiation	Involves the deconstruction of established hierarchies e.g. high/low culture, and the blurring of previously apparently clear-cut constructs e.g. philosophy/ religion or science/religion
Hyperreality	Involving the loss of a sense of authenticity and the tangibilizing of what was previously simulation. Examples would include theme parks, themed restaurants and computer games
Chronology	Comprising concern for the past, or representations of the past, in a retrospective, backward looking perspective
Pastiche	Consisting of the collage of available styles and mixing of existing codes. Examples include those from architecture, art, music and literature
Anti-foundationalism	Referring to the sense within postmodernism of deconstructionism. This is evidenced by an antipathy towards orthodoxy, the establishment and systematic generalizations in such areas as science and socialism. This factor refers to the discrediting, within postmodernism, of a search for universal truth and objective knowledge
Pluralism	Which Brown suggests should not be considered as a category on its own but reflects the sense in which postmodernists conclude that anything is acceptable, there are no rules and nothing is excluded.

Figure 8.2 Postmodern marketing
Source: adapted from Brown (1995)

consumers. This model is used to investigate an aspect of the contemporary hospitality industry, in Case Study 8.1, which considers the postmodern nature of one of the latest cruise ships developed by Royal Caribbean. Brown (1995; 2000) then simplified Firat and Shultz's model by combining a number of elements (see Figure 8.2). The result focuses the discussion on seven key themes he identifies as fragmentation, de-differentiation, hyperreality, chronology, pastiche, anti-foundationalism and pluralism, each of which is defined below.

Fragmentation of markets

As I have previously suggested in Chapter 7, the fragmentation of markets from mass-product led images to smaller individualized segments is a key feature of contemporary marketing. As a result, a massive array of goods and services are on offer to the consumer, within the fast-food market. For example, companies have increasingly moved away from a single product offering to one encompassing choice. Burger chains such as McDonald's now offer chicken and Burger King experimented with allowing customers to customize the product with their 'you want it, you got it promise'. This fragmentation and micro-segmentation has been reinforced by the growth in distribution and media channels. Distribution has grown as locations for hospitality retailing have altered from traditional town centre sites to out-of-town shopping malls, retail parks, ancillary locations (for example, at airports or hospitals) and the growth in shopping from home, both from printed media and television shopping channels (Parker, 1992).

The increased availability of complex technology has increased the possibility of *narrow casting* to replace previously utilized broadcasting strategies. Indeed, such are the possibilities offered by these technologies that it is becoming routine to talk of segments of one, and the mass customization of individual products and services (Schlossberg, 1991). Fragmentation can be seen to underpin much of the current debate on the disintegration of mass markets, including such aspects as micro-marketing, one-on-one marketing and the growth of software-based marketing databases.

De-differentiating markets

The effects of fragmentation, however, are to an extent at odds with a suggested trend towards de-differentiated markets, that is, the blurring of what were previously perceived as clear marketing boundaries. Examples of this blurring include such goods and services as Rock Island Diner restaurants, where service staff are expected to burst into song at programmed intervals, the tendency among hospitality companies to extend product range beyond traditional boundaries, for example, the recent purchase of a substantial shareholding in the Prêt-a-Manger chain announced by McDonald's (a company that recently purchased the Aroma coffee company) and the growth of shopping centres within theme parks, and vice versa. Adair (1992) suggests that the clearest example of de-differentiation is that found within television advertising, and in particular the growth of the advertisement as a television soap, for example, the OXO family, the Gold Blend couple or, most famously, Nicole and Papa's ongoing saga for Renault. These advertisements blur the distinction at the marketing boundary to such an extent that they have in the past been reported as news items, as if they were real events not simply product promotions (Brown, 2000).

De-differentiation, it is argued, can be evidenced in two areas of contemporary hospitality: first, the growth in strategic alliances, joint venture relationships and vertical marketing systems, and second, in the development of hospitality activities in cultural forums, for example, museums, places of religion and art galleries. A recent trend among fund-seeking museums and galleries, for example, has been the hiring out of these cultural bastions for corporate and social events. This clash of culture and Mammon is representative of postmodernism. A further example would be the recent advertisement for the Victoria and Albert museum in London, which promoted it as an excellent café, with a nice museum attached.

Hyperreality

Hyperreality refers to the movement away from marketing as providing product information to one in which consumer desires, wants and needs are routinely manipulated. As a result, meanings have become detached from products, to be replaced by alternative signifiers. The most obvious of these is sex, which has been used to signify a wide range of goods and services including chocolate (Cadbury's Flake), pensions (Scottish Widows), throat drops (Halls) and ice-cream (Haagen Dazs) (Harvey, 1989). It is also argued that hyperreality is evident in the development of themed food courts, such as those at Sheffield's Meadowhall (based on a Mediterranean town square) and Newcastle's Metro Centre (based on a Mediterranean village). Finally, hyperreality can be argued to be evident in a wide range of new product developments which imitate, while parodying, their origins, including decaffeinated coffee, butterless butter and alcohol-free alcohol (Brown, 1995).

Brown argues that hyperreality subsumes most areas of branding or product image, including as it does price, perception, atmospherics, etc. As Brown (1995: 140) suggests, however, some of the most extreme examples of hyperreality in contemporary hospitality are seen in the 'Scripts, schemata and dramaturgical roles played by participants in the service encounter'. Nowhere, is this more evident than in the actor-as-waiter encounters one receives in heavily themed restaurants. If we consider the role of bar staff in restaurants such as Whitbread's TGI Friday chain of themed restaurants, it is difficult to avoid the conclusion that the staff are based on the character Tom Cruise plays in the film *Cocktail*.

Chronology

Whilst hyperreality can be argued to have been responsible for a growth in artificiality, a consequent rise has been noted in the desire for 'authenticity' and a concern with chronology. As a result there has been a growth in demand for products which are perceived as being authentic, for example, real ale, real bread (with n'owt taken out), free range eggs and traditional holidays. The restaurant industry has seen demand for authentic foods cooked on traditional equipment, for example, Indian tandoori ovens, Italian pizza ovens and Chinese wok cookery. The development of the Indian meal Balti provides an interesting example: customers readily consume the product (which is cooked in a large wok-like bowl) in the belief that it is a traditional form of curry, despite it having been developed as a form of cooking by the families of migrant Indians in Birmingham in the mid-1980s. Within the public house retail sector the growth of the tavern-style pub can also be seen as an attempt to tap into the chronology aspect of postmodernism.

Branding can clearly be seen to be linked to this demand for authenticity as it provides security to consumers. As a result, producers in turn make extensive reference to their past in order to suggest stability. This has enabled a number of producers to market a range of goods that are complementary to their original brands and use the strength of the original brand to support the new product launch, including Persil washing-up liquid, the wide range of luxury confectionery based ice-creams, and the development of Guinness lager and bitter which has arisen out of the strength of the original Guinness stout brand. Virgin is a classic example of a company using its brand name in this way, with the Virgin brand now extending across numerous industries, not least hospitality, leisure and tourism. From its original record empire Virgin now encompasses such diverse activities as airlines, hotels, health clubs, cosmetics, resorts and holidays, publishing, the rail network, ballooning, Internet service provider, wine sales, etc.

Pastiche

It is argued that it is pastiche, more than any other factor, that is the defining feature of postmodernism (Brown, 1995), including as it does such aspects as irony, parody, imitation and quotation. Examples of marketing promotions utilizing these characteristics are widespread, including those for lager (Carling Black Label parodying Levi jeans), cigars (Hamlet parodying Andrex toilet rolls), Hovis's self-referential adverts for brown bread and Terry's chocolate orange (imitating the film *Raiders of the Lost Ark*). A final example of pastiche that sums up its influence in postmodern consumption is that of the promotion of Levi jeans during the late 1980s and early 1990s. As a result of linking retro music to a promotion for jeans, not only did the jeans product increase sales but the promotion was also responsible for a string of number one hits and a chart-topping album of the re-released music. In the licensed retail industry such adverts as those for Boddingtons, which ape Chanel, and Holstein Pils which parodies those for 'traditional' Irish ales such as Caffrey's are among the best known.

Retro-marketing, a feature of pastiche, is well founded in hospitality, J. Lyons coffee bars, for example, which disappeared in the late 1950s, are seeking to take advantage of the current trends in the coffee bar market by making a comeback, linking their long tradition in this market with the latest advances in coffee technology (Killgren, 1999). In a similar way pastiche, through adopting a seemingly quasi-retro (what Brown, 1999, refers to as a repro-retro) stance, allows the new to become the old. The case of Caffrey's ale (discussed in detail by Brown) provides a classic example of what we are referring to here. Launched in 1994 Caffrey's combines the features of lager (light, cool, refreshing) with traditional ales (mild, creamy, settlement). At its launch it was provided with an instant Irish heritage, with adverts featuring forgotten images of Ireland, for example, urchins playing in inner city streets, beautiful Irish maidens frolicking in the fields and a run-away horse galloping through the town centre. The truth is less whimsical, with the beer being a product of cutting-edge technology from a brewing plant in industrial West Belfast. However, the success of Caffrey's has led to numerous imitators, with Kilkenny being the most successful, all of which play on a neo-Celtic myth.

Anti-foundationalism

Examples of anti-foundationalism are often based on promotions perceived as being anarchist or subversive. For example, Benetton clothes have a history of producing shock promotional material including a poster of clothes from a dead soldier (complete with blood and bullet holes). Other examples would include the 'you've been Tangoed' advertisements for soft drinks, and the pirate broadcasting advertisements used by Sega computer games that seek to suggest that they are breaking into the genuine broadcast.

It could be argued that much of the original demand for restaurants such as Hard Rock Café were due to their links to rock bands perceived, as they were by authority, to be in some ways subversive. Similar claims could be made for Bass's It's a Scream chain of student pubs.

Pluralism

As we have previously suggested pluralism refers to the combination of many of the characteristics of postmodernism identified above, referring to the interweaving of these aspects that is evident in much of contemporary hospitality activity. Within the hospitality industry Centre Parcs, an example of a combined holiday camp, health club and theme park, exemplifies pluralism in the postmodern industry, combining as it does hyperreality and de-differentiation. Similarly the Disney corporation's Main Street USA is central to all four of its theme parks worldwide and Main Street USA can be seen to be a combination of an integral theme unit that unifies a diverse merchandising system. This in turn is formed from a retro situation – that of a street Walt Disney knew as a child growing up in Marceline, Missouri. Given such a scenario, it is not surprising that many commentators suggest that Disney and similar theme parks are the epitome of postmodernism (Kowinsky, 1985).

Postmodern hospitality: some examples

In order to explore in more detail a number of the aspects identified above we have incorporated two case studies, one of which investigates the postmodern implications which can be derived from the recent growth in the cruise ship market using the framework supplied by Firat and Shultz (1997). The second investigates the UK contemporary retail licensed house market, using Brown's (1995) model. Both of these case studies seek to identify the key issues that face operators in such markets in a postmodern marketplace.

Case Study 8.1 is not a definitive guide to postmodern consumption of cruises. These examples are only representative of the many features of postmodernism that can be drawn from the example used; many more are possible in this extensive industry.

Case study 8.1

Aspects of postmodernism and their significance to Royal Caribbean's latest cruise ship, *Voyager of the Seas*

To understand the implications of postmodernism on consumers of hospitality services we have chosen the example of the cruise line market. The nature of this rapidly developing, highly competitive and turbulent market is well documented (Dale and Robinson, 2001; Formica and Olsen, 1998; McAuley, 1998). In addition the literature has cited changes in consumer behaviour and

Hospitality, Leisure & Tourism Series

the blurring of traditional distinctions between the providers of such services and other mainstream hospitality company operators.

Background to the contemporary cruise market

The cruise industry worldwide is carrying more passengers than at any previous time. In 1970 only 1.5 million passengers were carried. By 1995 this had risen to 5 million and by 2000 10 million people took a cruise, and this figure is expected to rise to 22 million by 2010 (Dickinson and Vladimir, 1997). The USA market rose by more than 17 per cent in the year 1999 to 2000, to reach a volume that was double that of 1990. The UK, which is the second largest market behind the USA, saw increases in volumes of 400 per cent during the same period, spurred on by companies such as Thompson, Airtours and First Choice (Scull, 2001). The largest company, in fleet terms, is Carnival Corporation which operates forty-five ships through six brands, ranging from the largest ships, the Carnival brand, through to their motor-sailing ships, the Windstar brand. At the other end of the market, in shipping terms, is Disney which operates just two ships, *Magic* and *Wonder*; however, they do also have the theme park at the outboard stage and their own island stages, Port Orleans and Caribbean Beach. While at the current time the market is perhaps not as buoyant as it was previously, in total forty-four new ocean-going ships are on order to be delivered before 2004, although a number of these are due to replace old inefficient ships, many of which date back to the 1960s. The cruise market is seen as having huge unfulfilled potential – currently less than 13 per cent of Americans have taken a cruise holiday, and other markets such as Europe and Asia are considered underdeveloped.

Voyager of the Seas is Royal Caribbean's latest cruise ship and currently, albeit briefly, the worlds largest at 142 000 tonnes. It has a capacity of almost 4000 passengers and if stood on its end would be taller than the Eiffel Tower. It has expensively decorated rooms (many with proper baths), most of which have sea views and more than half of which have balconies. *Voyager of the Seas* has a shopping area, the Royal Promenade, which is longer than a football field, four decks deep and with two eleven-storey high atriums at either end.

We use Firat and Shultz's (1997) framework to identify the postmodern significance of ships such as *Voyager of the Seas*:

1 *Openness/tolerance*: an acceptance of different styles, ways of being and living and their impact on accommodation provision; the breakdown of traditional customer assumptions; an acceptance of the pre-eminence of the customer as the focus for all operational activities, which incorporates the removal of barriers to entry for all 'classes' of passengers. This market is exemplified by the breakdown of traditional social order, in that traditionally a series of 'social classes' would have been evident, ranging from first class (those who would be invited to the white tie event that is the Captain's Ball) through to stowage. Today on *Voyager of the Seas* everyone gets to go to the ball.

2 *Hyperreality*: the superseding of traditional functions of information provision by manipulation of customer desires, tastes and motivations; the routine development of fantasy worlds, which exploit by embellishment and exaggeration historical, media, etc. resonance's of cruise ships. *Voyager of the Seas* is a classic example of simulacrity and hyperreality, the loss of authenticity and the becoming real of what was previously a simulation, artefacts from a bygone age become part of the décor, with designers recycling them as sculpture and other art. Thematic elements, including photographs, ship's compasses and navigational equipment are pinned to the wall. *Voyager of the Seas* has a theatre called La Scala, it also has an art collection valued at some £7.5 million, and a shopping mall, the Royal Promenade, modelled on Burlington Arcade.

3 *Perpetual present*: the propensity to experience the past and the future in the present, allusions to history, authenticity and tradition, all in an environment which is superior to a romanticized original. *Voyager of the Seas'* employees dress in uniforms that evoke memories, real or imagined, of the 1920s. The ships plunder the past for images and, in using them, deny their history, making them a perpetual present. *Voyager of the Seas* has a main restaurant, incorporating décor from ships of a bygone age of teak and brass; an Italian restaurant, Portofino's, decorated to evoke images of an earlier more glamorous age; and a 1950s roadside diner, complete with vintage sports cars and waitresses performing choreographed routines of 1980s and 1990s music (YMCA, Respect, etc.)

4 *Paradoxical*: the propensity to juxtapose oppositional, contradictory and essentially unrelated items, for example, juxtaposing fully equipped health clubs and the availability of exercise classes with the provision of numerous eat-as-much-as-you-like meal events. Similarly, cruse ship operators juxtapose mini-golf and driving ranges, which should be associated with wide-open green spaces, with the stern of ships and their nautical surroundings. *Voyager of the Seas* has both a 'golf course' complete with sand bunkerettes, and a simulator that allows you to play courses from around the world. Customers are able to juxtapose visiting developing countries, with their need for export currencies, but purchasing representative 'local' products on board, products which may have been made anywhere in the world where cheap labour can be found – wherein the profits return to the ship's western owners.

5 *Fragmentation*: demonstrated by the fragmentation of markets into increasingly smaller and smaller segments, each with its own range of carefully positioned products. The multiplication of distribution channels and media sources, leading arguably (though not truthfully if my own junk mail is any example) to an ability to deliver highly focused messages to specific groups of people. Also included here are features of hyper-targeting, mass customization and micro-marketing. *Voyager of the Seas* divides its young customers, those between the ages of three and seventeen, into four segments, each with its own activities and play areas. In addition, Royal Caribbean has a range of promotional material for *Voyager of the Seas*,

targeted at different markets. The product is the same; it is just the message that is different.

6 *Loss of commitment*: a recognition that customers are unwilling to commit to single ideas, projects or grand designs, linked with a recognition that customers need to be able to identify a reason to be loyal, thus emphasizing the importance of the role of value to customers. Royal Caribbean is only one of six or seven such companies that operate more than ten ships each. In total the largest six companies operate around 112 ships. Cruise ships represent a new mode of perception fostered by an age of instant communication (Solomon, 1998), that is, television, cinema and radio. Viewing the world as a television camera views it, cruising reduces experience to a series of ten-second views. As a result, cruising becomes a carnival of arresting images and spectacles, the cruising experience best being described as a *perpetual montage*.

7 *Decentring subjects*: the blurring of previously clear-cut boundaries, for example class/status, high/low culture, advertising/information. This breakdown in order is further evidenced by the blurring of distinctions between leisure and consumption, wherein scrambled merchandising means that, on *Voyager of the Seas*, casinos, gift shops and fashion stores all occupy the same space. These ships are highly regulated, private commercial spaces that are expressly designed to make money. However, this purpose is somewhat disguised in order to avoid offending customers. A number of premium cabins on *Voyager of the Seas* look inwards to the Royal Promenade, removing any pretence that the experience is about 'seeing the world'. Decentring is also evidenced by the fact that, while a typical *Voyager* cruise incorporates three 'explorations' (off-boat excursions), more than half of the customers never leave the ship. Indeed, *Voyager of the Seas* is so big that most Caribbean islands, the Panama Canal and most of the Mediterranean ports are off limits; for passengers on the *Voyager* 'the ship's the thing'.

8 *Production/consumption*: the rapid growth of the cruise ship holiday market linked to the identification of markets and cultures, which are consumption driven, leading to a recognition of the importance of consumption to contemporary western society. The *Voyager of the Seas*, which was only launched at the end of 2000, has already been joined by two equal size siblings, and both Cunard and P & O have similar or even larger boats in the water or on the drawing board. Cunard, for example are currently awaiting delivery of the *Queen Mary 2* (the original *Queen Mary* has spent the last thirty years as a hotel, convention centre and visitor attraction at Long Beach, California) which will be the biggest ship ever built, more than 150 000 tons, twice the size of the QE2.

9 *Emphasizing form/style*: the increasing influence of form and style rather than content in determining satisfaction, as demonstrated by a focus on quantity over quality. In this market the emphasis is on the largest ships, the number of eating opportunities, the size of the restaurants, shops and bars. *Voyager of the Seas* has the only rock-climbing wall at sea, some 200 feet above the

water. In addition, while ice played an important part in the history of the *Titanic*, only *Voyager* has an ice rink on board, large enough, of course, to host full-size ice shows. Issues in respect of corporate image and perceived style also become important, as does the perception of service quality versus real quality. Royal Caribbean has leased a 260-acre promontory, annexed it from the rest of Haiti, and turned it into a luxury day at the beach. They are very proud of the vast sums of money they have spent restoring Labadee (they have renamed their part of Haiti in order to ease the worries of the predominantly US guests, who have bad perceptions of Haiti) to the same atmosphere Columbus experienced centuries ago.

10 *Disorder/chaos*: the importance of developing organizational structures which are able to cope effectively with states of crisis and disequilibria. For example, Royal Caribbean has to board almost 4000 passengers when *Voyager of the Seas* leaves Miami. It does this in part by placing boarding desks within most of the local hotels used by guests the night before departure. Developing an adaptable, flexible workforce and organization is also important; so multiskilling is commonplace on cruise ships such as *Voyager*.

Again, Case Study 8.2 demonstrates only a limited number of examples of postmodern consumption that can be found in the contemporary public house industry. Others that could valuably be discussed would be the growth of public houses engineered to be attractive to female customers (because, cynically, the public house companies know that where females go the males will follow), the growth of other national stereotyped public houses such as Springbok (South African) and Walkabout (Australian), (as a Welshman I often wonder what a Welsh themed public house would incorporate), the growth of children's public houses (where children and their parents are given separate rooms to eat in, thus avoiding them upsetting the drinkers), in-pub brew houses and many more.

Case study 8.2

Postmodernism and hyperreal pubs

It can be argued that many of the features that distinguish postmodernism are applicable to the contemporary public house environment, this case study considers the contemporary retail public house market utilizing the framework proposed by Brown (1995).

Changes to the nature, scope and structure of the contemporary pub industry are well documented and are increasingly being investigated (Clarke et al., 2000; Knowles and Howley, 2000; Williams, 2000). It is clear that as a result of such factors as government intervention, changes in society, technological developments and the growth of branding, managed development of the industry has replaced the traditional, organic development of public houses. Some of the repercussions of this change can be seen when we investigate the postmodern public house industry.

1 *Fragmentation*: can be evidenced in the growth of segmentation and the range of venues that are on offer to consumers. As a result of changes in their marketplace, public house retail companies invested heavily in the development of categorization schemes, in order to segment their estates. Typically estates are segmented on the basis of differentiation by situation, dominant age of customers, perceived social class of customers and dominant drinking habits. These categories are then utilized by managers to operationalize the outlets. For example, unit managers and other staff are selected using categorization as a criteria. However, this operationalization can extend further, with categorization determining the level of investment in pubs, etc. Fragmentation can also be seen in the proliferation of products available in public houses, along with the increasing number of public house types and brands, for example, those bars dedicated to selling single product ranges, such as the 'Revolution' vodka bar chain. This change is mirrored by the multiplication of distribution channels as the number of locational options has exploded; traditional high street locations have been supplemented by out-of-town centres, retail parks, airports, railway stations, etc.

2 *De-differentiation*: the effects of fragmentation are, to an extent, at odds with a suggested trend towards de-differentiated markets, that is, the blurring of previously clear marketing boundaries. De-differentiation can be evidenced in a number of ways in public houses, for example, in the sale of associated merchandise, such as T-shirts and sweat shirts, branded to the outlet. This merchandising can be a lucrative business in its own right; one only has to consider the number of 'Firkin' T-shirts on display on our streets to realize their potential sales. De-differentiation can also be seen in the growth of the staff as entertainer, with many bar staff required to perform set dance or acting schemata as an integral part of their employment. TGI Friday will, for a fee, offer companies a 'bar flair' course to train staff in the art of swinging bottles and drinks around, in order to better entertain the customer. A further example of de-differentiation in the public house market is the collapse in the boundary between art and everyday life, between high and mass culture. Several major companies have 'museums' dedicated to their history and development. For example in Leeds, Tetley operate a 'museum', which incorporates demonstrations of brewing technology through the ages, a tour of its stables, high-tech audiovisuals demonstrating Tetley's history and the opportunity to 'sample' the product in their 'Victoriana' public house. As Berger (1998: 95) argues: 'The notion that original works of art are what museums should show no longer has much currency in postmodern societies. We don't think originality matters that much anymore.' De-differentiation is also

seen in the wider public house retail environment, as evidenced by the growth in strategic alliances, joint venture relationships and vertical marketing systems (Parker, 1992).

3 *Chronology*: this can be noted in the desire for authenticity and a growth in demand for traditional products, as a result of which we have seen the development of the Taverns by public house groups, with their interiors decked out in 'old world kitsch'. This includes faux gas lamps, faux libraries, leatherette seating, etc., each public confronting the customer with an image of some old-style imagined public house of the past. They also offer a promise of traditional public house food, much of which is of course mass produced off site in food factories. Branding can also be seen to be linked to this demand for authenticity, as it provides security to consumers. As a result of such links, producers make extensive reference to their past in order to suggest stability. This has enabled a number of producers to market a range of goods and services that are complementary to their original brands, using the strength of the original brands to support the product launch. As a result, we have seen the advent of such items as Guinness lager that has arisen out of the strength of the original Guinness stout brand.

4 *Pastiche*: pastiche is available in a number of ways in the contemporary public house industry, ranging from the growth in themed evenings, for example karaoke and quizzes, through to the latest concepts from the retail companies such as Bass Taverns' 'Bacchus' theme, consisting as it does of a pastiche evoking a number of eras ranging from Jacobean through ancient Greek to Roman, Egyptian, etc. The City Limits outlets operated by Scottish & Newcastle are typical examples of the pastiche available within the public house industry. Early in 2000 Scottish & Newcastle announced their plan to spend £150 million developing the City Limits chain nationally. These are food-led venues that typically incorporate bowling alleys, restaurants, sports bars and coffee bars, with each site costing upwards of £6 million to open. In addition to the above, pastiche, which incorporates irony, parody, imitation and quotation, can be seen in advertisements for such drinks as Boddingtons Bitter, which apes Chanel, and Holstein Pils that parodies those for traditional 'Irish' ales such as Caffrey's.

5 *Anti-foundationalism*: in the public house sector this has been product led rather than environment led. Anti-foundationalism is seen to include such aspects as the growth of innovative and slightly 'risky' products such as alcopops and sachet spirits, along with developments such as drinking out of bottles. Anti-foundationalism is based on promotions perceived as being anarchistic or subversive, such as the advertisements for Lemonhead alcopop that incorporated a man in a dress. The subversion of a traditional soft drink, such as lemonade, is a clear example of anti-foundationalism. It can also be argued that the growth in premium brands such as Sol and Budweiser is linked to the way in which they are consumed straight from the bottle, never from a glass. The recent advertisements for Guinness can also be see to fit into this subversive category; they are certainly a long way away from the more traditional toucan adverts. Anti-foundationalism can also be

seen in public house environments, in examples such as Bass Taverns' 'It's a Scream' outlets. These public houses, themselves retro-modelled on an early 1980s 'fun pub' concept introduced by Whitbread Inns, offer customers a safe outlet for mildly subversive activities. They stress subversion as part of their culture and pursue activities, which promote this, such as showing cartoons all day and through the types of games and entertainment, which are offered.

6 *Pluralism and hyperreality*: these arguably best illustrate postmodernism in the contemporary public house sector. Hyperreality refers to the loss of authenticity, a tangibilizing of simulation wherein reality and simulation become interlinked. Hyperreality incorporates the movement away from marketing as providing product information, to one in which consumer desires, wants and needs are routinely manipulated. As a result of hyperreality, meanings have become detached from products to be replaced by alternative signifiers. Hyperreality has become routine in the public house retail industry, culminating in the development of such concepts as the 'Irish' bar. Irish bars such as Bass Taverns' 'O'Neil's' concept and Allied's 'Scruffy Murphy's' allude to an Ireland that does not exist, except in the marketer's imagination. An Ireland where horses run free in high streets, where every pub hosts a ceilidh every night, where everyone drinks Irish stout and eats champ. This is an Ireland where public houses are decorated with the labourer's tools of trade, and where customers sit around on wooden stools using upturned beer casks as tables. An Ireland where your beer comes with a shamrock drawn carefully into it, in other words a pub that introduces every stereotype of Irish nationalism imaginable. In order to make money, however, this reversion to tradition is supported by the latest technology including, sophisticated stock and financial control systems, technologically advanced entertainment systems and a full range of 'Irish' ales, beers and lagers (often brewed under licence in the UK). The traditional Irish food is mass produced, portion controlled and frozen or chilled off site at a large food processing plant, before being reheated on site. Such is the hyperreal pub in a postmodern market.

Criticisms of the postmodern perspective

It will become clear from what is written above and in the following chapters, that I am an advocate of the belief that contemporary consumers live in a society, which is rapidly changing from a modernist to a postmodernist perspective, within which they experience doubt, ambiguity and uncertainty. The modernist view of society, with its consumer-related assumptions of meaning, cohesion and transparency, is to me invalidated by what I see within the contemporary hospitality industry. However, there are those who are less convinced of the value of postmodernism in interpreting contemporary hospitality, for example, Peter and Olson (1993) and Hunt (1993). Indeed, it is very easy to be cynical about the value of postmodernism and many authors are available to aid such cynicism, including Connor (1989: 19) who defined it as, 'The Toyota of thought, produced and assembled in several different places and then sold everywhere', and Scruton (1994: 504) who refers to it as, 'The philosophy of inverted commas'. The lack of definition, within postmodernism, is cited as an obstacle to its application by Fielding (1992: 21) who states, it is 'Something that gets everywhere but no one can quite explain what it is'.

A more emphatic criticism is offered by both Beaumont (1993: 43), 'Never having to say sorry for not having an original idea in your head', and Thorne (1993: 199), 'A chaos of competing styles and cross-references transmitted by a free-market consumerist system that creates its own reality for its own ends'. While Butler and Brown (1994: 153) call into question the very concept of a postmodern society, suggesting, 'The question of postmodernism is surely a question, for is there, after all, something called postmodernism?', an argument supported by Patterson (1998: 68) who states: 'Postmodernism is less a unified body of knowledge and more a compilation of several themes with different starting points.'

Despite these criticisms, however, it seems clear that an appreciation of the concept of postmodernism offers a new perspective to our understanding of hospitality consumer behaviour. As Thomas (1997: 56) suggests, after questioning why a renowned professor of marketing, such as himself, has been caught espousing postmodern thoughts, 'if we fail to take the issue (postmodernism) seriously, then it may be difficult to differentiate our world from fable and fairy-tale'.

Summarizing postmodernism as it relates to hospitality

I have sought within this chapter to introduce some key aspects of postmodernism and the ways in which they can be seen to relate to a key feature of contemporary society, the role of consumption and, in particular, hospitality consumption. While it is accepted that there are problems with investigating postmodernism and its application to the study of hospitality consumption, nevertheless, it encompasses a broad range of developments within contemporary hospitality, many of which have been highlighted here.

As Firat and Shultz (1997: 204) suggest: 'We submit that postmodernism, so influential in other disciplines, has the potential to reframe our thinking about social trends and business practices in an increasingly global but fragmented marketplace, and thus to give to marketing managers insights that in turn can abet strategic decision making. Finally we suggest that a better understanding of the underlying macro social forces and micro human behaviour associated with postmodernism can ultimately be leveraged by marketers to obtain competitive advantages in an increasingly dynamic, unpredictable and unstable marketplace.' While many of the characteristics of postmodernism are clearly applicable to the contemporary hospitality industry it is argued that it is features of hyperreality and simulacrity that best illustrate postmodernism. Hyperreality, as we have previously discussed, refers to the loss of authenticity, a tangibilizing of simulation wherein reality and simulation become interlinked, with simulacrity referring to copies for which no original exists, and this feature of postmodernism is so prevalent in hospitality consumption that the whole of Chapter 9 is devoted to exploring it in more detail.

Hospitality implications of the revolution in consumption: marketing simulacrity and hyperreality

Key themes

- This chapter explores a number of the implications of the transformation from modern to postmodern societies for hospitality organizations and consumers.

- The chapter argues that postmodern consumers demand different types of hospitality products and use them in a variety of ways, thus presenting hospitality companies with new opportunities which can only be realized if marketers understand who these consumers are and how they think, feel and behave.

- Postmodern consumers change their self-concept over very short periods of time, and consequently it is essential that hospitality companies of the future recognize this characteristic of postmodern consumers and develop products that address their needs.

- One result of a move to postmodern consumption within hospitality is the increasing tendency among consumers to replace an extant reality with one that is simulated, or indeed one that is hyperreal.

- The new settings for hospitality consumption are important in themselves, in terms of what they say about contemporary hospitality consumers. However, they are also important because of the central role they play in sustaining the contemporary phenomena of hyperconsumption

The transformation to a postmodern hospitality industry

This chapter examines some of the ways in which deep societal and economic changes are transforming contemporary hospitality consumers, and will continue to do so in the future. It explores a number of the implications of the transformation from modern to postmodern societies for hospitality organizations and consumers, based on the premise that if the societies of developed countries are fundamentally changing then it follows that hospitality organizations, embedded as they are in social processes, will also have to be different, particularly in terms of the ways in which they understand hospitality consumer behaviour. The importance of this change is so significant because it represents a radical new way of viewing consumption, including that of hospitality products, as Baudrillard (1998: ix) states: 'it has to be made clear from the outset that consumption is an active form of relationship (not only to objects, but also to society and to the world), a mode of systematic activity and global response which founds our entire cultural system'.

As Burke (2000: 274) argues, 'as manufacturing societies, driven by production technologies, give way to service societies, driven by knowledge and information technologies, capitalism is being transformed into an economy of icons. New types of hospitality consumers are beginning to emerge'. Postmodern consumers demand different types of hospitality products and use them in a variety of ways, thus presenting hospitality companies with new opportunities, which can only be realized if marketers understand whom these consumers are and how they think, feel and behave. As we have seen in earlier chapters it is argued that traditional modernist consumers consume brands, goods and services in order to aid them in finding and reinforcing a unitary or essential self-concept, while postmodern consumers mix and match eclectic images in a variety of ways. Postmodern consumers change their self-concept over very short periods of time and, consequently, it is essential that hospitality companies of the future recognize this characteristic of post-modern consumers and develop products that address their needs.

If we can recap the previous chapter, we stated that marketing, being modernist in nature, perceives the consumer as an individual who is centred, self-conscious and committed to a reasoned and reasonable goal or end (Firat and Shultz, 1997). As such as Firat and Shultz (1997: 187) argue, 'modern marketing thought tends to hold that a unity of self or self-concept, a sense of one's identity and character, can and does exist'. In such a perspective the consumer, complete with this united concept of self, seeks satisfaction of identified needs for this self, suggesting a unity of purpose, orientation and behaviour. As a result we are able to develop segmentation models that describe their likely behaviour, and use them as marketing tools to communicate with them and similar consumers.

Postmodernism rejects the notions that have shaped such modern marketing thought, arguing that the marketing concept is simply one narrative among many and, therefore, ought to have no more a favoured status than any other. To post-modernists, the modernist narratives, which are suggestive of a unique quality and superiority, have to be challenged. As a result, postmodernism rejects the modernist view of the consumer as a knowing subject, and replaces it with a view of the consumer as someone who 'actively communicates the social reality she or he prefers to live rather than passively inheriting one constructed without his/her participation' (Firat and Shultz,1997: 188). If we accept such a view, hospitality organizations have to be tolerant of the non-traditional demands communicated by contemporary consumers.

The simulated reality of postmodern hospitality

The themed environments of everyday hospitality

One result of a move to postmodern consumption within hospitality is the increasing tendency among consumers to replace an extant reality with one that is simulated, or indeed one that is hyperreal. Ritzer (1999: x) suggests that contemporary society has undergone radical change and argues, 'a revolutionary change has occurred in the places in which we consume goods and services, and it has had a profound effect not only on the nature of consumption but also on social life'. He goes on to list activities today's consumers can undertake, that they could not do a couple of decades ago, many of which are directly or indirectly connected to aspects of the hospitality industry, and incorporate elements of simulacrity. Thus Ritzer discusses shopping malls that incorporate themed amusement parks, casinos that incorporate themed hotels, cruise ships that dock at 'artificial' islands, themed restaurants and theme parks. All of these settings for the consumption of hospitality products incorporate simulated environments where contemporary consumers can play at experiencing the hyperreal. As Ritzer (1999: 146) states: 'if I had to choose only one term to catch the essence of the new means of consumption . . . it would be simulations'. Such simulation is not in itself a new phenomenon, it has been used extensively throughout the history of the hospitality industry, however, there are two characteristics of the current scene that are new and significant. The first is the extent to which simulation has become an all-embracing feature of contemporary hospitality consumption. As Debord (1994: 16) argues, 'the spectacle is the chief product of present-day society . . . the world the spectacle holds up to view is the world of commodity ruling all lived experience'. The second characteristic of the contemporary scene is that these simulations are no longer an end in themselves; they are designed for the sole purpose of encouraging mass consumption.

The extensive use of simulations in the consumption of hospitality goods and services contributes to the erosion of distinction between 'reality' and 'imagination', to the extent that Baudrillard (1983: 324) argues that we exist in 'an age of simulation' where the 'real' and 'true' have disappeared under a sea of simulacrity. This is supported by Huxtable (1997: 64) who argues the 'unreal has become the reality . . . the real now imitates the imitation', and suggests that consumers appear to prefer simulated rainforests, volcanoes and rocks to the real thing, before concluding that 'real architecture has little place in the unreal America'. However, it is not simply the settings in which hospitality interactions take place that are increasingly simulated, many of the interactions themselves are similarly unreal. The staff that deal with the customers at venues such as Walt Disney World, McDonald's, Royal Caribbean and TGI Friday's, whether wearing a costume or not, are all playing roles and simulating interactions. These host companies and many, many more, have well-developed guidelines which dictate how employees should look, sound, behave, etc. Employees in such hospitality scenarios are not expected to be creative or act as individuals. As such the series of interactions that take place between staff and consumers in many contemporary hospitality settings are as simulated as the settings themselves. As Ritzer (1999: 116) states: 'employees follow scripts, and customers counter with recipe responses, that is those responses they have developed over time to deal with such scripted behaviour'. In many contemporary hospitality settings simulated interactions have become so routine that they have entered mainstream dialogue. For example, it is common when stereotyping a 'brain-dead' youth to cite the McDonald's mantra 'do you want fries with that', to the extent that any understanding of a distinction between the simulated and the reality is lost.

There are a number of reasons why hospitality has so quickly and completely taken on board simulation as a means of consumption, and the most important of these are likely to be:

1 *Control.* It is far easier to control simulated environments than it is real ones. For example Ocean World, the pinnacle of the 6-mile long Seagaia (Ocean and Land) resort complex which is located on Kyushu, the southernmost of Japan's main islands, is a tropical island with beaches, waterfalls, caves and trees. However, in this simulated environment the air is a constant 30 °C, and the water 28 °C, it never rains, there is a perfect cloudless sunset every night and the surfers and boarders are guaranteed exactly 2.5 metre waves every time. Ocean World, the world's largest indoor water park is capable of hosting 10 000 people at any time, it has a retractable roof and incorporates a number of activities to keep its visitors amused, such as Polynesian shows and its famous Ocean Dome illusion, which tells the story of the ocean and its mystery (for more information see www.seagaia.com). A similar picture is told by the Akita Sky Dome, a 12 000 square metre indoor sports dome, which has been built in Akita, on the north-west coast of Honshu, Japan's largest island. The complex which incorporates ice rinks, downhill and cross-country skiing, among many other activities, was built because residents of the city of Akita experienced such severe winters and snowfalls that the authorities felt they needed an environment which could overcome such local conditions. A key feature of the Akita Sky Dome is that it is fully glazed, that is, roof and walls, making it difficult to identify where the sky dome ends and reality starts (www.akita.com).

2 *Repair.* It is far easier to repair and update simulations than it is 'reality', at its most extreme. For example, there are plans to develop faux stones in a visitor centre at Stonehenge, which when combined with a multimedia display, will mean that visitors do not have to go up to the site to see the actual stones

themselves, thus avoiding damage to them. In a similar way, visitors are not generally permitted to see the original prehistoric cave paintings in the caves at Lescaux, due to possible damage to the caves and paintings, so simulations have been painted in simulated caves close to the site. The Jorvik centre in York is another example, built close to the site of an exposed Viking settlement, when opened it contained state of the art multimedia displays including animatronics and smell-around (visitors on the ride through the display were exposed to the simulated smells of a Viking settlement). A number of years later the displays are no longer state of the art; however, as they are only simulations they are being repaired and updated with the latest in media display systems.

3 *Hyperreality.* A third reason why there has been a move to replace reality with simulation in the hospitality industry is that it is possible to make the simulations more real than the original, to make them hyperreal. If we take the example of the Luxor casino and hotel in Las Vegas (www.luxor.com) which seeks to simulate the world of ancient Egypt, we find a thirty-storey pyramid, adorned with such artefacts as obelisks, a sphinx (which at ten-storeys high is taller than the original) and Cleopatra's Needle. Unlike the real pyramids, however, inside the Luxor is a modern casino hotel which cost more than US$650 million to develop. Here the bedrooms have whole walls of sloping glass, lifts travel at 40 degrees to the vertical, a shopping complex themed around a Cairo bazaar is included along with a treasure chamber and a scarab shop and finally a 315 000-watt beam of light is emitted from the point of a huge beacon. In the Luxor bazaar it is possible to purchase genuine Egyptian artefacts, alongside simulations of the same artefacts, many of which are more popular because to the consumers they look more 'genuine'.

The world pavilion in Walt Disney World's Epcot centre is another such example, where else can visitors sample the delights of Great Britain, Norway, China and many other countries all within a few minutes walk of each other. Visitors can partake of a traditional English ale in the Rose and Crown public house, served to them by staff wearing beefeaters' outfits, before going on a raid with the bloodthirsty Viking warriors of Norway, and finish up with dim sum and tea while watching a traditional lion-dance in the Chinese gardens. Clearly this is much more convenient than trying to find such a range of activities in the original countries.

4 *The role of the media.* There are many examples of the way that media images have encouraged the rise of simulation through-out the hospitality industry, reflecting the importance that the

media, particularly films and television, play in contemporary society. The most explicit of such examples are the themed restaurants that have become common in recent years, many of which are directly or indirectly linked to media images. Hard Rock Café, a music-industry based restaurant and one of the originals within this genre, founded in 1971 at Hyde Park Corner, London, took American-style food and drink as understood by the British, when interpreted through film and television images. Thirty years later the fifty or so restaurants are awarded icon status by consumers, who covet the merchandise which includes T-shirts, sweatshirts, baseball caps and even leather jackets costing more than £200. Indeed, the merchandise is so highly coveted that sales account for almost half of the company's turnover, pirate copying is rife and ironic merchandise is widely available touting locations where no restaurant exists or is likely to. The brand is now so powerful that as Wolitz (1996: 25) argues, 'most people who wear the T-shirts never even sit down to have a meal there, they simply walk into the apparel stores to look at and purchase Hard Rock buttons, caps and sweatshirts. What in the world compels these people to buy memorabilia from a restaurant in which they have never eaten'. Other examples include Planet Hollywood, developed by Robert Earl after he sold Hard Rock to Rank, a similar venue to Hard Rock, this time film inspired, the ill-fated Fashion-models inspired restaurant, which was recently wound up and Football-Football, inspired by the massive growth in media coverage of football worldwide. Ritzer (1999: 22) identifies a number of other media-inspired restaurants available to US consumers including 'the Apple Café (a cyber café from Apple Computer), Bubba Gump Shrimp Co. (based on the movie Forest Gump), Club Kokomo (inspired by the Beach Boys' song), Marvel Mania (comic book theme), Motown Café (inspired by the music and stars of Motown records), and so on'.

The links between the media and simulated hospitality are not limited to restaurants, of course. For example, we have already considered the case of hotels such as the Luxor. In addition, one of the major vehicles for simulation within the wider hospitality environment is that of the film-company inspired theme parks. We will consider the case of the best known of these, the Disney empire, later in this chapter; however, here we will briefly discuss the example of Warner Brothers. Warner Brothers has a number of film-related theme parks worldwide, including the Warner Brothers Movie World theme park near Cologne in Germany (www.movieworld.de). The site incorporates thirty-five different

Hospitality, Leisure & Tourism Series

rides themed on various Warner movies and animations, and a working film lot with two studios. The main visitor attraction, however, is the Bermuda Triangle, where computer technology and special effects escort visitors through subterranean rapids, over tumbling waterfalls, through fire-spitting volcanoes, to a land of alien creatures. Such theme parks have become so common a feature of contemporary hospitality that even the oddest examples elicit little comment, and one of the oddest must be that of Volkswagen Werke, in Wolfsburg, Germany (www.au-tostadt.de). This theme park, inspired by the manufacture of Volkswagen vehicles, is on the site of the world's largest car factory, some 16 million square metres in the town of Wolfsburg, where more than 80 per cent of cars are Volkswagens. The Autostadt park includes restaurants, a Ritz Carlton hotel, themed pavilions dedicated to the Volkswagen divisions (which whisper to you as you pass through them), simulators which allow you to drive all manner of Volkswagens in various scenarios, a 360-degree cinema showing car-related movies and a series of 40-metre high glass towers filled with vehicles, which are disgorged to customers every 60 seconds.

Simulation: the new means of consuming hospitality

As we have stated previously, the role of simulation and hyperreality is prevalent within the contemporary hospitality industry. What we intend to do at this point is to look at some of the main industry sectors and identify examples of these new settings of hospitality consumption, before going on to consider their implications for the contemporary industry. The sectors we will pay particular attention to, are:

- the restaurant and bar sector
- theme parks
- cruise ships
- hotels
- heritage sites.

Restaurants and bars

The restaurant and bars sector of the industry has seen massive developments in terms of simulated settings for consumption, exaggerated by the fact that they are also often incorporated in many of the other simulated settings we will discuss, such as theme parks, hotels, cruise ships, heritage sites, etc. We have already considered a number of examples of themed restaurants, including Hard Rock Café and Planet Hollywood; however, there are many more available for consumers. Ritzer (1999) describes the themed restaurant sector as 'eatertainment', emphasizing the trend towards entertainment as an integral part of the offer. Early examples of themed restaurants such as Pizzaland, which sought to represent Alpine Italy through the use of pine furniture and painted murals of Alpine scenes, seem very unsophisticated when set against the elaborate theming of many contemporary restaurants. For example, the Rainforest Café restaurants seek to extemporize a tropical rainforest scene by incorporating waterfalls and cascades, tropical rainstorms complete with thunder and lightning, live tropical birds such as parrots and macaws, and other rainforest animals, flora and fauna such as crocodiles, butterflies, elephants and trees, which use the latest in animatronics to move and vocalize. The menus are themed to the décor as is the music, staff uniforms, etc. Everything is in place to make consumers imagine they are eating in a tropical rainforest. To support the restaurant there is an extensive retail area selling merchandise ranging from clothing, to toy animals and stationery, all of which incorporates the Rainforest Café logo. In addition, the brand has become so popular that supermarkets are now stocking a range of Rainforest Café foods based on actual menu items in their refrigerator sections.

One of the earliest examples of the heavily themed restaurant brands to take off in the UK was that of TGI Friday's, which was brought to London by Whitbread in 1981. This American diner, with its central bar area, revolutionized restaurant-going for many people in the early 1980s, by combining what were then relatively exotic menus with a style of service which had not been seen before in the UK. If we consider the service styles of the bar staff, for example, it is difficult to avoid the conclusion that their actions, which include throwing bottles and drinks around the bar, pouring drinks behind their backs, etc. are based on the character Tom Cruise plays in the film *Cocktail*. Other examples of simulated environments within the themed restaurant sector include chains such as Chiquita's, a Mexican brand which seeks to ape a typical Texas/Mexico border cantina, as envisaged in Clint Eastwood films such as a *Fistful of Dollars*, the numerous sports bars such as the Red Café brand, which is themed to the sanctity of Manchester United Football Club, and the once very successful Pierre Victoire chain of French restaurants, where staff were dressed in stereotypical French waiter/waitress outfits, menus used recognizably French language and descriptions and the décor was liberally sprinkled with representations of recognizable French landmarks.

It is not only in the area of themed restaurants, however, that simulation is used to entice hospitality consumers. Fast food restaurants also have a part to play, with their vibrant colours, play areas, give-aways and film tie-ins. Fast-food restaurants find it difficult to compete on the basis of food, price or service style and, as a result, increasingly need to introduce simulation in order to compete. As Collins (1997: 1) suggests: 'the competition among fast-food giants has always been as much about appearances as reality ... with ever new, ever more flashy show stoppers needed to keep the crowd coming in ... toy giveaways, movie tie-ins, glitzy ad campaigns and new food products have all done the job'. As fast-food restaurants become increasingly alike their use of simulations becomes more important as a means of gaining competitive advantage. As a result, for example, we are seeing increasingly sophisticated play areas introduced within many McDonald's and Burger King restaurants. However, fast food also uses simulation extensively within its product range, through the watering down of traditional dishes such as hamburgers, tacos, pizzas and chicken. For example, it could be argued that the chicken nugget perfectly represents Baudrillard's (1983) idea of simulation as a copy for which no original ever existed; the chicken nugget clearly cannot in any way be said to represent chicken.

This link to the food product is important, as simulated foods are in many ways the very essence of the fast-food industry, as well as many other parts of the restaurant sector. Many of the foods we consume at the range of ethnic restaurants that are now available can be seen as simulations of their genre, many of which are not even good simulations. Pizza, for example, is variously represented as an example of fine Italian cuisine to be served with quality salads and other Italian breads (the Olive Garden brand), or an example of a hot baked Chicago-style sandwich, to be consumed using your hands while watching sport on wide-screen television (the Chicago Pizza Pie Factory way). During the 1990s the Balti grew to be one of most popular dishes served in restaurants; derived from the Indian subcontinent (replacing the previously ubiquitous tikka dishes), customers readily consume the product (which is cooked in a large wok-like bowl) in the belief that it is a traditional form of curry, despite it having been developed as a form of cooking by the families of migrant Indians in Birmingham in the mid to late 1980s. Many other foods have been similarly misrepresented, or simulated, including the Mexican tacos, the hamburger, sushi (see yo sushi and compare it to the ritualized consumption of Japanese food as described in Case Study 5.2 for the most extreme example of this feature of contemporary consumption), Chinese foods, and the bagel.

As well as restaurants, bars have increasingly become simulated settings for hospitality consumption, with décor ranging from sports (bars dedicated to particular sports, all-sports or sporting heroes), to national identity (e.g. Walkabout [Australian] or Springbok [White South African]), to adults' play areas (It's a Scream, Dave and Busters) and traditional heritage (Taverns, etc.). If we consider the range of bar offers as described by Six Continents Retail (formerly Bass Taverns) on their own web site, we can see the simulated nature of many of the outlets (see Case Study 9.1).

Case Study 9.1

Six Continents' Hyperreal bars

Six Continents is a leading global hospitality group focusing on hotels, restaurants and bars. Six Continents Hotels operates a portfolio of international brands (for example, Holiday Inn and Inter-Continental) with over 3200 hotels across 100 countries. Six Continents Retail manages a network of over 2000 outlets, over 900 of which are branded. Since 2000, Six Continents has undertaken a clear strategy of repositioning its estate to higher take branded outlets. The retail business is organized into two groups; first, the Restaurant Group, with over 500 branded restaurants and food-led high street outlets (average weekly takes of over £18 000 each) and, second, the Pubs and Bars Group, with over 350 branded outlets (average take £16 000 a week each), together with approximately 1000 unbranded pubs which provide future conversion opportunities. The current portfolio consists of the following themed and branded outlets.

1 *Edward's*: light, airy, spacious café-bars that seek to follow a pattern of moods from speciality coffees for early morning risers through to lunchtime pub food, afternoon coffees and pastries and, finally, early evening serious music and a faster pace for the evening pre-club scene. The décor is café-bar chic, as are the menus. Edward's aims to evoke a sense of a perceived continental style, using stereotypical images and décor which represent such an atmosphere to its customers.

2 *O'Neill's*: one of the largest Irish bar chains in the world, where you can enjoy a 'real' Irish experience including Irish entertainment, Irish beers and ales such as Caffrey's and Guinness, and traditional Irish wholesome public house food such as champ and sausages. It is a place to have fun, meet friends and enjoy the 'craic'. The décor includes upturned beer kegs as tables and picks and shovels as ornaments.

3 *It's a Scream*: a concept designed to appeal especially to students or those who prefer the student way of life. These are located in towns and cities mainly close to colleges or universities with a large student population. These adult games venues show cartoons and music videos all day, have numerous games machines and offer student-orientated entertainment. The décor is 'student digs shabby'.

4 *Hollywood Bowl*: uses the latest tenpin bowling technology combined with café, licensed bar and an extensive video games and amusements collection. It is decorated throughout in brash, bright colours and hard materials, evoking the macho sports feel, but softened up for all the family.

5 *Ember Inns*: traditional local public houses furnished with comfortable leather sofas, wooden floors, easy chairs, real fires, faux libraries and lots of cosy corners. Ember Inns are places to meet for a relaxing drink in a warm, comfortable atmosphere. Intended to appeal to a wide range of age groups, Ember Inns seek to create a real 'home from home' feel.

6 *Flares*: a themed, 1970s bar, described and outfitted to evoke images which are funky and groovy. The bars open late for drinking and dancing, undertaken within a retro 1970s-style music bar.

7 *Arena*: bright friendly public houses offering an alternative to the 'big night out' away from the city centre. These bars offer a seven-night programme of activities including quizzes, Premiership football, karaoke, discos and live music.

8 *All Bar One*: designed as replicating the best of contemporary bar environments, they have a modern, open airy design, which is seen as appealing and safe, especially by women. Soft furnishings, including leather sofas, internal plants and natural colours, along with décor of stripped, antiqued pine and brass create All Bar One's contemporary atmosphere. The bars are meant to evoke perceptions of security, comfort and familiarity for women customers in particular.

9 *Harvester Restaurants*: the home of the char-grill and help-yourself salad cart, they have a relaxing country farmhouse atmosphere and décor intended to inspire images of wholesome, hearty meals made from quality, farmhouse-fresh ingredients.

10 *Vintage Inns*: a more food-led version of the Ember Inns, which incorporate much of the décor and style, for example, comfortable sofas, wooden floors, easy chairs, real fires, faux libraries and lots of cosy corners.

Source: www.sixcontinents.com

Theme parks

The most famous example of this genre is obviously the Disney empire, which, in terms of theme parks at least, began with the development of Disneyland in California in 1955. This was followed by Walt Disney World (WDW) in Florida, which opened in 1971, Tokyo Disneyland, which opened in 1983, and Euro-Disney (now renamed Disneyland Paris) in 1992. Each of the parks is modelled around the same series of activities and operations, with difference accounted for only by the age of the locations, and for this reason we can use Walt Disney World as representative of the other parks. Walt Disney World starts with the Magic Kingdom, which is entered through Main Street USA, before splitting up into the six themed 'lands': Tomorrowland, Fantasyland, Adventureland, Frontierland, Liberty Square and Mickey's Toontown Fair. Alongside the Magic Kingdom are three other theme parks; the Epcot Centre, which incorporates the World Showcase, the Disney-MGM studios and the recently added fourth theme park, the Animal Kingdom, opened in 1998, which incorporates the Oasis, Safari Village, Dinoland and Africa. In addition to the land parks there are also three themed water parks – Blizzard Beach, Typhoon Lagoon and River County – themed mall areas, Downtown and Broadwalk, and a number of themed hotels. Each of the highly successful Disney parks is in effect nothing more than a complex merchandising system, a means by which consumers are encouraged to spend in many and diverse ways. However, it is the way in which that merchandising system is set out that is of interest to us, as clearly the whole of the Disney structure is a simulation, albeit in the case of Disney a simulation that has become one of the world's most important icons. Thus in the Magic Kingdom and beyond we find a huge range of restaurants, bars and hotels/resorts, all of which use simulation to create settings for hospitality consumption. These include the Liberty Tree Tavern, which 'celebrates the American spirit in a recreation of a Colonial Inn, where everything is authentic right down to the 18th century style windows'; the Crystal Palace with 'food prepared in our on-stage kitchen' and Tony's Town Square restaurant 'a Lady and the Tramp inspired Italian restaurant' (WDW website). Similar restaurants are available in the Epcot park, including the Rose and Crown Dining Room, 'a jubilant replica of the pubs that have become a mainstay of British life . . . includes a jolly English sing-along in the bar' (WDW website) and the Restaurant Marrakech, a mosaic-adorned restaurant, which one finds by wandering along the winding alleyways of an ancient Moroccan village and in which one can enjoy typical Moroccan hospitality such as belly-dancing. The Animal Kingdom park includes a Rainforest Café and other simulated settings such as the Flame Tree Barbecue, a thatched building with views of the 'Nile' and the Restaurantosaurus, which has typical American cuisine, but served by student palaeontologists. Finally, in terms of restaurants, the Disney/MGM Studios has restaurants such as the 1950s Prime Time Café, where customers eat in the kitchen of a vintage 1950s sitcom and the Toy Story Pizza Planet, a classic example of simulacrity, a pizza restaurant which re-creates the artificial pizza restaurant from the cartoon *Toy Story*. When we consider hotels and resorts, examples include the All-Star Movies Resort, which is themed around classic Disney films such as *Fantasia* and the *Mighty Ducks*;

the Swan Hotel, which has five-storey high swan statues and murals of waves and bananas; the Polynesia Resort, with its waterfalls and lush gardens; Port Orleans, a replica of the French Quarter of New Orleans and Fort Wilderness 'the heart of the great outdoors' (WDW website). All these examples, and many more that exist on the site of WDW, are simulations designed to encourage hospitality consumption. Huxtable (1997: 50) describes Disney as 'expertly engineered, standardized mediocrity, end-lessly, shamelessly consumerized, a giant shill operation with a Mickey Mouse façade' and the consumers love it.

Of course, Disney is not the only example we could have chosen, it is simply the most all-encompassing. Others would include Warner Brothers, the Asterix theme park outside Paris, Busch Gardens and, in the UK, Alton Towers, Chessington World of Adventure and Camelot. I have included two other examples as illustrations within this chapter, which, while not theme parks in the traditional sense, discuss many of the same issues (see Case Studies 9.2 and 9.3).

Case Study 9.2

Aspects of simulation and their significance within the hospitality industry: New Orleans, the theme park city

To understand the implications of simulation on consumers of hospitality services we have chosen to look at how cities, such as New Orleans, are increasingly becoming simulations of themselves, and thus becoming theme park cities.

The French Quarter is just like it is represented in the films, full of wrought-iron balconies, faded wooden shutters of Creole cottages, Mardi Gras decorations hanging from ornate lamp-posts, and the shopping is everything one could wish for. On Decatur Street alone there are more than thirty souvenir stores, each packed with New Orleans merchandise such as T-shirts, ashtrays and Mardi Gras masks. The ornate, historical buildings on this street have been transformed into highly effective merchandising units, which use all possible representations of the past to turn a profit, including artefacts from Voodoo, to which whole shops are given over, selling love potions, tarot cards and grigri dolls among other items. Other shops in the area use representations from the days of slavery, selling artefacts such as irons and whips – in New Orleans even slavery is simulated and themed.

Jackson Square is another area, which represents the theming of New Orleans, with the cobbled plaza outside the St Louis Cathedral a mainstay of the area. The plaza is always filled with fortune-tellers, portrait painters, acrobats and mime artists, while bands play 'traditional' local tunes such as 'When the Saints Go Marchin' In' on ukuleles, and dancers tap-dance to 'Way Down Yonder in New Orleans'.

Attractions and trips available to visitors to New Orleans include steamboat trips down the Mississippi River on the steamboat Natchez, where calliopes (a musical instrument powered by steam atop the boat) call visitors to the wharves, 'traditional' Dixieland bands play the tunes associated with the area and the all-you-can-eat buffet includes such local dishes as shrimp, gumbo and beignets, washed down with Pernod. Or visitors can take carriage rides around the French Quarter in carriages drawn by decorated mules, go on a swamp tour to see the haunts of long-gone pirates, and hopefully to spot the legendary 'Bigfoot' and handle live Mississippi alligators (including feeding them their traditional diet of marshmallow, which is used to draw them to the boats), have their palms read, have their caricatures drawn, ride the streetcars to St Charles Avenue or the river road and visit the mansions and plantation houses (many of which have made numerous appearances in film), go to the Treasure Chest Casino or stay at any number of guest houses that were the original 'House of the Rising Sun'. A must for all visitors to New Orleans is a visit to the Cities of the Dead, the cemeteries of New Orleans, with their above-ground and exposed tombs. New Orleans is known as the most haunted city in the USA, and numerous ghost and haunting tours, which go around the Cities of the Dead, are available – after all, this is the city with the ghostly singing rain, a mystical haunting noise that occurs whenever it rains in New Orleans.

If any single area represents the theming of New Orleans, however, it is Bourbon Street, block after block of continual Mardi Gras, where the streets are so crowded with tourists people are forced to push their way through the crush. Here the good-time music combines with the heat, noise and swampy air, to produce an atmosphere that even Disney cannot replicate, although of course it tries in its Port Orleans resort. The party never ends in Bourbon Street, even during the height of the day men in tight T-shirts drink cocktails and blow kisses from the windows and balconies. However, it is at night that the party really gets going. The whole street is blocked solid with bodies, all of them holding their go-cups, everyone drinking mint julep or bourbon with the intention of getting very drunk. Music blasts from all the bars, restaurants and street corners, and within some of the clubs contemporary vaudeville includes strippers and simulated sex scenes. This street is the epitome of New Orleans as a theme park.

Sources: Cohn (2001); *Time Out* (2001); www.experienceneworleans.com

Cruise ships

In recent years the cruising industry has undergone dramatic changes, not least that in the contemporary market the ship is largely seen as the holiday, rather than the means of getting to interesting locations. As a result, the cruise industry is currently carrying more passengers than at any previous time, up from 5 million in 1995 to more than 10 million in 2000, with predictions that volume will rise to over 20 million by 2010 (Dickinson and Vladimir, 1997). The largest market is still the USA, which accounts for almost 70 per cent of current volumes; however, the UK with 750 000 passengers, a 400 per cent rise in ten years, is also a significant market. The largest operator is Carnival Corporation, which operates six brands, and has a total of forty-five ships at sea, twice as many as its nearest competitor Royal Caribbean; however, there are currently more than forty ships on order for delivery in the next three years. The cruise market is in many ways still seen to be in its infancy. For example, despite the USA being the largest market for cruise holidays, only 13 per cent of Americans have taken a cruise holiday, and this position is replicated and exaggerated in many other markets, especially mainland Europe and Asia. Case Study 8.1 in Chapter 8 discusses in detail how the characteristics of cruise ships, using *Voyager of the Seas* as an example, can be seen as simulated means of consumption. However, we will consider some further examples here. The *European Vision*, which is owned by Festival Cruises, and was recently host to a G8 summit, is a classic example of the genre. It incorporates all of the European stereotypes imaginable in a 60 000-tonne ship; for example, it offers Le Flamenco (Spanish-style) discotheque, the Vivaldi piano bar, the Goethe library and reading room and the White Lion English-style public house. For entertainment it has health spas, casinos, a 7.5-metre climbing wall, cinemas, etc. Other cruise ships such as the *Grand* and *Golden Princess* have Skywalker nightclubs hanging from the backs of the ships, with whole glass walls giving dancers the perception they could dance straight into the sea. The Wind-jammer line of sailing cruisers, offers customers the opportunity to join in and hoist the sails, as does the Royal Clipper, which has no casinos or Las Vegas style shows, but opts for the Windows Net – a huge hammock slung across the ship. Disney, of course, have the ships *Magic* and *Wonder*, with dedicated children's areas incorporating Mickey Mouse shaped pools, and their own island.

The main reason these ships are important to us, however, is that they are means of encouraging hospitality consumption – all of the facilities and extras on the ships are payable separately. For example, Festival Cruises, who operate the *European Vision*, suggest that almost 35 per cent of its income is generated from additional spending on its ships, that is, spending over and above the cost of the holiday. As Ashworth (2001: 47) suggests: 'whatever you pay for your cruise, you will end up spending a third as much again . . . generating further profits for the cruise ship operator'. So significant is this spend that many operators are happy to offer free and budget trips, for example, two-for-one offers, as they know that on average in 2000 customers spent more than £70 per day on additional items, such as drinks, excursions, spa treatments, on-board shopping, gambling and gratuities (Scull, 2001: 46). As Ritzer (1999: 19) suggests, 'the modern cruise ship is a highly effective means for getting people to spend large sums of money and consume an array of services and goods' many of which, of course, are hospitality products.

Hotels

As with restaurants, bars, theme parks and cruise ships, hotels have increasingly used simulation as a means of increasing consumption, often in conjunction with other venues such as theme parks, casinos, sports stadiums, etc. The most notable examples of the genre are those in locations such as on the strip in Las Vegas and attached to the theme parks of Disney. On the strip in Las Vegas, for example, we have the Luxor Hotel, which incorporates the largest pyramid in the world, a monolith, a replica of the sphinx, which is larger than the original and rooms that get smaller and smaller as one reaches the pinnacle of the pyramid. The hospitality provision within the Luxor is similarly themed, and includes the Sacred Sea Room, where murals, mosaics and hieroglyphics combine to suggest dining at sea. We also find Excalibur, designed to represent a medieval castle, and incorporating Sir Galahad's Rib House, a Tudor-style eating house; New York, New York which represents a New York skyline, and incorporates Times Square, a statue of Liberty 150 feet tall and the Chin Chin restaurant, a replica of New York's China town area; the Paris Casino Hotel, with a fifty-storey Eiffel Tower, and an Arc de Triomphe, which has a 'traditional' gourmet French restaurant in the interior; the Mirage, with an exploding volcano outside, a 50-foot aquarium in the reception area, and a dolphin habitat, and which incorporates Kokomos rainforest restaurant and the Caribe Café, Caribbean-style restaurant; Treasure Island, which incorporates a sea battle and sinking ship, and which offers the Kahunaville tropical restaurant and bar, and Bellagios, with its indoor fountains and gardens, which completely change for each of the seasons, and which offers the Picasso Mediterranean style restaurant, complete with millions of pounds worth of original Picassos.

In the UK the Alton Towers hotel, attached to the theme park of the same name, offers its customers similar simulations and extravaganza, including the Secret Garden Restaurant, with foods discovered by Sir Algernon (?) on his many journeys around the world, and the Pirates Lagoon Spa and Pool. Alton Towers also offers a range of themed hotel accommodation, including the Peter Rabbit room, with characters drawn from the children's books; the Arabian Knights room, with a canopied bed and marble jacuzzi; the Princess room, with satin sheets and roses around the windows and doors; the Cadbury's chocolate room, with a chocolate dressing table and a machine that continually spouts out chocolate and the Coca-Cola room, which offers a cola fountain and a room full of bubbles. All these hotels are examples of highly effective means of encouraging hospitality consumption, and promoting all the activities associated with them, whether these are theme parks, casinos or whatever.

Heritage sites

Heritage is increasingly becoming a means of hospitality consumption, especially in theme park Britain, where heritage is stereotyped and simulated until it no longer resembles the original it stands for (Hewison, 1987). Museums, art galleries, industrial heritage sites, political history, have all been ransacked in order to simulate consumption, including that of hospitality services. As Goulding (2000: 835) suggests we have a 'culture industry which substitutes escapist commodified leisure for authentic experience and by doing so have fostered conformity, passivity and political indifference amongst participants turned spectators'. Such a view is supported by Featherstone (1991: 96) when he states 'the general expansion of the cultural sphere . . . not only points to the enlarged markets for cultural goods . . . but also to ways in which the purchase and consumption of commodities is increasingly mediated by cultural images'. This commodification means that we increasingly view culture as a leisure activity and evaluate it in terms of its value as trade. The result of this is that culture has to go through a series of staged authenticity, where the experiences of the past are reconstructed to suit the tastes of modern visitors before being packaged and sold as authentic. As Featherstone (1991: 96) states: 'this is evident in the forms of leisure consumption in which the emphasis is placed upon experiences and pleasure and the ways in which more traditional forms of high cultural consumption become revamped to cater for wider audiences . . . with an emphasis on the spectacular, the popular, the pleasurable and immediately accessible'.

When Baudrillard (1988) discussed the levels of simulation that are experienced, he suggested that just below hyperreality, exemplified by products such as WDW, was a level wherein simulation masked the absence of a reality, and one of the best examples of this is Williamsburg, Virginia, USA. Williamsburg and its surrounding area is known as 'the largest living museum in the world', and is described thus: 'Williamsburg – the centre of monumental clashes of minds, ideas, wills and finally armed conflict ... think of Williamsburg and the images that come to mind are colonial life, American independence and the new model for Democracy ... as more than 4,000,000 visitors discover there's more than history waiting' (www.williamsburg.com). 'History' is related through the scenes replayed at:

- Jamestown – representations of the times, trials and lives of the earliest European settlers
- Yorktown – simulations of the battle for democracy
- Williamsburg – the history area, the land of taverns, colleges and the constitution.

While the extras include:

- world-class theme parks with some of the largest roller coasters in America
- golf courses that have hosted many USA presidents, including 'possibly' the very first
- taverns where the likes of Jefferson and Patrick argued over the fate of the colony
- the opportunity to tap your toes to 'authentic' balladeers when you visit Ireland, home of many of the early settlers
- 'authentic' replicas of boats like the *Susan B. Constant*, which brought the settlers across the ocean
- 'authentic' reconstructions of the battle scenes of some of the region's bloodiest days
- the opportunity to serve on a jury trying the area's bloodthirsty pirates.

Nowhere does the oxymoronic nature of phrases such as 'authentic replicas' or 'authentic reconstructions' cause any discomfort to the organizations involved in selling Williamsburg to the public ('authentic' being defined as conforming to fact or reality, not imaginary, false or imitation; while 'replica' is defined as a close copy or reproduction and 'reconstruction' is defined as a mental or physical representation [*Longman Dictionary*]).

One aspect of the commodification of culture and history such as museums and art galleries has been the development of increasingly sophisticated hospitality services, such as the authentic taverns in Williamsburg, leading, for example, to a recent advertisement suggesting the Victoria and Albert Museum was a great café, with a nice little museum attached. It is also possible in today's cultural market to hire the halls and foyers of our museums and galleries in order to host company or private parties, or to hire many of our most historic houses for similar purposes. At the Royal Armouries Museum in Leeds, for example, it is possible to organize your function in 'A venue where hospitality can be provided amongst the world's finest collection of arms and armour. Within the Royal Armouries Museum five themed galleries we can offer anything from an intimate dinner for sixteen in the Edwardian Gun Room to a formal dinner for 150 in the War Gallery', all of which can be accompanied by 'historical live interpretations by the Royal Armouries Museum's interpretation team to enhance your evening to create an extra special memory, from men in full armour demonstrating their sword skills to a narrative depicting Florence Nightingale in the Crimea' (www.armouries.org).

Case study 9.3

Heritage theme parks: the Magna experience

To understand the implications of simulation on consumers of hospitality services we have chosen to look at how it is increasingly being used to produce cultural and heritage theme parks.

Magna is a lottery funded 'science adventure centre' housed in a disused steelworks in Templeborough, near Rotherham, South Yorkshire, and was the recipient of the British Architecture Best Building of the Year Award for 2001, beating, among others, Portcullis House and the Eden Project. It cost £46 million pounds to develop and opened in June 2001.

Gosh, what a hectic week! Only Thursday, and already I have dynamited a quarry cliff, shifted a pile of rocks with my trusty JCB, tonked up a hydrogen rocket, recycled a couple of million gallons of water, winched a ton of scrap metal with a few deft flicks of my electro-magnetic crane, and popped down t'pit to check on progress at the coal face. So what is all this? Is this part of a one-man campaign to revive the golden age of Britain's heavy industries? I wish it were. But unfortunately for the battered populace of South Yorkshire, everything I experienced this week – yes, even the trusty JCB – was as much make believe as Alton Towers' log flume. What I had visited was Magna, the science adventure centre at Templeborough. It is housed in what was, back in 1916, the biggest building in the country: 40 yards long, 10 double-decker buses high, dark and cold as a mausoleum, and with many of its vast, blackened cauldrons, crane hooks and pulleys still in place. In its heyday 10 000 people worked here, in temperatures that frequently hit three figures; even in the late 1970s it was breaking world records for tonnage produced each week. The transformation into South Yorkshire's largest tourist attraction has been brilliantly conceived. Essentially it has been kept exactly as it was, grimy and derelict, but now a high, wide viewing platform runs through it like a spine, giving access to four giant interactive exhibition pods, Earth, Air, Fire and Water.

It isn't hard to see why Magna has become such a smash hit; the place is as much about entertainment as education. The Water area for instance, enlivens its ecological stance with an array of giant taps and 'Super-Soaka' canons, which do exactly what the name suggests. And in Air you can feel the force of a tornado or experience what it was like to stand on the notoriously wobbly Tacoma suspension bridge in Seattle, just before it collapsed in high winds in 1930. All over the building, electric wires high above your head crackle, fizz and spark. Steam rises from the cavernous bowels. And best of all is a remarkable one-minute *son et lumière* show called the Big Melt which gives the impression that the giant electric arc-furnace, once the world's biggest, is belching and roaring back into life in a spectacular display of smoke, flames and fireworks. Some museum! Yet as I walk around I feel curiously uneasy. Is it me? Or is Britain turning into one gigantic heritage theme park? More than fifty new museums have open in the past twenty years, and most seem to be converted factories, docks or mines. There is surely something odd about a country that is so obsessed with long-faded industrial glories. It is as if the past has become Britain's comfort blanket; we cling to it because, like Peter Pan, we do not want to grow up and face the big world. You particularly feel this desperate nostalgia in South Yorkshire for, despite the spinning of various government departments, it is quite apparent that new jobs in the much vaunted 'sunrise' and 'dot-com' industries have not materialized in sufficient numbers to replace the mass employment lost when the pits and steelworks were killed off. Far from deflecting attention away from this community tragedy, Magna seems almost to flaunt it. As you enter the building, five huge cinema screens play out the history of the steelworks in contemporary newsreels, culminating in the last-ditch clashes of the early 1980s between pickets and police, as you watch the furnace with its pyrotechnic party tricks a voice recites an elegiac commentary about the steelworks' past, ending with the mournful 'but that was yesterday, today you're looking at a dragons' graveyard'. I started to wonder about the wisdom and morality of recycling the savage demolition of northern England's industrial heritage, with all the misery and wasted lives which that entailed, as the backing to a neat package of entertainment. But what do I know? Nearly 20 000 people have visited Magna since April and they seem to love it. Clearly Magna must be pressing the right culture buttons with lots of folk.

Source: adapted from Morrison (2001)

Other examples include the Metropolitan Museum of Art, which incorporates a shopping mall and food emporium within its ground floor area and the Louvre, which again has a shopping mall and restaurant areas, within its site. Crawford (1992: 30) when comparing the National Gallery of Art in Washington to a shopping mall stated: 'potted plants, lavish use of marble and brass, and the fountains, shops, and fast-food counters make the resemblance even more striking'.

As we have seen in an age dominated by simulacrum and hyperreality, the heritage and culture industries are increasingly incorporating simulation as a means of encouraging consumption, and in many cases hospitality products are a key element of this consumption.

Transforming relationships between buyers and sellers: some conclusions

This chapter has sought to identify the fact that, within hospitality consumption, settings are becoming increasingly simulated and hyperreal in order to attract consumers who are themselves increasingly expecting extravaganza and simulation to be an integral part of the hospitality offer. These new settings are important in themselves, in terms of what they say about contemporary hospitality consumers, but they are also important because of the central role they play in sustaining the contemporary phenomena of hyper-consumption. However, the very demand for spectacle, simulation and hyperreality from hospitality consumers is also one of its main difficulties. As Ritzer (1999: 174) argues: 'spectacles tend to grow dated and boring quite quickly, the already spectacular . . . are under constant pressure to create ever more spectacular settings . . . and yesterday's spectacle falls to the wrecking ball'. This can be seen already to be happening within hospitality; theme parks such as Alton Towers and Chessington World of Adventure need to constantly update their rides in order to maintain their share of the market. For example, for the 2002 season Alton Towers is introducing AIR 2002, a multi-million pound new-generation roller coaster, while Chessington World of Adventure will compete with its New Vampire, a multi-million pound swinging, suspended, floorless coaster. In the restaurant sector chains such as the Fashion café have closed due to lack of demand for its products, while one of the more glamorous themed restaurants of the late 1990s, the Rainforest Café, has had to cut its losses and close its store in the Trafford Centre, Britain's largest shopping centre. A similar picture can be seen in the hotel, fast-food and bars sectors, at enormous cost to companies operating within them.

As we enter a postmodern world the changes we are beginning to witness in consumer behaviour call for a perplexing variety of products and services within single locations. The rationale for the development and placing of these will have to come from new ways of researching consumer behaviour. Previous models which sought to understand consumers through treating them as automatons reacting to stimuli, whether at a micro or macro level, will not be appropriate for today's hospitality consumers. What are needed are new postmodern and more subjective research methodologies, which look for difference and uniqueness rather than similarity and pattern in the behaviour of hospitality consumers. It calls for a more radical, individual customer-centred approach to relationship marketing and less reliance on traditional market segmentation strategies. The way forward is radically to rethink our consumer research methodologies in order to better understand how to market meanings and sell significations to postmodern consumers, rather than market and sell products and services. This aspect will provide the focus for the final chapter.

CHAPTER 10

Researching contemporary hospitality consumer behaviour

Key themes

- The methodological issues confronting those researching hospitality consumers are daunting, as the rationale for the development of hospitality products in contemporary markets will have to come from new ways of researching consumer behaviour.

- Previous research models, which sought to understand consumers through understanding their reaction to stimuli, will not be appropriate for today's hospitality consumers.

- What is needed in today's markets are new and more subjective research methodologies, which look for difference and uniqueness rather than similarity and pattern in the behaviour of hospitality consumers.

- This chapter considers a set of research methods suitable for inquiry into the behaviour of contemporary hospitality consumers.

Interpreting hospitality consumer behaviour

The significance of research is well understood by most hospitality academics and practitioners, and while many may be sceptical about its practical value it is generally taken for granted that it is a beneficial activity. Johns and Lee-Ross (1998: vii) for example state that 'research is increasingly significant at all levels of service industry management, particularly the hotel, tourism and leisure sectors'. Despite this, however, few researchers within hospitality management explicitly describe and evaluate a range of available research methods. Indeed, it could be argued (Gore and Riley, 2000), that academics have only recently made serious attempts to explain methodology as it specifically relates to hospitality research. Publications by Clark et al. (1998) and Brotherton (1999) are welcome additions to this area and can be seen as long overdue. Brotherton (1999) is worthy of particular highlighting, as he seeks to provide insights into current methodological practice and to add to the development of a research culture within the hospitality sector.

However, as we have discussed, in today's hospitality industry we are beginning to witness significant changes in the ways consumers behave, changes that require new ways of researching consumer behaviour. Previous models which sought to understand consumers through treating them as automatons reacting to stimuli, whether at a micro or macro level, will not be appropriate for today's hospitality consumers. What are needed are new interpretive and more subjective research methodologies, which seek out difference and uniqueness, rather than similarity and pattern, in the behaviour of hospitality consumers. These changes call for a more radical individual customer-centred approach to marketing research and less reliance on traditional market concepts such as segmentation and positioning strategies. In order to be effective in understanding hospitality consumers in the future, we need radically to rethink our consumer research methodologies in order better to understand how to market meaning and signification to postmodern consumers rather than, as at present, market and sell goods and services.

In recent years some progress has been made in this area, however, it is clear that much consumer research in hospitality still follows a traditional scientific model. For example, at the CHME (Council for Hospitality Management Education) research conference in 2000, all but two of the forty-five conference papers utilized traditional scientific methods for researching activities such as customer and organizational behaviour, labour turnover, organizational strategies, etc. This despite Johns and Lee-Ross's (1998: 14) argument that 'the level

Hospitality, Leisure & Tourism Series

of focus (required for scientific research) is frequently counter-productive in management research'. As we have seen, the consumption of hospitality goods and services is the result of complex, multifaceted interactions between consumers, suppliers and others within the macro and micro environment. Traditional research methodologies are not sufficiently holistic nor sufficiently flexible to deal with such scenarios, and thus alternative models need to be introduced. However, within hospitality such research is the exception rather than the norm, as Gore and Riley (2000: 31) argue: 'Despite increased and prolific reporting of methodological considerations in the field of management, few researchers within hospitality management explicitly describe and evaluate the validity of their research methods. Hospitality academics have only recently made substantive attempts to fill the methodological void for hospitality research audiences.'

The 1980s and 1990s has generally seen a growing application of qualitative research methods to problem scenarios within hospitality, and this trend is evident within what limited consumer behaviour research there is. However, these methodologies still tend to be 'scientific' or positivist in nature, as if researchers are fearful of the criticisms often levelled at qualitative research, for example, issues in respect of orientation, clarity, transgression and method mixing (Goulding, 1999: 859). This position replicates that found in the wider research arena. For example, Hirschman (1993) compared themes and ideologies used in articles published in the *Journal of Consumer Research* in the 1990s and found that the most dominant themes were still the construction and testing of consumer behaviour, using positivist, quantitative models. Similar findings are revealed if one looks at the CHME research conference proceedings for the decade it has been in existence.

In the wider domain consumer behaviour research is becoming increasingly interdisciplinary, and established paradigms and traditional positivist philosophies are under attack. Within hospitality Roper and Brookes (1999: 174) argue that 'interdisciplinary research is not a new phenomenon; a number of authors have been advocating the need for using an interdisciplinary approach for some time', going on to name Slattery (1983) and Littlejohn (1990), among others. Such a view is supported by Lashley (1998: 295) who argues: 'traditional research that tends to focus on single independent variables that will supposedly alter a dependent variable, does not recognize the interdependence of inter-factional influences in hospitality'. This raises the questions of what is meant by interdisciplinary research and the extent to which hospitality research has been inter-disciplinary in the past. Nilles (in Roper and Brookes, 1999) defines interdisciplinary research as 'the joint, co-ordinated and continuously integrated research done by experts with different disciplinary backgrounds, working together producing papers etc., which are so tightly woven that the specific contribution of each research tends to be obscured by a joint product'. The intention of such a research model, according to Roper and Brooks is to achieve a holistic, synergistic understanding of the subject being investigated. However, within hospitality research Johns and Lee-Ross (1998: ix) suggest that they 'feel that far too often "interdisciplinary" is really interpreted as multidisciplinary, in which accepted approaches from established disciplines are brought to bear upon problems identified within service industries'. What authors such as this wish to see is more innovation within the methodology of hospitality research. Again if we consider the wider consumer behaviour research domain we can see such innovation. For example, Gould (1995) rejects the concept of objectivity in research and argues that researchers should be allowed introspection. Other authors such as Thompson, Locander and Pollio (1990), McQuarrie and McIntyre (1990), Goulding (1999) and Johns and Lee-Ross (1998) argue the case for phenomenological approaches to research, and Holbrook and Hirschman (1993) advocate the merits of hermeneutics and semiotics in research, while Firat and Venkatesh (1995) and Brown (2000) argue the case for postmodernism. All these disparate models have one thing in common – unlike positivist models they accept that consumer behaviour is a complex, non-rational, unpredictable phenomenon, whereas Goulding (1999: 860) states, it is necessary to take a position that 'not only focuses on the process of buying, but gives equal significance to the experiential and meaningful aspects which underpin consumption'.

The problem with many of the approaches currently utilized are summed up by Thomas (1997: 58) when he states: 'survey research, based on simplistic questionnaires, are in my opinion outdated and methodologically mechanistic. Standardized inflexible questionnaires will not capture tastes and meanings. But we knew that all along'. There is clear evidence that the causal links between attitudes and behaviours are at best soft. What we say and what we do are complex equations. This leads us to a number of fundamental questions with regard to consumer behaviour, including:

- To what extent are groups homogeneous in any real way?
- Are we able to analyse lifestyles that are in a constant state of flux?
- Do the discriminators we have been using have currency in the contemporary hospitality environment?

- What, if anything, does your work, job, career or vocation say about you?
- Does where you live have anything to say about the hospitality goods and services you consume, especially at the level of individual postcodes?
- What are the implications of the new means of communication, media and connectivity for researching hospitality consumers?
- What is the value of prescriptive, positivist data such as SIC codes in a world where goods and services are constantly converging, being redefined, and reinvented.

It is clear from a consideration of these questions that the problems encountered in understanding hospitality consumers are numerous and significant, prompting us to reconsider the approaches we are using. If accepted methods are currently under question, as suggested above, then a reappraisal of the methodologies which support the old thinking is required, and studies based on a more phenomenological approach are likely to give greater insight.

Options available to hospitality consumer behaviour researchers

Brown (1995) suggests that it is possible to visualize consumer research as a grid, using epistemology (the grounds of knowledge) and ontology (the nature of the world) as its axis, which are subdivided along realist and relativist lines (see Figure 10.1). The top left-hand cell, which represents many of the earliest attempts

EPISTEMOLOGY / ONTOLOGY	REALIST	RELATIVIST
REALIST	'Traditional' consumer research	'Traditional' quantitative research
RELATIVIST	Interpretive consumer research	Postmodern consumer research

Figure 10.1 Options available to hospitality consumer researchers
Source: adapted from Brown (1995: 171)

to model hospitality consumption, assumes that consumers have direct access to the 'real' world and thus it is possible to obtain hard, objective knowledge about this single external reality. Typical examples would include empirical attempts to understand the consumer behaviour of Japanese tourists (Ahmed and Krohn, 1992), market segmentation strategies for fast-food restaurants (Grazin and Olsen, 1997) or the study of preferred hotel attributes among business travellers (Kattara, 2000).

The top right-hand cell also represents consumers having direct access to an external reality. However, here it is assumed that the consumer's knowledge of that reality is individual and, therefore, subjective, difficult to access and quantify, and thus best investigated through the use of 'traditional' qualitative methods such as focus groups, in-depth interviews, group interviews, etc. This model of research has been a significant area of development within hospitality, and examples are too numerous to mention; one simply needs to consider any issue of the *International Journal of Contemporary Hospitality Management* or the *Journal of Travel and Tourism Marketing* to see the preponderance of qualitative studies within this area. However, as Brown (1995: 172) suggests, too often 'such studies not only provide hypotheses for subsequent empirical test, but for some researchers, they also form the basis of meaningful generalizations and model development', this despite the known limitations of such approaches when applied to the external environment in general.

The bottom left-hand cell does not presuppose that individuals have direct access to an external reality, but that characteristics such as language, semiotics and culture interpose. However, research within this set does accept that the consumer's knowledge of their perceived world is meaningful in its own terms, and thus can be understood using the appropriate naturalistic or ethnographic methods, even though any findings cannot be applied more generally. Hospitality research within this area is much more difficult to find, although it is slowly being discovered as increasing numbers of 'new school' researchers begin to investigate the complexity of the industry. Recent research by authors such as Gillespie and Morrison (2001), Clarke et al. (2000) and Bowen (1998) are representative of this set.

The final cell, the one at the bottom right-hand side, represents the postmodern position, which, as we have seen, rejects any notion of consumers having access to an external reality but also questions the concept of consumers being freethinking subjects whose behaviour is open to interpretation. Postmodernism suggests that, far from having perfect knowledge, the knowledge consumers have is unreliable, fragmented and 'an epiphenomenon of language' (Brown, 1995: 172). As such, undertaking any form of meaningful empirical research in a postmodern era, becomes problematic. This raises the question, where does hospitality consumer research go from here? And the answer would seem to be increasingly in favour of both interpretive and postmodern methodologies. It is clear that attempts to understand the behaviour of a complex phenomenon such as the consumption of hospitality goods and services through prescriptive, mechanistic, positivist approaches such as have often been advocated in the past are doomed to failure. Tests of empirical significance, whether quantitative or quasi-qualitative, but rooted in a modernist perspective, are increasingly insignificant in an era when consumers live in a world of doubt, ambiguity and uncertainty. In such an era consumer research has to be capable of answering the questions, how do we understand the consumption of hospitality products

- in a world which has no concrete social construction?
- where reality is not a pre-existent idea that has outside language?
- where the cultural construction of respondents' worlds are encoded in their responses?
- where each consumer comprises a number of different consumers, all of whom require different brand or product solutions?
- where consumption is so clearly dependent on context and circumstance (Thomas, 1997)?

The answer to such questions is that hospitality consumption in today's world can be investigated only through a range of methodologies, which respect the divergent perspectives of consumers, some of which will be considered in the next section of this chapter. Investigations into postmodern hospitality consumers offer little comfort for researchers. Indeed, given the three key themes we identified earlier, that is, the disintegration of universal forms of knowledge, the rise of simulacrity and hyperreality, and the move to an era of conspicuous consumption, it is difficult to imagine how a research agenda for investigating postmodern consumer behaviour could be determined. There is at present no well-used paradigm for consumer behaviour that allows hospitality organizations to investigate postmodern consumption. Traditional concepts drawn from marketing and consumer behaviour are increasingly seen to be invalid in understanding contemporary hospitality consumption. As a result, when hospitality researchers using postmodern concepts seek to address the so what/now what questions, they often stumble and pass on to other issues (Crotty, 1998). As we have seen in Part Two of this book, models of consumer behaviour have as a dominant paradigm a mix of cognitive and social psychologies, the legacy of which is that consumer research, particularly in the hospitality field, lacks a systematic framework of conceptualization and analysis for the explanation of situational influences on consumer choice. When post-modernists turn to research a number of questions arise, including: what kind of envisaged world forms the backdrop for postmodern research? What assumptions does postmodernism bring to it? What is the postmodernist take on the human scene? In addition we need to consider the extent to which an acceptance of postmodernism condemns people to keep reinventing themselves endlessly. Do they never achieve an identity, that is, some sense of a coherent personality and sense of self? Does postmodernism generate identity-less people, caught up in continually changing fads and fashions and identities? Given what has been discussed above, we know that no simple, tidy answer exists for these questions. Nevertheless, if we are to understand the consumption of contemporary hospitality, an appropriate research agenda must be identified.

Methodological approaches and issues in contemporary (postmodern) hospitality consumer research

This section introduces a range of methodologies that may be suitable for investigating hospitality consumer behaviour in contemporary settings, and advocates the need for understanding the diversity of the consumer experience. It is an attempt to address some of the problems and issues that are raised by postmodern consumers, and at best seeks to sensitize hospitality researchers to the various methods that are available. It is not intended to be a definitive research methods chapter, but simply provides a number of guidelines, which seek to address the issues raised in Part Three of this book. Those involved in research within this area, and who share some of the concerns I have expressed about traditional approaches to research, are directed to the texts referenced throughout this chapter, where they will be able to gain a better understanding of some of these approaches than I am able to offer here.

Alternative paradigms for researching postmodern hospitality consumption: paradigmatic pluralism

One approach which has begun to be identified in other research areas, and which might offer some scope in investigating postmodern hospitality consumption, is the embrace of a pluralist tradition in terms of identifying different paradigmatic orientations and their respective knowledge claims. It is argued (Thompson, Arnould and Stern, 1997) that a postmodern conception of pluralism could foster interparadigmatic dialogues that would contribute to a richer theoretical account of consumption. In essence paradigmatic pluralism would seek to heighten sensitivity to differences of interpretation, to offer a place to less conventional perspectives and to explore a range of understudied dynamics and interests that exist in consumer culture. Such pluralism offers the opportunity to investigate the tensions between different paradigms that may harbour the potential for transforming consumer research conventions. In terms of a postmodern framework, paradigmatic pluralism manifests a dynamic between inclusion and exclusion and, as such, certain assumptions assume a primary position in an account while others are marginalized. Thus, each paradigm manifests unique theoretical narratives that address only a subset of the range of research issues that could be defined as dimensions of a given consumer phenomena. What does this mean in practice, that is, how do we move from philosophical abstraction through to research methodology? Two strategies have been proposed which seek to move this discussion on.

Paradigmatic boundaries ● ● ●

The first strategy which has been proposed operates through the specification of paradigmatic boundaries (Thompson, Arnould and Stern, 1997), wherein it is argued that the nature of a paradigm is most clearly revealed by contrasting it to other paradigms. Within this, framings are thus recognized as assumptions when they are placed in contrast to other framings drawn from alternative paradigms. As a result the differences between paradigms become constitutive and create meaning, rather than being seen as a source of polemical stagnation. As Thompson, Arnould and Stern (1997: 169) argue, 'implicit to all research paradigms are conceptual and methodological legacies that have arisen from philosophical genealogy'. These legacies have led to a focus on rebuttal, critique and synthetic solutions; a dynamic of paradigmatic diversity offers the opportunity of more explicit and systematic investigation of the features that comprise hospitality consumer behaviour. The presentation of paradigmatic difference creates a narrative space for the expression of alternative voices and expands definitions of mainstream or relevant consumer research issues.

Dialogical retextualization • • •

The second approach highlighted here is that of dialogical retextualization, which refers to reformulating a research narrative in light of another paradigmatic orientation. In essence it considers research propositions, focusing on the different issues, social positions and cultural aspects that would be forwarded through a range of paradigmatic narrative. Retextualization revisits an existing set of research propositions but focuses on the different issues, social positions and cultural issues that would be voiced by different paradigmatic narratives. The implication inherent in the methodology is that dialogue between different paradigms creates a new interpretation that offers a new way of understanding what is happening. Thus it offers a conceptual and empirical means of advancing theory development through more inclusive and innovative explanations of consumer behaviour in hospitality. In addition, it calls attention to the dynamic and contingent nature of theoretical proposition.

As can be seen both of the methodologies highlighted above fit well within a postmodern research agenda; after all, postmodernism is not about satisfying a quest for an idealized rational form. In truth, the opposite is the case; postmodernism manifests itself through parody and reappropriation. As Thompson, Arnould and Stern (1997: 173) argue, postmodern consumer research 'does not privilege one paradigmic form over another, it allows many types of expressive, creative, symbolic forms to emerge'. The main advantage of these methodologies is that these approaches enable access to a wide range of interpretive, what Hirschman and Holbrook (1992: 29) refer to as 'the linguistic construction of reality', and other subjective, referred to by the same authors as 'the individual construction of reality' (Hirschman and Holbrook, 1992: 9) research procedures. For example:

1 *Hermeneutics*. Hermeneutics emerged from the efforts of classical scholars seeking to understand texts such as those in Greek literature and the Bible. The interpretation of research using hermeneutics involves the concept of the hermeneutic circle, a sense in which the interpretation of the whole text guides the exegesis of its parts, which in turn shape an understanding of the whole (Hirschman and Holbrook, 1992; Makkreel, 1975). Within hermeneutics the validity of the interpretation rests on forming a tentative interpretation of the whole (which can be regarded as a hypothesis) and then testing this overview against a detailed investigation of the sub-elements (considered as the evidence) before altering the original interpretation in the light of the findings (revising the

theory). The value of hermeneutics to an understanding of hospitality consumption is that it grounds meaning in more than semantic significance, account has to be taken of characteristics such as the intention and history of the authors, the relationship between author and interpreter, and the relevance of texts for readers. As Crotty (1998: 110) suggests 'researchers looking to get a handle on people's perceptions, attitudes and feelings, may be best placed to find useful insights if they look to hermeneutics'.

2 *Semiotics*. Semiotics, a concept introduced by Saussure (1916), is the study of signs, symbols and systems, defined by Echtner (1999: 50) as 'concerned with examining a system of signs in order to uncover the recurring patterns (determine structure) and the various layers of meaning (delve deeper). Therefore the aim of the semiotic approach is to uncover the deep structure of meaning'. Semiotics consider the critical role played by signs in shaping the meaning within consumption, including words, brands, pictures, music, objects, products, etc. Semiotics, as an interpretive approach, seeks to develop an intertextuality, which brings the plurality of the text to the fore, a structuring of the evidence in a manner that supports a general reading of its meaning. As Hirschman and Holbrook, 1992: 34) state, researchers can 'view the semiotics of any symbolic system, including consumption ... as a text that shapes its own hermeneutic interpretation via a series of binary oppositions, differences, or contrasts'.

3 *Phenomenology*. Phenomenological approaches seek to attempt to understand the interactions between individuals and external objects in order to achieve knowledge structures that compose an individual's construction of reality. It suggests that if we set aside the prevailing understanding of phenomena, and only consider our immediate understanding of them, possibilities for new meaning emerge or former meanings can be authenticated and enhanced (Crotty, 1998). They are primarily psychological in nature, focusing on the individual, rather than social groups and the impact of culture. Phenomenology suggests that, after being co-constituted by the interaction between an individual's consciousness and the social world, the individual's construction of reality resides mainly in the mind (Hirschman and Holbrook, 1992). Crotty (1998: 96) refers to phenomenology as 'an attempt to return to the primordial contents of consciousness, that is, to the objects that present themselves in our very experience of them prior to our making any sense of them at all'. The value of taking a phenomenological approach to the study of hospitality consumers is that it encourages us to set aside the tendency to

immediately interpret, based on our understanding as a result of culture, etc., and to revisit our immediate experiences.

4 *Ethnography.* Ethnography originates in the field of anthropology, and involves the use of a rigorous style of participant observation, which allows the researcher to use the participants' socially acquired, shared knowledge to account for observed behaviour (Johns and Lee-Ross, 1998). Within ethnography, researchers interpret behaviour in ways that are compatible with the ways that members of the participant group would interpret it and, as such, it holds that interactions can only be studied in the field. Ethnography as a research method encourages the researcher to observe the participants as closely as possible, attempt to be assimilated within those being observed and, thus, to seek out the participants' perspective. As Hammersley (1985: 152) states: 'ethnography is a form of research in which the social settings to be studied, however familiar, must be treated as strange, and the task is to document the . . . perspectives and practices of the people in these settings, the aim is to get inside the way each group of people sees the world'.

5 *Existentialism.* Put very simply, existentialism argues that the fundamental basis for knowledge is existence itself, and that once comprehension of one's own existence is achieved, this leads to self-understanding and this can then be directed outwards to aid comprehension of other entities. It predicates only the existence of the individual, ignoring the external world and focusing on the individual. As such as Hirschman and Holbrook (1992: 40) argue, 'if people cannot be reduced to a set of common essences or constituent attributes, each person become unique and noncomparable'. As a research method, existentialism is seen to encourage individual subjective interpretation, while rejecting the relevance of external meaning. Criticisms of the existential approach suggest it lacks value as 'everyone is trapped in a private world of perception and interpretation . . . one cannot even talk of validity' (Seung, 1982: 198). However, in reality researchers do not form interpretation in a vacuum; they possess common meaning with others from the community of researchers. As we have discussed, society and interaction is central to the generation of self-identity and meaning.

Alternative perspectives to hospitality consumer research, such as those outlined in this chapter, offer a number of desirable outcomes, they can provide more critical insights into assumptions previously taken as fact and they allow a greater sensitivity to aspects such as class, ethnocentric conceptions and biases due to features such as gender. In addition, they encourage intellectual dialogue between formally separate disciplines and allow less conventional perspectives, not least postmodernism itself, into mainstream research. Finally, they achieve a truly interdisciplinary approach to the researching of the disparate characteristics of hospitality consumer behaviour, supporting the arguments of Shaw and Nightingale (1995) that hospitality's knowledge base should draw on multiple disciplines in management as well as related fields in the behavioural and social sciences.

Summarizing the role of research in aiding our comprehension of hospitality consumption

I would argue that hospitality consumer research has to begin to look at the ways in which we seek to understand consumer behaviour, and to try to investigate as many approaches as possible, including the ones highlighted above. This book and others advocating similar themes are simply the beginning of such a process. A number of studies have been undertaken in order to investigate consumer behaviour in purchase decisions (Buttle, 1989; 1992; Tauber, 1972). However, much of the research in this area, including those studies highlighted above, has tended to focus on the consumption of goods and to consider consumption as an internalized state. Future research has to focus specifically on the hospitality industry and has to be grounded in a constructionist rather than a positivistic assumption, considering motives not as internalized states but in terms of descriptive or ascriptive accounts of contextualized acts. A constructionist framework would accept that individuals could be seen as both products and producers of their individual social world. As Buttle (1992: 353) suggests, 'any one person stands at a particular map reference with respect to a multiplicity of social systems . . . each of which may construe in different ways'.

Contemporary hospitality consumer behaviour, including that of the postmodern phenomenon, has not been studied in depth by consumer researchers. Too often the machine metaphor, which sees consumers as automatons or instruments, is still prevalent. In addition, while not as popular as was previously the case, the assumption of economic rationality and utility maximization are still seen in descriptions of hospitality consumer behaviour. If hospitality marketing and consumer research is to continue to be relevant a macro societal perspective needs to be adopted, and approaches such as postmodernism may be the means by which this perspective is promoted.

This raises a number of questions that I will not attempt to answer, but simply leave for further consideration. First, if stances such as postmodernism are undermining the foundations of the hospitality environment, what directions should hospitality marketing and consumer research take to help the discipline retain a measure of relevance? As McLarney and Chung (1999: 295) suggest: 'in light of the ferment in the cultural landscape of society, researchers may do well to re-examine their ontological and epistemological assumptions'. If the ideology of concepts such as postmodernism is ontologically inconsistent with the current dominant ideology within hospitality, that of positivist inquiry, leading to demand for a more humanistic perspective, in practical terms how does hospitality and, in particular, hospitality consumer research further develop such a perspective?

Second, of what relevance are the theories and concepts imparted in hospitality marketing courses and texts if the foundations on which they are based are ideologically unsound? Such is the preponderance of hospitality marketing texts, and so central are they to most hospitality courses that it is a safe assumption that most managers within hospitality companies have been exposed to marketing's conceptual techniques. As a result it is argued (Brown, 1995) that hospitality practitioners are employing marketing concepts and acting on their predictions, even though the concepts themselves are far from proven. As Brown continues, the implications of the centrality of marketing concepts in contemporary hospitality organizations are that they do not simply reflect events in the marketing environment, they directly affect marketing behaviour. As Brown (1995: 27) concludes, 'theory is not neutral, it influences and alters the phenomena to which it pertains'.

Third, in an era when image and symbolism are increasingly dominant, how are these images, which seem to demonstrate contextual and situational preference, constructed? This is a question that needs to be addressed alongside consideration of how participation by consumers, hospitality organizations and other cultural institutions in the process of signification and representation of the images can be determined. At a time when consumers are choosing hospitality products in order to produce their self-image in multiple contexts, how do consumers select those images that represent different situations? As we have seen, hospitality consumers are increasingly fragmented and, consequently, they represent multiple images fashioned for individual occasions. This requires them to manage this multiplicity, as it forms and reforms.

Finally, as a result of the changes taking place within the hospitality industry, what changes are happening to the nature of the product and its marketing? It is moving from one of marketing products, to one where process and experience become the marketing focus. This points to the need for substantive changes to what hospitality marketing and consumer research is and what it needs to become in the future, requiring both a general and conceptual rethink, along with a rethink of the practical role of hospitality marketing and consumer research.

Goulding (1999: 869) summarized the common themes of approaches such as those advocated above, and they are worth repeating here, as in many ways they also sum up much of Part Three of this book. She stated that contemporary approaches to hospitality consumer research should:

- acknowledge the consumer in relation to their own culturally constructed world
- recognize the importance of language, symbols and gestures in relation to life experience
- understand that time and space have different meanings and are not universal rigid concepts, but are fluid and negotiable
- demonstrate humility regarding notions of 'truth' and recognize that observations are part of a process and a product of interpretation
- understand that interpretivist and subjectivist approaches to hospitality enquiries can offer rich and valuable insights, and contribute to the debate regarding contemporary hospitality consumption.

If companies are to be effective in the highly competitive marketing environment that comprises the contemporary hospitality industry, it is imperative that they understand contemporary consumers and consumer decision-making. As we have seen, it can be suggested that many of the research approaches that are currently being undertaken are based in, arguably, flawed models. The industry has to recognize that in contemporary western society consumers do not adopt consistent recognizable lifestyles, but opt to experiment with an eclectic combination of goods and services in order to experience a range of, often conflicting, identities. Contemporary consumer research needs to develop research strategies that recognize such eclecticism and focus on critical and self-reflexive interests. The way forward would seem to be radically to rethink consumer research methodologies in order to offer a better understanding of how contemporary consumers buy and use hospitality products. Concepts such as postmodernism have the potential to reframe our thinking about the hospitality industry in an increasingly global, but fragmented marketplace, giving managers insights that will aid their decision-making. As Firat and Shultz (1997: 204) argue, 'a better understanding of the underlying macro social forces and micro human behaviour associated with postmodernism can ultimately be leveraged by marketers to obtain competitive advantage in an increasingly dynamic, unpredictable and unstable marketplace'.

Simply to continue in both hospitality theory and practice to expound the theories inherent in traditional marketing concepts without question, will not in the long term offer our industry the progressive marketing developments it needs to succeed in the new century. If the industry is to develop and grow, it is imperative that some of the issues raised within this chapter are addressed by researchers within the field of hospitality marketing. As Brown (1995: 178) concludes: 'this implies that the fundamental issue to which we should address ourselves is not marketing myopia, but the myopia of marketing'.

Bibliography

Adair, G. (1992). *The Postmodernist Always Rings Twice*. Fourth Estate.

Adorno, T. W. (1977). The actuality of philosophy. *Telos*, **31**, Spring, 120–133.

Ahmed, Z. U. and Krohn, F. B. (1992). Understanding the unique customer behaviour of Japanese tourists. *Journal of Travel and Tourism Marketing*, **1** (3), 73.

Alford, P. (1998). Positioning the destination product. *Journal of Travel and Tourism Marketing*, **7** (2), 53–68.

Allen, D. E. and Anderson P. F. (1994). In consumption and social stratification: Bourdieu's distinction (C. T. Allen and D. J. Roedder, eds), *Advances in Consumer Research*, **21**, 70–74.

Appignanesi, R. and Garratt, C. (1995). *Postmodernism for Beginners*. Icon.

Armstrong, G. M. and Brucks, M. (1988). Dealing with children's advertising. *Journal of Public Policy and Marketing*, **7**, 93–113.

Ashworth, J. (2001). A ship that thinks it's a conference centre, *The Times*, 14 July, p. 47.

Assael, H. (1998). *Consumer Behaviour & Marketing Action*. Southwestern.

Baker, M. J. (1995). *Marketing Theory & Practice*. Macmillan.

Ball, S. (1994). Establishing staffing levels. In *The Management of Foodservice Operations* (P. Jones and P. Merricks, eds), Cassell.

Bareham, J. (1995). *Consumer Behaviour in the Food Industry*. Butterworth-Heinemann.

Baron, S. and Harris, K. (1995). *Services Marketing*. Macmillan.

Bateson, J. (1996). *Managing Services Marketing*. Dryden.

Baudrillard, J. (1983). *Simulations*. Semiotext(e).

Baudrillard, J. (1988). Simulacra and simulations. In *Baudrillard: Selected Writings* (M. Postner, ed.), Stanford Press.

Baudrillard, J. (1993). *The Transparency of Evil: Essays on Extreme Phenomena*. Verso.

Bazerman, M. (1998). *Judgement in Managerial Decision Making*. Wiley.

Beardon, W. O. and Etzel, M. J. (1982). Reference group influence on product and brand purchase decisions. *Journal of Consumer Research*, **9**, September, 178–196.

Beaumont, P. (1993). Postmodernism. *Observer*, 9 May, p. 43.

Belk, R. (1987). A child's Christmas in America: Santa Claus as deity, consumption as religion. *Journal of American Culture*, **10**, Spring, 87–100.

Belk, R. W. (1988). Possessions and the extended self. *Journal of Consumer Research*, **15**, 139–168.

Belk, R. W. (1995). Studies in the new consumer behaviour. In *Acknowledging Consumption* (D. Miller, ed.), Routledge.

Benson, J. (1994). *The Rise of Consumer Society in Britain*. Heinemann.

Berger, A. A. (1998). *The Postmodern Presence*. Sage.

Berry, L. (1980). Services marketing is different. *Business*, **30**, 24–29.

Best, S. and Kellner, D. (1991). *Postmodern Theory*. Guilford.

Bitner, M. (1992). Servicescapes: the impact of physical surroundings on customers and employees. *Journal of Marketing*, **56**, 57–71.

Blythe, J. (1997). *The Essence of Consumer Behaviour*. Prentice-Hall.

Bocock, R. (1993). *Consumption*. Routledge.

Bonomo, T. V. and Shapiro, B. P. (1984). Evaluating market segmentation approaches. *Industrial Marketing Management*, **13**, 257–268.

Bourne, F. S. (1989). Group influence in marketing and public relations. In *Some Applications of Behavioural Research* (R. Likert and S. P. Hayes, eds), UNESCO.

Bowen, J. T. (1998). Market segmentation in hospitality research: no longer a sequential process. *International Journal of Contemporary Hospitality Management*, **10** (7), 289–296.

Brotherton, B. (ed.) (1999). *The Handbook of Contemporary Hospitality Management Research*. Wiley.

Brotherton, B. and Wood, R. (2000). In *In Search of Hospitality: Theoretical Perspectives & Debates* (C. Lashley and A. Morrison, eds), Butterworth.

Brown, S. (1993a). Postmodern marketing. *European Journal of Marketing*, **27** (4), 19–34.

Brown, S. (1993b). Marketing as multiplex: screening post-modernism. *European Journal of Marketing*, **28** (8/9), 27–51.

Brown, S. (1995*). Postmodern Marketing*. London, Routledge.

Brown, S. (1999). Retro-marketing: yesterday's tomorrows, today. *Marketing Intelligence and Planning*, **17** (7), 363–376.

Brown, S. (2000*). Postmodern Marketing 2*. London, Routledge.

Brownlie, D. and Saren, M. (1992). The 4 P's of the marketing concept: prescriptive, polemical, permanent and problematic. *European Journal of Marketing*, **26** (4), 34–47.

Burke, K. (2000). Marketing meaning and signification. Unpublished proceedings of the CHME research conference, Huddersfield.

Butler, P. and Brown, S. (1994). Broadening the concept of relationship marketing, in *Marketing: Unity in Diversity* (J. Bell et al., eds), Marketing group conference proceedings, Coleraine.

Buttle, F. A. (1986). Unserviceable concepts in service marketing. *Quarterly Review of Marketing*, **11** (3), 94–102.

Buttle, F. A. (1989). Why do people shop? A constructivist perspective. Unpublished working paper, Department of Hotel Restaurant and Travel Administration, University of Massachusetts.

Buttle, F. A. (1992). Shopping motives, *Services Industries Journal*, **12** (3), 349–367.

Buttle, F. A. (1994). New paradigm research in marketing. *European Journal of Marketing*, **28** (8/9), 8–11.

Calver, S. (1994). *Marketing in Hospitality & Tourism*. Cassell.

Campbell, C. (1995). The sociology of consumption. In *Acknowledging Consumption* (D. Miller, (ed.), Routledge.

Carlson, L. (1994). Family communication patterns. *Journal of Consumer Affairs*, **28** (1), 25–53.

Carlsson, T. (1987). *Moments of Truth*. Ballinger.

Carpenter, G. S., Glazer, R. and Nakamoto, K. (1997), *Reading on Market-Driven Strategies*. Addison-Wesley.

Cattell, H. B. (1989). The 16PF: personality in depth. Institute for Personality and Ability Testing campaign, Illinois.

Chisnall, P. M. (1994). *Consumer Behaviour*. McGraw-Hill.

Clark, M. A., Riley, M. J., Wilkie, E. and Wood, R. C. (1998). *Researching and Writing Dissertations in Hospitality and Tourism*. International Thomson Business Press.

Clarke, I., Kell, I., Schmidt, R. A. and Vignali, C. (1998). Thinking the thoughts they do. *Qualitative Market Research*, **11** (3), 132–144.

Clarke, I., Kell, I., Schmidt, R. and Vignali, C. (2000). Thinking the thoughts they do, symbolism and meaning in the consumer experience of the British pub. *British Food Journal*, **102** (9), 692–710.

Cohn, N. (2001). A city that sold its soul. *Sunday Times*, 9 December, p. 5.

Collins, G. (1997). Egg McMuffins, priced to move. *New York Times*, 4 April, p. 18.

Connor, S. (1989). *Postmodernist Culture, an Introduction to the Theories of the Contemporary*. Blackwell.

Cova, B. and Badot, O. (1995). Marketing theory and practice in a postmodern era. In *Marketing Theory & Practice* (M. J. Baker, ed.), Macmillan.

Cova, B. and Svanfeldt, C. (1992). Marketing beyond marketing in a post-modern Europe: the creation of societal innovations. In *Marketing for Europe – Marketing for the Future* (K. G. Grunert and D. Fuglede, eds) pp. 155–171, EMAC.

Craig, C. S. and Douglas, S. P. (2000). *International Marketing Research*. Wiley.

Crawford, M. (1992). The world in a shopping mall. In *Variations on a Theme Park* (M. Sorkin, ed.), Hill and Wang.

Crawford-Welch, S. (1994). *Marketing in Hospitality & Tourism*. Cassell.

Cross, G. (1997). *Kids Stuff: Toys and the World of American Children*. Harvard University Press.

Crotty, M. (1998). *The Foundations of Social Research*. Sage.

Curwen, P. (1995). EuroDisney: the mouse that roared (not!). *European Business Review*, **95** (5), 15–20.

Czepiel, J., Solomon, M. and Surprenant, C. (1985). *The Service Encounter*, Lexington Books.

Dale, A. and Robinson, B. (2001). The theming of tourism education, *International Journal of Contemporary Hospitality Management*, **13** (1), 30–35.

Dawes, R. M. (1988). *Rational Choice in an Uncertain World*. Harcourt Brace Jovanovich.

Debord, G. (1994). *The Society of the Spectacle*. Zone Books.

Denison, T. and McDonald, M. (1995). The role of marketing past, present and future. *Journal of Marketing Practice: Applied Marketing Science*. **1** (1), 54–76.

Dickinson, B. and Vladimir, A. (1997). *Selling the Sea: An Inside Look at the Cruise*. Wiley.

Dubois, B. (2000). *Understanding the Consumer: A European Perspective*, Prentice-Hall.

Echtner, F. (1999). The semiotic paradigm: implications for tourism research. *Tourism Management*, **20** (1), 47–57.

Eco, U. (1987). *Travels in Hyper-Reality*. Picador.

Ekstrom, K. M., Tansuhaj, P. S. and Foxman, E. (1987). Children's influence in family decisions and consumer socialisation: a reciprocal view. In *Advances in Consumer Research* (M. Wallendorf and E. Arnould, eds), vol. 14, Scott Forseman.

Elliot, R. (1993). Marketing and the meaning of postmodern consumer culture. In *Perspectives on Marketing Management* (M. J. Baker, ed.), vol. 3, Wiley.

Engel, J. F., Blackwell, R. D. and Miniard, P. W. (1995). *Consumer Behaviour*. Dryden.

Enis, B. M. and Roering, K. J. (1981). Services marketing: different products, similar strategy. In *Marketing of Services* (J. Donnelly and W. George, eds), AMA.

Eurostat (1996). *Living Conditions in Europe*. Office for Official Publications of the EC.

Evans, M. J. and Moutinho, L. (1999). *Contemporary Issues in Marketing*. Macmillan.

Evans, M. J., Moutinho, L. and Van Raaij, F. (1996). *Applied Consumer Behaviour*. Addison-Wesley.

Eysenck, H. J. and Eysenck, S. B. G. (1964). *Manual of the Eysenck Personality Inventory*. University of London Press.

Featherstone, M. (1991). *Consumer Culture & Post-Modernism*. Sage.

Festinger, L. (1982). *A Theory of Cognitive Dissonance*. Tavistock.

Fielding, H. (1992). Teach your-self postmodernism. *Independent on Sunday*, 15 November, p. 21.

Firat, A. F. (1991). Postmodern culture, marketing and the consumer. In *Marketing Theory and Application* (T. Childers, ed.), AMA.

Firat, A. F. and Shultz, C. J. (1997). From segmentation to fragmentation. *European Journal of Marketing*, **31** (3/4), 183–207.

Firat, A. F. and Venkatesh, A (1993). Postmodernity; the age of marketing. *International Journal of Marketing*, **10** (3), 227–249.

Firat, A. F. and Venkatesh, A (1995). Liberatory postmodernism and the re-enchantment of consumption. *Journal of Consumer Research*, **22** (3), 239–267.

Fischer, E. and Arnold, S. J. (1990). More than a labour of love: gender roles and Christmas shopping. *Journal of Consumer Research*, **17**, December, 333–345.

Fisher, R. J. and Price, L. L. (1992). An investigation into the social context of early adoption behaviour. *Journal of Consumer Research*, **19**, December, 477–486.

Fisk, R., Brown, S. and Bitner, M. J. (1993). Tracking the evolution of services marketing literature. *Journal of Retailing*, **69** (1), 61–103.

Formica, S. and Olsen, M. D. (1998). Trends in the amusement park industry. *International Journal of Contemporary Hospitality Management*, **10** (7), 297.

Foucault, M. (1977). *Discipline and Punish: The Birth of the Prison*. Penguin

Foucault, M. (1980). *Power, Knowledge and Other Writings 1972–1977*. Harvester Wheatsheaf.

Foxall, G. R. (1980). *Consumer Behaviour.* Croon Helm.

Foxall, G. R. (1992). The behavioural perspective of purchase and consumption. *Journal of the Academy of Marketing Science*, **20** (2), 189–198.

Foxall, G. R. and Goldsmith, R. E. (1994). *Consumer Psychology for Marketing.* Routledge.

Frank, R. E., Massey, W. F. and Wind, Y. (1972). *Market Segmentation*, Prentice-Hall.

Fraser, N. and Nicholson, L. (1990). Social criticism without philosophy: an encounter between feminism and postmodernism. In *Feminism/Postmodernism* (L. Nicholson, ed.), Routledge.

Freidman, M., Abeele, P. V. and De Vos, K. (1993). Boorstin's consumption community concept: a tale of two countries. *Journal of Consumer Research*, **16** (1), 35–60.

Fullerton, R. (1990). Tea and the Viennese: a pioneering episode in the analysis of consumer behaviour. *Advances in Consumer Research*, **21**, 201–214.

Gabbott, M. and Hogg, G. (1998). *Consumers and Services.* Wiley.

Gabriel, Y. and Lang, T. (1995). *The Unmanageable Consumer.* Sage.

Gellner, E. (1992). *Postmodernism, Reason & Religion.* Routledge.

Giddens, A. (1979). *Studies in Social and Political Theory.* Hutchinson.

Gillespie, C. and Morrison, A (2001). Commercial hospitality consumption as a live marketing communication system. *International Journal of Contemporary Hospitality Management*, **13** (4), 183–188.

Goodman, E. (1997). Zapping Xmas. *Washington Post*, 20 December, p. 14.

Gore, J. and Riley, M. (2000). Methodology in question: experiencing cognitive task analysis. *Proceedings from CHME Research Conference 2000*, Huddersfield.

Gould, S. (1995). Researcher introspection as a method in consumer research. *Journal of Consumer Research*, **21** (4), 719–722.

Goulding, C. (1999). Consumer research, interpretive paradigms and methodological ambiguities. *European Journal of Marketing*, **33** (9/10), 859–873.

Goulding, C. (2000). The commodification of the past. *European Journal of Marketing*, **34** (7), 835–853.

Grazin, K. L. and Olsen, J. E. (1997). Market segmentation for fast-food restaurants in an era of health consciousness. *Journal of Restaurant & Foodservice Marketing*, **2** (2), 1–20.

Green, R. T. (1983). Societal development and family purchasing roles: a cross-national study. *Journal of Consumer Research*, **9**, March, 107–123.

Greene, P. E. and Kreigner, A. M. (1991). Segmenting markets with conjoint analysis. *Journal of Marketing*, October, 20–31.

Greene, P. E., Tull, D. S. and Albaum, G. (1988). *Research for Marketing Decisions*. Prentice-Hall.

Gronroos, C. (1990). *Service Management and Marketing: Managing the Moments of Truth in Service Competition*. Lexington Books.

Gummerson, E. (1987). The new marketing – developing long-term interactive relationships. *Long Range Planning*, **20** (4), 10–22.

Gummerson, E. (1996). Relationship marketing and imaginary organisations. *European Journal of Marketing*, **30** (2), 31–44.

Haley, R. J. (1968). Benefit segmentation: a decision orientated tool. *Journal of Marketing*, July, 30–35.

Hammersley, M. (1985). Ethnography: what it is and what it offers. *Research & Evaluation Methods in Special Education*. NFER-Nelson.

Harvey, D. (1989). *The Condition of Postmodernity*. Blackwell.

Hebdige, D. (1986). Postmodernism and the other side. *Journal of Communication Inquiry*, **10** (2), 78–98.

Hewison, R. (1987). *The Heritage Industry*. Methuen.

Hirschman, E. (1993). Ideology in consumer research: a Marxist and feminist critique. *Journal of Consumer Research*, **19**, March, 537–555.

Hirschman, E. C. (1981). American Jewish ethnicity: its relationship to selected aspects of consumer behaviour. *Journal of Marketing*, **45**, Summer, 102–105.

Hirschman, E. C. (1982). An examination of ethnicity and consumption using free response data. In *A.M.A. Educators' Conference Proceedings*. AMA.

Hirschman, E. C. and Holbrook, M. B. (1992). *Postmodern Consumer Research*. Sage.

Hofstede, G. (1984). *Culture's Consequences: International Differences in Work-Related Values*. Sage.

Holbrook, M. B. and Hirschman, E. C. (1993). *The Semiotics of Consumption*. Mouton de Grayter.

Holt, D. B. (1998). Does cultural capital structure American consumption. *Journal of Consumer Research*, **1**, June, 1–25.

Hooley, G. (1980). The multivariate jungle: the academic's playground but the manager's minefield. *European Journal of Marketing*, **14** (7), 379–386.

Horkheimer, M. and Adorno, T. W. (1972). *Dialectic of Enlightenment*. Continuum.

Horner, S. and Swarbrooke, J. (1996). *Marketing Tourism, Hospitality and Leisure in Europe*. Thompson.

Horney, K. (1958). *Neurosis & Human Growth*. Norton.

Howard, J. A. and Seth, J. N. (1969). *The theory of Buyer Behaviour*. Wiley.

Hoyt, F. B. (1991). We don't do marketing here anymore. *Marketing News*, **25** (1), 4.

Hui, M. and Bateson, J. (1991). Perceived control and the effects of crowding and consumer choice on the service experience. *Journal of Consumer Research*, **18** (2), 174–184.

Hunt, S. D. (1993). Objectivity in marketing theory and research. *Journal of Marketing*, **57** (2), 76–91.

Huxtable, A. L. (1997). *The Unreal America*. New Press.

Jacoby, J., Speller, D. E. and Kohn (1974). Brand choice behaviour. *Journal of Consumer Research*, **1** (8), 33–42.

Jameson, F. (1985). Postmodernism and consumer society. In *Postmodern Culture* (H. Foster, ed.), Pluto Press.

Jameson, F. (1991). *Postmodernism or the Cultural Logic of Late Capitalism*. Verso.

Jeannet, J. and Hennessey, D. (1998). *Global Marketing Strategies*. Houghton Mifflin.

Jenkins, M. and McDonald, M. (1997). Market segmentation: organisational archetypes and research agendas. *European Journal of Marketing*, **31** (1), 17–32.

Jenkins, M., Le Cerf, E. and Cole, T. (1994). How managers define consumer markets. In *Advances in Consumer Marketing* (M. Jenkins and S. D. Knox, eds) pp. 185–197, Kogan Page.

Jennings, D. and Wattam, S. (1998). *Decision Making: An Integrated Approach*. Pitman.

Johansson, J. (2000). *Global Marketing*. McGraw-Hill.

Johns, N. and Lee-Ross, D. (1998). *Research Methods in Service Industry Management*. Cassell.

Joint Hospitality Industry Congress (1996). *Hospitality into the 21st Century: A Vision for the Future*. JHIC.

Kassarjian, H. H. (1971). Personality and consumer behaviour, a review, *Journal of Marketing Research*, **8**, pp. 409–419.

Kassarjian, H. H. and Sheffet, M. J. (1981). Personality and consumer behaviour. In *Perspectives in Consumer Behaviour* (H. H. Kassarjian and T. S. Robertson, eds), Scott Foreseman.

Kattara, H. S. (2000). A study on preferred hotel attributes among business travellers, *Proceedings from the 9th Annual CHME Research Conference*, Huddersfield, pp. 275–290.

Keith, R. J. (1960). The marketing revolution. *Journal of Marketing*, January, 35–38.

Kellner, D. (1988). Postmodernism as a social theory: some challenges and problems. *Theory, Culture and Society*, **5**, 239–269.

Kelly, K. J. (1998). Hello young buyers. *New York Daily News*, 22 January, p. 6.

Killgren, L. (1999). Joe Lyons makes comeback. *Marketing Week*, 17 June, p. 5.

King, R. L. (1965). The marketing concept. In *Science in Marketing*, (G. Schwartz, ed.), Wiley.

Klaus, A. (1985). Quality epiphenomenona: the conceptual understanding of quality in face-to-face encounters. In *The Service Encounter* (J. Czepiel, M. Solomon and C. Surprenant, eds), Lexington Books.

Knight, D. (1991). A problem of market definition. *Marketing*, **25**, July, 17.

Knowles, T. and Howley, M. J. (2000). Branding in the UK public house sector. *International Journal of Contemporary Hospitality Management*, **12** (6), 366–370.

Kotler, P. (1980). *Marketing Management: Analysis, Planning, Implementation & Control*. Prentice-Hall.

Kotler, P. (1994). *Marketing Management*. Prentice-Hall.

Kowinsky, W. S. (1985). *The Malling of America*. Morrow.

Lash, S. and Urry, J. (1994). *Economics of Signs & Space*. Sage.

Lashley, C. (1998). Action research: an essential tool for hospitality management education. *Proceedings from the 7th Annual CHME Research Conference*, Glasgow, pp. 294–310.

Lashley, C. (2000). *Hospitality Retail Management*. Butterworth-Heinemann.

Lashley, C. and Morrison, A. (2000). *In Search of Hospitality: Theoretical Perspectives & Debates*. Butterworth-Heinemann.

Lazer, W. and Wykham, R. G. (1961). Perceptual segmentation of department store marketing. *Journal of Retailing*, **45**, 3–14.

Leach, P. (1995). The importance of positive customer service to Ansells. *Managing Service Quality*, **5** (4), 31–34.

Lee, C. K. and Collins, B. A. (2000). Family decision-making and coalition patterns. *European Journal of Marketing*, **34** (9), 1181–1198.

Leong, S. M. (1989). A citation analysis of the journal of consumer research. *Journal of Consumer Research*, **15**, March, 492–497.

Levinson, S. et al. (1992). Halloween as a consumption ritual. In *Advances in Consumer Research* (J. F. Sherry and B. Sternthal, eds), vol. 19, Provo.

Levitt, J. (1976). The industrialisation of services. *Harvard Business Review*, **37**, 117–119.

Levitt, T. (1981). Marketing intangible products and product intangibles. *Harvard Business Review*, May, 94–102.

Levitt, T. (1986). *The Marketing Imagination*. Free Press.

Lewin, K. (1935). *A Dynamic Theory of Personality*. McGraw-Hill.

Lewis, R. C. and Chambers, R. E. (1989). *Marketing Leadership in Hospitality*. Van Nostrand Reinhold.

Littlejohn, D. (1990). Hospitality research: philosophies and progress. In *Managing and Marketing Services in the 1990s* (R. E. Teare, L. Moutinho and N. Morgan, eds), Cassell.

Littler, D. (1995). Marketing segmentation. In *Marketing Theory & Practice* (M. J. Baker, ed.), Macmillan.

Lockwood, A. and Jones, P. (2000). Managing hospitality operations. In *In Search of Hospitality: Theoretical Perspectives & Debates* (C. Lashley and A. Morrison, eds), Butterworth-Heinemann.

Lovelock, C. (1981). Why marketing management needs to be different. In *Marketing of Services* (J. Donnelly and W. George, eds), AMA.

Lovelock, C. (1996). *Services Marketing*. Prentice-Hall.

Lyotard, J. F. (1984). *The Postmodern Condition – a Report on Knowledge*. Manchester University Press.

Lyotard, J. F. (1990). *Mode of Information*. Polity Press.

McAuley, A. (1998). Editorial. *Journal of Marketing Practice*, **4** (3), 1.

McCraken, G. (1981). Culture and consumption: a theoretical account of the structure and movement of the cultural meaning of consumer goods. *Journal Of Consumer Research*, **13**, June, 31–36.

McDonald, M. and Dunbar, I. (1998). *Market segmentation*. Macmillan.

McGregor, L. (1995). Consumer behaviour. In *Marketing Theory & Practice* (M. J. Baker, ed.), Macmillan.

McGrew, A. G. and Wilson, M. J. (1982). *Decision Making: Approaches and Analysis*. Manchester University Press.

MacKay, K. J. and Fesenmaier, D. R. (1998). A process approach to segmenting the gateway travel market. *Journal of Travel & Tourism Marketing*, **7** (3), 1–39.

McKenna, R. (1991). Marketing is everything. *Harvard Business Review*, **69** (1), 65–79.

McLarney, C. and Chung, E. (1999). Post-materialism's silent revolution. *Marketing Intelligence and Planning*, **17** (6), 288–297.

McNeal, J. U. (1991). Getting 'em while they're young. *Business Week*, 9 September, 94.

McQuarrie, E. and McIntyre, S. (1990). What the group interview can contribute to research on consumer phenomenology. In *Research in Consumer Behaviour* (E. Hirschman, ed.), JAI Press.

Makkreel, R. A. (1975). *Dilthey: Philosopher of the Human Studies*. Princeton University Press.

Marrion, G. (1993). The marketing management discourse: what's new since the 1960s. In *Perspectives on Marketing Management* (M. J. Baker, ed.), vol. 3, Wiley.

Maslow, F. (1954). *Motivation & Personality*. Harper and Row.

Mazanec, J. A., (ed.) (1994). *Marketing in Hospitality and Tourism*. Cassell.

Miles, S. (1998). *Consumerism as a Way of Life*. Sage.

Mill, R. C. (1986). Upping the organisation. *Cornell Quarterly,* February, 30–37.

Miller, D. C. (1991). *Handbook of Research Design and Social Measurement.* Sage.

Miller, G. and Real, M. (1998). Postmodernity and popular culture. In *The Postmodern Presence* (A. A. Berger, ed.), Sage.

Milner, A. (1991). *Contemporary Cultural Theory: An Introduction.* Allen and Unwin.

Mitchell, A. (1994). New generation marketing. *Marketing Business: The Magazine of the Chartered Institute of Marketing,* February, 11–14.

Morrison, A. and Wensley, R. (1991). Boxing up or boxed in: a short history of the BCG matrix. *Journal of Marketing Management,* **7** (2), 105–129.

Morrison, R. (2001). Some museum. *The Times,* 25 October, p. 7.

Mort, F. (1989). The politics of consumption. In *New Times, the Changing Face of Politics in the 1990s* (S. Hall and M. Jacques, eds), Lawrence and Wishart.

Moschis, G. P. (1985). The role of family communication in consumer socialisation. *Journal of Consumer Research,* **11**, March, 898–913.

Nelson, M. C. (1988). The resolution of conflict in joint purchase decisions. *Advances in Consumer Research,* **15**, 436–441.

Nicosia, F. (1966). *Consumer Decision Processes.* Prentice-Hall,.

Nightingale, M. (1985). The hospitality industry: defining quality for a quality enhancement programme. *Service Industries Journal,* **5** (1), 9–22.

O'Brien, S. and Ford, R. (1988). Can we at last say goodbye to social class? *Journal of the Market Research Society,* **30**, 289–332.

O'Guin, T. and Belk, R. (1989). Heaven on earth: consumption at Heritage Village, USA. *Journal of Consumer Research,* **15**, 227–238.

Ogilvy, J. (1990). This post-modern business. *Market Research Today,* February, 4–22.

Oh, H. and Jeong, M. (1996). Improving marketers' predictive power of customer satisfaction on expectation based target market levels. *Hospitality Research Journal,* **19** (4), 65–85.

Oliver, G. (1986). *Marketing Today.* Prentice-Hall.

Park, C. W. and Lessig, V. P. (1977). Students and housewives: susceptibility to reference group influence. *Journal of Consumer Research,* **4**, September, 102–110.

Parker, A. J. (1992). Retail environments into the 1990s. *Irish Marketing Review,* **5** (2), 61–72.

Patterson, M. (1998). Direct marketing in postmodernity: neo tribes and direct marketing. *Marketing Services,* **1** (3), 8–14.

Peracchio, L. A. (1992). How do young children learn to be consumers. *Journal of Consumer Research*, **18**, March, 25–40.

Peter, J. P. and Olson, J. C. (1993). Is science marketing. *Journal of Marketing*, **47**, Fall, 111–125.

Pfeifer, Y. (1983). Small business management. In *The Management of Hospitality* (E. H. Cassee and R. Reuland, eds), Pergamon.

Piercy, N. F. (1992). *Market-Led Strategic Change*. Butterworth-Heinemann.

Piercy, N. F. and Morgan, A. (1993). Strategic and operational market segmentation. *Journal of Strategic Marketing*, **1**, 123–140.

Prasad, V. K. (1975). Socio-economic product risk and patronage preferences of retail shoppers. *Journal of Marketing*, **39**, July, 42–47.

Quall, W. J. and Jaffe, F. (1992). Measuring conflict in household decision behaviour. In *Advances in Consumer Research* (J. F. Sherry and B. Sternthal, eds), pp. 522–531, Association for Consumer Research.

Rapp, S. and Collins, T. L. (1990). *The Great Marketing Turnaround: The Age of the Individual and How to Profit from It*. Prentice-Hall.

Reisman, D., Glazer, N. and Denney, R. (1960). *The Lonely Crowd*. Yale University Press.

Reynolds, W. H. (1965). More sense about market segmentation. *Harvard Business Review*, September/October, 107–111.

Ritzer, G. (1999). *Enchanting a Disenchanted World*. Sage.

Roberts, S. D. (1992). Beyond the family life-cycle. In *Developments in Marketing Science* (V. L. Crittenden, ed.), Coral.

Robertson, T. S. (1971). *Innovative Behaviour and Communications*. Rinehart and Winston.

Robson, I. and Rowe, J. (1997). Marketing: the whore of Babylon? *European Journal of Marketing*, **31** (9/10), 654–666.

Rockeach, M. J. (1968). The role of values in public opinion research. *Public Opinion Quarterly*, **32**, Winter, 547–549.

Rook, D. W. (1985). The ritual dimensions of consumer behaviour. *Journal Of Consumer Research*, **12**, December, 251–264.

Roper, A. and Brookes, M. (1999). Theory and reality of interdisciplinary research. *International Journal of Contemporary Hospitality Management*, **11** (4), 174–179.

Roscoe, A. M., LeClaire, A. and Schiffman, L. G. (1997). Theory and management applications of demographics in buyer behaviour. In *Consumer and Industrial Buyer Behaviour* (G. Woodside, ed.), Wiley.

Rosenau, P. M. (1992). *Postmodernism & the Social Sciences*. Princeton University Press.

Rue, L. (1994). *By the Grace of Guile*, Oxford University Press.

Rushton, A. M. and Carson, D. J. (1989). The marketing of services: managing the intangibles. *European Journal of Marketing*, **23** (8), 23–44.

Rust, R. T. and Oliver, R. L. (1994). *Service Quality: New Directions in Theory and Practice*. Sage.

Sasser, W., Olson, R. and Wyckoff, D. (1978). *Management of Service Operations*. Allyn and Bacon.

Saunders, J. (1987). Marketing and competitive success. In *The Marketing Book* (M. J. Baker, ed.), Macmillan.

Saussure, F. (1916). *Cour de linguistic generale*. McGraw-Hill.

Scanzoni, J. and Szinovacz, M. (1980). *Family Decision-Making*. Sage.

Schaninger, C. M. and Danko, W. D. (1993). A conceptual and empirical comparison of life cycle models. *Journal of Consumer Research*, **19**, March, 580–594.

Schlossberg, H. (1991). Health club T.V. targeting an audience that can't click back. *Marketing News*, **25** (21), 1–15.

Schmidt, R. A. and Sapsford, R. (1995). Women's views of pubs. *Journal of Managerial Psychology*, **10** (2), 18–25.

Scrutton, R. (1994). *Modern Philosophy – an Introduction and Survey*. Sinclair-Stevenson.

Scull, T. (2001). Cruise operators steer clear of recession. *The Times*, 14 July, p. 46.

Seidman, S. (1990). Substantive debates: moral order and social crisis. In *Culture & Society* (J. C. Alexander and S. Seidman, eds), Cambridge University Press.

Seidman, S. (1994). *The Postmodern Turn – New Perspectives on Social Theory*. Cambridge University Press.

Seidman, S. and Wagner, D. (1991). *Postmodernism & Social Theory*. Basil Blackwell.

Seung, T. K. (1982). *Structuralism & Hermeneutics*. Columbia University Press.

Shaw, M. and Nightingale, M. (1995). Scholarship reconsidered: implications for hospitality education. *Hospitality Research Journal*, **19** (1), 81–93.

Shepherd, R. (1989). *Handbook of the Psychophysiology of Human Eating*. Wiley.

Sheth, J. N. (1974). A theory of family buying decisions. In *Models of Buyer Behaviour* (J. N. Sheth, ed.) pp. 17–33, Harper and Row.

Shostack, L. (1977). Breaking free from product marketing. *Journal of Marketing*, **41**, April, 73–80.

Shostak, G. L. (1982). How to design a service. *European Journal of Marketing*, **16** (1), 49–63.

Sivadas, E., Mathew, G. and Currey, D. J. (1997). A preliminary examination of the continuing significance of social class to marketing. *Journal of Consumer Marketing*, **14** (6), 463–479.

Slattery, P. (1983). Social scientific methodology and hospitality management. *International Journal of Hospitality Management*, **2** (1), 9–14.

Smart, B. (1992). *Modern Conditions, Postmodern Controversies.* Routledge.

Solomon, J. (1998). Our decentred culture: the postmodern worldview. In *The Postmodern Presence* (A. A. Berger, ed.), Sage.

Solomon, M. R. (1996). *Consumer Behaviour.* Prentice-Hall.

Spiro, R. L. (1983). Persuasion in family decision-making. *Journal of Consumer Research*, **10**, March, 393–402.

Statt, D. A. (1997). *Understanding the Consumer.* Macmillan.

Stern, B. (1990). Literary criticism and the history of marketing thought. *Journal of the Academy of Marketing Science*, **18** (4), 239–336.

Swarbrook, J. and Horner, S. (1999). *Consumer Behaviour in Tourism*, Butterworth-Heinemann.

Tauber, E. M. (1972). Why do people shop. *Journal of Marketing*, **30**, October, 46–72.

Teare, R. E. (1990). An exploration of the consumer decision process for hospitality services. In *Managing and Marketing Services in the 1990s* (R. E. Teare, L. Moutinho and N. Morgan, eds), Cassell.

Teare, R. E. (1994). The consumer decision process: a paradigm in transition. In *Marketing in Hospitality & Tourism: A Consumer Focus* (R. E. Teare, J. Mazanec, S. Crawford-Welch and S. Carver, eds), Cassell.

Teare, R. E. (1995). *Services Management.* Cassell.

Teare, R. E. (1998). Interpreting and responding to customer needs. *Journal of Workplace Learning*, **10** (2), 76–94.

Teare, R. E., Mazanec, J. A. and Crawford-Welch, S. (1994). *Marketing In Hospitality & Tourism.* Cassell.

Tharp, M. and Scott, L. M. (1990). The role of marketing processes in creating cultural meaning. *Journal of Macro-Marketing*, Fall, 7–60.

Thomas, M. J. (1993). Marketing in chaos or transition. In *Rethinking Marketing* (D. Brownlie, ed.), pp. 114–123, Warwick Business School.

Thomas, M. J. (1997). Consumer market research: does it have validity/some postmodern thoughts. *Marketing Intelligence & Planning*, **15** (2), 54–59.

Thompson, C. J., Arnould, E. J. and Stern, B. B. (1997). Exploring the difference. In *Consumer Research* (S. Brown and J. Bell, eds), Routledge.

Thompson, C. J., Locander, W. B. and Pollio, H. R. (1990). The lived meaning of free choice. *Journal of Consumer Research*, **25** (2), 139–153.

Thorne, T. (1993). *Fads, Fashion & Cults: The Definitive Guide to (Post) Modern Culture*. Bloomsbury.

Usunier, J. C. (2000). *Marketing across Cultures*. Prentice-Hall.

Van Raaij, W. F. (1993). Postmodern consumption. *Journal of Economic Psychology*, **14**, 541–63.

Venkatesh, A. (1995). Ethnoconsumerism: a new paradigm to study cultural and cross-cultural consumer behaviour. In *Marketing in a Multicultural World* (J. Costa and G. J. Banussy, eds), Sage.

Venturi, R. (1995). Distorted imagination. In *Postmodernism for Beginners* (R. Appignanesi and C. Garratt, eds), Icon.

Vuchinich, S., Emery, R. E. and Cassidy, J. (1988). Family members as third parties in dyadic family conflict. *Child Development*, **59**, 1293–1302.

Wallendorf, M. and Arnould, E. (1992). We gather together: consumption rituals of Thanksgiving Day. *Journal of Consumer Research*, **18**, June, 13–31.

Ward, S. (1990). Consumer socialisation. In *Perspectives in Consumer Behaviour* (H. H. Kassarjian and T. S. Robertson, eds), Scott Foresman.

Wearne, N. and Morrison, A. (1996). *Hospitality Marketing*. Butterworth-Heinemann.

Weber, M. (1946). Class, status, party. In *From Max Weber* (H. H. Gerth and C. Wright Mills, eds), Oxford University Press.

Weir, D. (1996). Trawlers, snoopers and branding popes, *Times Higher Education Supplement*, 13 September, 28.

Wells, W. A. and Guber, G. (1966). The life-cycle concept in marketing research. *Journal of Marketing Research*, **3**, November, 353–363.

Wells, W. D. (1993). Discovery-orientated consumer research. *Journal of Consumer Research*, **19**, March, 489–504.

Wilkes, R. E. (1995). Household life-cycles. *Journal of Consumer Research*, **22** (1), 27–42.

Wilkie, W. L. (1994). *Consumer Behaviour*. Wiley.

Williams, A. J. (2000). Consuming hospitality: learning from postmodernism. In *In Search of Hospitality* (C. Lashley and A. Morrison, eds), Butterworth-Heinemann.

Williams, A. J., Demicco, F. J. and Kotschevar, L. (1997). The challenges that face restaurants in attracting and meeting the needs of the mature customer. *Journal of Restaurant & Foodservice Marketing*, **2** (4), 49.

Wolin, R. (1992). *The Terms of Cultural Criticism*. Columbia University Press.

Wolitz, D. (1996). Hard Rock absurdity. *San Francisco Daily online*, 15 August.

Wright, L. T., Nancarrow, C. and Kwok, P. M. H. (2001). Food taste preferences and cultural influences on consumption. *British Food Journal*, **103** (5), 348–357.

Yankelovich, C., Clancy, S. and Shulman, Y. (1990). Young consumers, perils and powers. *New York Times*, 11 February, p. 14.

Zaichkowsky, J. L. (1985). Measuring the involvement contract. *Journal Of Consumer Research*, **12**, December, 408–411.

Zeithaml, V. and Bitner, M. J. (1996). *Services Marketing*. McGraw Hill.

Index